A Psychoanalyst in the Classroom

SUNY series, Transforming Subjects:

Psychoanalysis, Culture, and Studies in Education

Deborah P. Britzman, editor

A Psychoanalyst in the Classroom

On the Human Condition in Education

DEBORAH P. BRITZMAN

Published by
STATE UNIVERSITY OF NEW YORK PRESS
Albany

© 2015 State University of New York

All rights reserved

Printed in the United States of America

No part of this book may be used or reproduced in any manner whatsoever without written permission. No part of this book may be stored in a retrieval system or transmitted in any form or by any means including electronic, electrostatic, magnetic tape, mechanical, photocopying, recording, or otherwise without the prior permission in writing of the publisher.

For information, contact
State University of New York Press
www.sunypress.edu

Production, Eileen Nizer
Marketing, Fran Keneston

Library of Congress Cataloging-in-Publication Data

Britzman, Deborah P.
 A psychoanalyst in the classroom : on the human condition in education / Deborah P. Britzman.
     pages cm. — (Transforming Subjects: Psychoanalysis, Culture, and Studies in Education)
 Includes bibliographical references and index.
 ISBN 978-1-4384-5733-8 (hc : alk. paper)—978-1-4384-5732-1 (pb : alk. paper)
 ISBN 978-1-4384-5734-5 (e-book)
 1. Learning, Psychology of. 2. Psychoanalysis and education. I. Title.

BF318.B785 2015
370.15—dc23   2014035447

10 9 8 7 6 5 4 3 2 1

Contents

	Acknowledgments	vii
1.	A Psychoanalyst in the Classroom: Character Studies in the Human Condition of Education	1
2.	"An Unexpected Novelty": Freud's Technique Papers Go to the University	29
3.	What Is the Use of Theory?	49
4.	The Adolescent Teacher	67
5.	On the Madness of Lecturing on Gender	87
6.	The Untold Story of the Writing Block	105
7.	The Psychopathologies of Everyday Education: Sleeping, Falling, Forgetting, Lateness, and the Professor's Mistakes	129

Notes	151
References	161
Index	173

Acknowledgments

It almost goes without saying that having education is a good idea, that it is both a social and individual imperative, and we do have to put mass populations of very young children, adolescents, and young adults—to say nothing of daycare workers, teachers, professors, among others—somewhere and give them something to do. Yet education is not a waiting room for real life, though it often feels that way. Even as we hope that the many years spent in classrooms become the psychological glue (and not the psychological zoo) for the social bond, the problem with things that go without saying is that they are quickly forgotten. And this creates particular difficulties to presenting what needs to be said about the education we forget.

Something is happening in the pedagogical relation that involves not only why the industrial metaphor of factory has given way to the faceless bureaucracy and then, to the multitasking, high-speed technological corporation. Part of what has happened is this: Students are urged to become clients with "takeaway knowledge"; professors are urged to deliver the goods without too much affect; and this thumbs-up/ thumbs-down education seems to justify the idealization of accountability, evidence-based practice, quality assurance, professionalization, and standardization. Mainly, we are asked if we like education. Neither is satisfaction nor education like that since each pedagogical exchange, each desire, each mistake, and all confusion that hold sway lead us to question the inexplicable occurrences of psychical life, its creative and mad procedures. Despite the overfamiliarity of education and the feeling that we have been there before and so must be able to predict and control what should happen again, learning is not like that. None of our normative measures help us encounter the human fact of dependency, the questions of love and hate, what learning feels like, why ideas make us nervous, what the contingencies of emotional life have to do with the ways in which thinking goes missing, and how one makes sense of discontentment in and desire for attaching to an education we know nothing about. And so the paradox this book opens begins with the idea that what we do not know, as well as what we do not want to know anything about, instructs the knowledge we thought we already had. Here I try to describe unconscious education, a character world of teaching and learning that gives permit to the liberties of psychoanalytic sensitivity and its disquieting imagination. Do we have time to listen to the human condition of education?

The novelties of practicing and writing from the psychoanalytic and pedagogical fields form the basis of this present volume's formulation of education as our human condition and have affected the style of communicating this work. While I place in the background my clinical practice in psychoanalysis, it is the traces of this intimate life world that deeply affect my sense of pedagogy, the choice of the subject, the objects amassed, and the flavor of writing. In listening to and associating with how individuals handle and disperse their matters of love and hate, fragile configurations of the human condition gradually emerge. There are moving questions of freedom of expression and anxieties over its loss. But it is with sorting through the urgencies of libidinal commitments and its flout of phantasy that bring us all to matters of the effervescent unconscious. When least expected the sotto voce phantasies of teaching and learning have sway. So throughout this volume I ask, how are we to advance theories of pedagogy with a capacious understanding of learning that recommends emotional life as our significant resource for thinking anew? May we write psychoanalytically and use the psychodynamics of pedagogical exchange as our best specimen?

In my view the affecting approach to analyzing the destiny of phantasy life in the panorama of teaching and learning involves the study of tiny details that present a meeting of the meant and the unmeant. Details come to life in throwaway lines, the trailed-off thought, the unexpected reply, the "I don't remember," and the missed encounters and leads me to question what else occurs between the lines of thought and communication. So it is that I turn to the analysis of my practices in university teaching and the difficulties education presents to a psychoanalyst in the classroom. In the pages that follow I invite your consideration for the idea that a generous recognition of the vulnerabilities and responsibilities of listening can create an affectionate and forgiving theory of learning that can stand the slow work of changing one's mind with attention to times when frustration, anxiety, and inhibitions seem to carry us away. I stay in contact with the throwaway lines.

It is typical when narrating learning matters to note a little warning, which is another word for anxiety: there is no endpoint to phantasies of teaching and learning, and, at times, they present as a vicious cycle that affect the writing. While much remains unconscious and while depth psychology may only scratch the surface, should we care to notice the significance of the symptomatic acts of quibbling learning and teaching, we find a great happening. Characters emerge in words and deeds and search for the genesis of neurosis. They may grate on one's nerves or be mistaken for one's nerves. I include in this mix the character of the psychoanalyst in the classroom.

I am gratified to know that psychoanalysis and education may travel together. Many of these chapters began with conference and workshop invitations in Toronto, Vancouver, Istanbul, Jyväskylä, Manchester, London, and Dublin. I am grateful to friends and colleagues who helped move this project along. I thank Dawn Skorczewski, Lewis Kirshner, Jane Miller, Sharon Sliwinski, Oren Gozlan, Michelle Flax, and the students I teach and learn from at York University in Toronto. I thank Lucy Angus for assistance with manuscript preparation and Dr. Beth Bouloukos of State University of New York Press for her interest in this work.

Most of all, I thank Alice Pitt.

A grant—The Emotional World of Teaching and Learning: A Psychoanalytic Inquiry—funded by the Social Science and Humanities Research Council of Canada supported this project. The views, mistakes, and limits of this study are my own. In this sense, I take seriously Freud's remark that behind the scenes, the analyst and professor's complexes and resistances will be a part of the work.

Some of the chapters were published in earlier versions and revised for this book. A shorter version of chapter 3 appeared as "What Is the Use of Theory?: A Psychoanalytic Discussion," in *Changing English: Studies in Reading and Culture* 19, 1 (2012): 43–56. An earlier version of chapter 4 appeared under the title "The Adolescent Teacher: A Psychoanalytic Note on Regression in the Helping Professions," in *Journal of Infant, Child, and Adolescent Psychotherapy* 11, 13 (2012): 272–238, and an earlier version of chapter 5, under the title "On the Madness of Lecturing on Gender: A Psychoanalytic Discussion," appeared in *Gender and Education* 6 (2010): 633–646. And a shorter version of chapter 7 appeared as "That Other Scene of Pedagogy: A Psychoanalytic Narrative," in *Changing English: Studies in Reading and Culture* 12, 2 (2014): 122–130. I thank Taylor and Francis—www.tandfonline.com—for granting permission to draw upon and expand this previously published work.

—Deborah P. Britzman
Toronto

I

A Psychoanalyst in the Classroom

Character Studies in the Human Condition of Education

> As a psychoanalyst I must take a greater interest in affective rather than intellectual processes, more in the unconscious than in the conscious life of the psyche.
>
> —Sigmund Freud, "On the Psychology of the Grammar-School Boy"

Necessities

A sixty-year-old Freud (1914b) declared his abiding interest in the unconscious a few paragraphs into his brief essay on memories of his childhood schooling, a contribution to a celebration of the fifty-year anniversary of the founding of his elementary school in Vienna.[1] He was asked to write on his influences in choosing a profession. It must have been a strange assignment since he discovered not only the impossible profession that affected him but also its theory made to question the destiny of the human's utter susceptibility to the other. Influence, for Freud, is a middle term, somewhere between unconscious impressions and the address of the transference. It would be the unknown influence that binds the urgencies of the inner world to our relations with the external one, and this affects not only the psychoanalyst but also what can be said about the vicissitudes of education. Is this the reason Freud must care more for the unknown than the known, more about the unconscious than the conscious?[2] And why for the psychoanalyst is education an exemplary frame? Freud tells us there are undercurrents that destroy the progression of time: "It gives you a queer feeling if late in life, you are ordered once again to write a school essay.... It is strange how readily you obey the orders, as though nothing in particular had happened in the last half century" (1914b, 241). How then does one grasp uncanny influence if it is both conscious and unconscious? In looking back on his childhood of education and feeling again the ripples of affective affairs as if they have never left, he remembers his intense studies of the teacher's character and cannot decide what impressed him the most: the teacher's knowledge or what the teacher was like. He admits that the roots of both desires were already entwined in earlier relations and the phantasies that arise from the family romance. His essay concludes by assigning his schoolmasters a little memory lesson: to understand your own student learning antics, return to the nursery. Only then will you too be able to ask, but what then influences the desire for an education one knows nothing about?

Learning antics are almost impossible to imagine in university life, though the oddest details of our earliest years seem to repeat in the currency of students and the professor's feelings toward teaching and learning. The indivisible influence behind the scenes—the unconscious education—that Freud pulls this reader closer to is unexpected: namely, the human's utter susceptibility to love's impressions and its loss enacted in forgotten scenes of learning and teaching. So the psychoanalyst in the classroom must care more for the elusive impressions of education, not as culmination but as ongoing dynamics composed from our human condition. It is these intimacies—of being influenced by both psychoanalysis in the clinic and a life in education—that bring me to write from the excess of their affective matters. Pathos and pleasure with the subject of learning leads to my thinking more about Freud's other understanding of influence: long after the events of childhood recede into memories and fracture in forgetting, the shudder of our earliest education persists. It has a second act in the drama and comedy of teaching and learning, and over the course of this chapter I introduce its third act: the psychoanalytic difficulties and pleasures of writing toward unconscious life in education. The work is a little like reading Luigi Pirandello's (1921) play, *Six Characters in Search of an Author*, that begins with the first line of complaint, "I can't see." The psychoanalyst receives this negation and takes away the "no."

When Freud looked back upon his affective world, he had to admit something he could not see. The present seemed to vanish and the past too was felt as a rather strange land. Freud (1914b) called childhood and youth an "extinct civilization" (241) akin to a buried archeological site containing fragments left behind in the form of side-by-side contrary feelings, termed "emotional ambivalence" (242), that we all require to detach from the childhood sense of the father and mother as omnipotent. It is at this crossroad of emotional life that Freud is sent to school to meet his teachers, who oddly resemble his emotional attitude toward his parents. Teachers appear as already complete, all knowing, and as mind readers. His study of influence as both a goodnight kiss and a wake-up call reckon with what could not be acknowledged at the time: that the play of love, hate, and ambivalence created in family life are transferred into any relation of learning. Freud names this practiced emotional logic as the rough draft of our psychology, another word for influence. So the dynamics of psychical reality and external demands meet without invitation. Their interplays are felt before known and learned before they can be understood.

For the contemporary psychoanalytic field, contentious and diverse as it is, good and bad influences come in many guises: from the other, the unconscious, the touch of communal bonds, the transference love and hate, the advent of guilt, the mysteries of the dream, the misheard words, gaps in theory, the history we have never lived but may wish for, and our vulnerability to and recoil from dependency in self/other relations. Influence, it turns out, carries on what we cannot see coming. It is a delicate matter that quickly turns on anxiety, paranoia, mania, phantasies, and the urge to act that continues to be a difficult venture for thinking about any narrative. More than a few psychoanalysts ask what inhibits their invention of psychoanalysis and how they may face the play of their unconscious education. Why, more often than can be admitted, does learning stall midsentence? At what point does the touch of the other's words feel heavy-handed? How does the desire to be original leave us in tatters? And what to make of our school assignments? When analysts today write about school memories, they consider their transference to education through new approaches to their old conflicts with dependency, helplessness, authority, knowledge, and love and hate.

"Few of us feel," write Gabbard and Ogden, "that we really know what we are doing when we complete our formal psychoanalytic training" (311). We can also add that during the learning of psychoanalysis, or learning anything for that matter, few of us feel we know what we are doing. Nor are we really clear about what we imagine our teachers or their theories are doing to us. Gabbard and Ogden suggest that learning reminds us of our immaturity, dependency, vulnerability, and precocity. And in the learning relation, phantasies of the other's knowledge involve anxiety over what the other holds back from us. It is indeed a curious dilemma. If we imagine we are only being told what to do, we feel impingement. If we are left too long in our regard, we feel abandoned. Gabbard and Ogden stay close to these affective dilemmas by exploring how the unconscious force of being educated throughout their lives affects the rules they thought they had to follow and note how difficult it is to break these rules open and live creatively with doubt. It is a brave admission to trace their many years of education with the force of their phantasies of learning and with their defenses against being affected while wondering more how the desire to be influenced collapses into fear of compliance and not measuring up. Gabbard and Ogden recall a stringent comment Wilfred Bion made to other analysts during one of his many clinical seminars:

> It is only after you have qualified [as an analyst] that you have a chance of becoming an analyst. The analyst you become is you and you alone; you have to respect the uniqueness of your personality—that is what you use, not all these interpretations [these theories that you use to combat the feeling that you are not really an analyst and do not know how to become one]. (Qtd. in Gabbard and Ogden 311, with their added comments)

So there really are complexes of qualifying problems that urge us to overuse our theories of self-doubt. And much boils down to the subjective fact that personality leans on taking personally the self's difficulties in trying to know. The analyst learns more about the self than is wanted, and some of the defenses against psychoanalysis include a range of resistances: clinging to idealizations of theory or clinical experience, getting a headache from the pounding voice of previous analysts, and falling into a phantasy of an indigestible education and an empty self.

One might consider these conflicts in learning as a crisis between affects and ideas. But they also take us to a question of time. Quinodoz and colleagues (2006) extend the becoming of an analyst to the capacity to influence the future of psychoanalysis that

> depends, to a great extent, on us psychoanalysts and our ability to transmit in a lively way both to our patients and colleagues the specific nature of the psychoanalytic experience. This demands of us a great deal of inner freedom; how are we to find the courage necessary to acquire that liberty, to hold on to it and pass it on? . . . [and] to find the audacity to be a psychoanalyst. (329–330)

It is a paradoxical demand that inner freedom be assumed before it can occur. And how to express the frustration that keeps company with that liberty? There are, after all, inexplicable times when freedom itself is destroyed by one's emotional logic and phantasies of irreparable loss. And yet, these analysts write from their everyday audacity as notice to the future of inner freedom. Only by accompanying their difficulties can they create a new relation: "the fact of freedom of expression goes hand in hand with the ability to listen attentively to what others have to say" (330). Much depends upon the liberty of listening for what is not said but nonetheless conveyed. Jurgen Reeder (2008) places this future of conflicts into the presence of our political scene: "The fate of psychoanalysis is inextricably bound up with the future development of democracy" (121). That fragile freedom makes way for the right to a symbolic and the fate of democracy too must call upon the audacity of free association.

Now these demands for the capacity to be a self, for a subjective position in the work, for an interest transmitting all that work, and for the audacity of freedom of expression as tied to the other's care, are not so far away from Freud's essay on the difficulty of remembering his schoolboy psychology and our inquiry into the stirrings of depth education. Inside each view one can find the insistence on the situation of the human condition, susceptible as it is to what is most incomplete and difficult for us to know. And what insists is our vulnerability, often experienced as depression, anxiety, inhibition, and fear of emotional life. In university education symptoms of affect go unremarked, and what is unspeakable is brushed under the vagaries of mental health without wondering why. More than a few professors feel helpless. Some may believe that by the time one comes to the university, all of the problems of emotional life should have been solved, and they turn away from pressing intimacies of learning with the defense that only their knowledge is important or, when their knowledge fails, complain that no one prepared them to be in contact with the difficulties of teaching and learning. Still others believe that education is impersonal. Few would consider these plaints as well-schooled emotional attitudes and as symptoms of our educational malady, flowering as crisis between affective relations and intellectual engagement in university life.

Freud's statement that opens this chapter gives us a clue as to one dimension of the difficulties we in university education face. His insistence may be understood as anticipating an intellectual and affective crisis that tears the soft tissue of both psychoanalysis and education. It concerns questioning what people learn about the life of the mind as human condition by asking how the genesis of learning may be apprehended, and then, whether any theory of learning can make something more from the dissipations of unconscious life and its relation to lost love, memory, desire, and phantasies of authority. Accepting a greater interest in affective processes challenges our understanding of the social bond, what we believe happens in the exchange of knowledge, and what must be disillusioned to meet the other. It brought Freud to an affectionate theory of learning. In his "autobiographical" study of his work, Freud (1925c) noted what changed for him:

> Even the most brilliant results were liable to be suddenly wiped away if my personal relation with the patient became disturbed. It was true that they would be re-established if a reconciliation

could be effected; but such an occurrence proved that the personal emotional relation between doctor and patient was after all stronger than the whole cathartic process, and it was precisely that factor which escaped every effort at control. (27)

Freud's choice for a greater interest in the destiny of his psychical life however begins with a narcissistic blow: lovely knowledge is "suddenly wiped away" with the other's reply. And it is the challenge of creating a new relation with the other that escapes controlling knowledge.

Throughout this chapter I use Freud's greater interest in the unconscious and the conflicts entailed in encountering the emotional world of self and other to introduce the emergence of education as human condition and to ask why matters of teaching and learning rely on the fragilities of a social bond, largely conveyed in the transference. As both a psychoanalyst and university professor, I wonder what else occurs behind the curtain of any education and why, when working with others, a change of heart becomes our greatest challenge. The graduate and undergraduate students and the professors I meet are curious about this combination of professions, though at first many worry what I will do to them, only asking how they feel and ignoring what they know and want to know. These sticky anxieties are not such a far cry from what I felt during my many years of learning in a psychoanalytic institute. There is no easy technique for taking our teaching and learning personally. Nor is there an easy method for transmitting to the other how it is that our work is taken personally. Also difficult to convey is my interest in psychoanalyzing phantasies of education—the fate of the ideas we love and hate, the presuppositions unconsciously exchanged in knowledge, authority, and our transferences—that do go on to affect our reading and writing lives and our sense of self with others. Freely associating with these interests does, however, invite phantasies of education onto the couch.

I must wonder how the mix-up of a history of ideas and personal events made from trying to learn affects me. I must be curious about my role in pedagogical catastrophes and ask what else is being communicated when relationships to students feel significant or insignificant. As a psychoanalyst in the classroom, my associations to teaching and learning occur during times when anxiety irrupts in the other's unexpected reply, with accidents of desire, and with the wish to write of education psychoanalytically. While clinical and pedagogical work may not be equated, each may be taken personally. Both activities depend upon getting to know the emotional situation of trying to narrate the human condition. And characters enter and exist in these rooms. The psychoanalytic field provides me with some vocabulary to sensitize the feel of contact; words such as libido, phantasy, transference, countertransference, and desire and neurosis, open the ritualized meanings of my psychological events to new beginnings. And the archives of clinical case studies that document this work serve as my model for writing. Here too conflicts emerge between affective and intellectual yearnings that play as emotional ambivalence toward affective life in university learning and teaching and that seems reparable in writing from this emotional life.

Let us concede that in presentation, logic, style, and reach the unconscious is difficult to know. It is one of those thorny terms André Green (2005a) names as "an epistemological break" (97). Psychoanalysts still lean upon Freud's dynamic definition for the unconscious: that *it* comes without the cover of intentions; follows the emotional logic of the wish and the pleasure principal; welcomes contradictions; works through equation, substitution, and displacement; and is timeless. There are also the procedures of condensation, where objects lose their boundaries and displacement creates new signs (Türcke 2013). Even if the unconscious is in agreement with itself, it takes the other to do its work. The unconscious, then, is not a possession but a relation to both intrapsychic affairs and the currency of intersubjective ties. When we are requested to say what is furthest from the mind or asked to name what we would never think, a fight is sure to follow or rather an improbable conflict occurs for the psyche between memory and forgetting, reality and phantasy, self and other, and between the work of lifting forgotten meaning and repressing intolerable thoughts.

Keep in mind that when questioning the density of well-worn and tattered desires, a greater investment in the unconscious does not abolish consciousness. Conscious life, after all, is an instance of the psychical, ostensibly closest to the world of others near and far, yet also partly unconscious. The psychoanalyst's obligation is to accompany these passions for knowledge and ignorance wherever they lead. "As a psychoanalyst, I must . . . ," writes Freud (1914b, 355). And his patients demanded this of him. For words to give birth to a new narrative, Freud must change his affections, tact, and style of communication. He must learn to wait. It is no longer a matter of deciding what is wrong with someone else and telling the person how to fix it. "The procedure," writes Freud, "is laborious and time-consuming. It presupposes great interest in psychological happenings, but personal concern for the patients as well" (Freud and Breuer 1893–1895, 265). We have as well a good enough description of education.

The writing also takes time and, as "psychological happening," the writer must care for words and their deferrals. Freud (Freud and Breuer 1893–1895) admitted as much quite early in his studies in hysteria. These case studies read like short stories, or unfinished dreams. They have the feel of a poetical undertaking. Something happens to language, and, indeed, throughout his opus readers join a lively parade of unforgettable characters. They transform his theory and his mode of practice and have their say. Yet as figures of writing, the characters are not immune from the writer's conflicts. Sometimes they turn up in Freud's dreams, only to appear as composite characters on improbable missions and serve as emissaries of garbled words. Colleagues too appear and disappear. There are friends and enemies, patients and collaborators, family members and lost loves. Some are banished in a few sentences, while others, even when erased, hover in the margins of his ideas. The case is never closed.

With hysteria come the characters called Fräulein Anna O., Frau Emmy Von N., Miss Lucy R., and Fräulein Elisabeth Von R. The phobias, the obsessions, infantile sexuality, and the psychosis follow from the *I must* of Little Hans, Dora, the Rat Man, the Wolf Man, Schreber, the nameless female homosexual, and Professor Freud. Concepts as well have character: his majesty the baby, the royal family, the crumpled giraffe, and the hat, for instance. And all of them stand in for something else. There are also casts of characters borrowed from creative writers, poets, artists, theater, ancient myths, and more than once, the biblical figure of Moses. In an early defense of the necessities of taking a literary approach as his model for writing, Freud (Freud and Breuer 1893–1895) wrote:

> *I must* console myself with the reflection that the nature of the subject is evidently responsible for this, rather than any preference of my own . . . [but] to obtain at least some kind of insight into the course of that affection . . . namely an intimate connection between the story of the patient's sufferings and the symptoms of his illness. (160–161; italics added)

Yes, Freud had to disguise the actual identities of his patients, though even if today many of their names are known, their destiny, now as archive figures, holds more in store. But it is not much of a question to ask who each patient really is. No one can answer to that and besides, each character stands in for someone else and there are too many of him or her. Each treatment is unique and unrepeatable, while much is lost in the ether of exchanging words. The clinical reports themselves become character studies of "psychological happenings"—accounts of where frustration erupts, the method fails, the patient walks out, and an impasse is noticed too late. And the case studies may offer a sense of the dimensions of reparation made when people are understood as more than their symptoms or walking instances of a theory. The more interested question is why our cast of characters must rummage through their personal effects, why we worry about what has gone missing, and how, in speaking to another, we too transfer memories from the inside to the story yet to be told.

In combing over Freud's close and missed encounters, many commentators have noted that in order to touch readers, patients, analysts, students, professors, and the general public, Freud had to take the side of affect and go beyond the limits of personal preference and that, "nature of the subject is responsible for this" (Freud and Breuer 1893–1895, 161). To write of psychoanalysis is to write psychoanalytically.[3] How else may we explain the desire to write against all odds? Character studies, along with the speculative theories that pressure and release their hold, invite the writer's own character to emerge from the work and thus create a means to grasp the transference and call upon it. Even with Freud's notion of "some kind of insight into the course of that affection" (Freud and Breuer 1893–1895, 160), one may only find the fault lines and latency of intimate knowledge. The influence is too unwieldy to posit a final cause. And so if we readers are to give our attention over to these affective affairs and learn from their affiliations and afflictions, we too must take interest in the unconscious overturning of meaning.

Over the course of this book the overturning of meaning takes many forms: the ego's resistance, the splitting of intellect and affect, the anxieties and phantasies that lean on and agonize the self's defenses against being affected, and the writer's efforts to express what has happened. These revolts bring me to relate our emotional logic in learning to the guts of the human condition of education. Learning with others is, after all, as much a process of digestion as it is vulnerable to regurgitation. And regurgitation, a consequence of feeling force-fed, is one of the central anxieties reported by students in the university. Inside these anxieties one can find what holds the story back. The metaphor of digestion is beholden to Bion (1993), who likened the mind to the stomach and thought that knowledge could then only signify getting to know or tolerate the taste of emotional experience by linking one's thoughts to the apparatus of thinking.[4] In reconsidering one of his early essays, "On Arrogance," Bion tried again to relate curiosity, stupidity, and arrogance, not from the words of the patient but from the valance of the Oedipal myth. The problem years later was that Oedipus felt as disastrous the ethic of curiosity. He really did not want to know what others thought and in arrogance felt others were liars and stupid. In the clinical setting Bion came to think that arrogance, stupidity, and curiosity are not easily linked, though they are conflated (161) and present as disqualified mental pain when pride and self-respect are equated and when the patient throws out these words as if they are meaningless, or only have to do with others. Bion may be one of the first psychoanalysts to create a method for introducing discontentment into communicating the psychoanalytic experience. The textual descriptions, he maintained, are always more stable than what the work feels like, and, properly speaking, the case study is not to be used as a security blanket against one's own defense mechanisms. Training to be an analyst, Bion thought, may be the psychoanalyst's greatest defense against the emotional world.⁵ May we say the same about the preparation for teaching?

Three years after writing his schoolboy psychology, Freud (1917) continues to ponder the heart of memory as both the elemental tie to the other and, more surprisingly, as bound up in the forgetting and resistance that form "a difficulty in the path of psychoanalysis" (137). If separation is so difficult for the subject, so too is our other necessity for passionate bonds to others. The queer feelings and estrangements walk hand in hand, and Freud will go so far as to note that the difficulty is between affect and ideation. So while the ideas of psychoanalysis may be intellectually accepted, he thought this must be a way of fobbing off the difficulty that is "an affective one—something that alienates the feelings of those who come into contact with it" (137). All this resistance to resistance will return in one of his (1940) last unfinished essays, written in exile, "Some Elementary Lessons in Psycho-Analysis":

> It is not merely that much of what it has to say offends people's feelings. Almost as much difficulty is created by the fact that our science involves a number of hypotheses—it is hard to say whether they should be regarded as postulates or as products of our research—which are bound to seem very strange to ordinary modes of thought and which fundamentally contradict current views. But there is no help for it. (282)

A century later Kristeva (1998) will ask why apprehending psychical life causes such a disturbance. Is the trouble with trying to understand the mind or does the threat belong to the question of what kind of relation is at stake when disquieting imagination meets with the psyche's vulnerability and suffering? For the Lacanian Bruce Fink (2014) understanding is the problem. After all, we may know the cause of our sufferings, but that bit of knowledge may only bring us to our knees. Psychical change is of a different order, far slower, easily reversed, and subject to what we do not know. "The desire to know that a new patient comes to analysis with," Fink observes, "is not yet, in effect, a will to discover where his own satisfactions come from, but rather a will to be provided with and a willingness to be satisfied with already formulated knowledge" (82). How close this feels to our first encounters with students or our own encounter with analysts and teachers. We want and don't want them to tell us what they know. The analyst, however, only has questions and wants more speech. Kristeva

(2000) takes the difficulty from the side of desire and as a matter of revolt: "psychoanalysis ultimately communicates this: happiness exists only at the price of a revolt. None of us has pleasure without confronting an obstacle, prohibition, authority, or law that allows us to realize ourselves as autonomous and free" (7).

Kristeva (1998) considers "choice" as a question of "freedom of psychical representation" (6) animated through "the fact that human desire is realized in psychoanalysis from within the relational bond" (10). The bonds are many: with actual people, with phantasies, with thought and sexuality, with object relations, with natality, with beautiful apprehensions, and with a history that gives birth to my own, provided that I symbolize the drives, affect, and the other. Her formulation on these ties is elaborate: "Let us say it without false modesty: no other modern experience, apart from psychoanalysis, offers such a prospect for recommencing psychic life, and thus, in a sense, life as such—in the opening up of choices that secures the manifold capacity for relationships (liens)" (12).

But we should also ask, can education too recommence psychical life? With our acknowledgment of libidinal bonds and their restraints, we are back to the human condition of education. There, the professor too has a share in the conflicts that belong to recommending psychic life and choosing what matters the most: the student's attraction to my intellectual ideas, or her or his cathexis to characters in search of learning. Reminiscent of Freud's memory dilemmas, the professor may wonder: Is something more required for me to be given over to an interest in remembering subterranean, buried matters? Might wishes for the smooth surface of intellectual exchange be just as easily understood as a defense against getting to know the enfoldments of the learning bond? Freud's obligation to the unconscious and Kristeva's formulation of choice and freedom are both the psychoanalyst and professor's challenge: follow the unconscious, permit the freedom of association, and become affected by transference life. Taking these liberties and reading between the lines of presence and absence is our first approach to meeting the characters that make up education as our human condition.

Intimacies

For the psychoanalyst in the classroom fleeting impressions, accidents, and mishearing contain the material that breaks open the cover of a story. Within the intimacies of experience in education, where the flurry of sad and happy associations weigh in as eventuality; where our sense of time, place, situation, and others scatter through the sieve of desire; where the unconscious dream work of condensation, substitution, displacement, and reversal into its opposite permit phantasy and reality to intermingle; and there, where our susceptibility to the dust of unknown and forgotten events slips into our moods and perceptions, the stray thought whisks away our intentions. The rough drafts of learning are being written, erased, and revised. We are involved in the intensities of the human condition and efforts to picture its object world of mental representations, much of them unconscious.

A psychoanalyst in the classroom greets these catches of psychical life and the vagaries of learning with more questions. In listening to the gap between words, the unmeant reply, the sexual innuendo, off-the-cuff remarks, and inscrutable questions; in watching the raised eyebrows and sudden frowns; in being rattled by the student hiding behind the computer, or, the one madly texting as if communication only happens beyond the seminar; in noticing the intake of breath and the deflated sigh; and, in noticing a great deal is happening but not yet known, a psychoanalyst in the classroom learns to wait. Communication does not give itself easily, and contact comes when least expected. By asking what else is being conveyed when we teach and learn and by becoming curious about what the student or teacher wants, the question occurs to this psychoanalyst, what passes off as education? How does it come to be that the force of education appears through the figure of a subject-supposed-to-know? And might this subject be inseparable from the anticipations, wishes, ideas, phantasies, and beliefs held for education?

At first, when people speak of what education has missed, one may listen for the symptoms of broken stories of learning, through secret plots and lost time. Many narratives of education carry the convictions of paranoia, anxiety, and depression, and one wonders what happened before the story of abandonment could be told. There are stories of a missed future beyond the subject's reach. Setbacks serve as a terrible reminder that nothing can happen. They come in the form of writing inhibitions and guilty worries one will accidentally plagiarize or be accused of doing so. They come when learning is assumed to be an unchanging possession or a thing held back by someone else. They come with the wish for certainty when choosing a profession, or they carry on the anxiety that one mistake or one bad grade will follow the subject into perpetuity. In these broken stories one has the feeling that an injustice is being written as in Nathaniel Hawthorne's *The Scarlet Letter*, a novel of social ruins, signs of unaccountable cruelty, and moral anxiety over the nature of love. With the phantasy of the eternal grade comes the closed off thought that nothing can ever change and that all of the treasures or jobs have already been taken. In the broken-off stories of education there are only winners and losers.

In imagining the adolescent syndrome of ideality, Kristeva (2009) is interested in how "the incredible need to believe" leads to the wish for perfection, the absolute, or paradise, an area of suffering from ideals: "Thus impelled, the *narcissism* of the ego, tied to its *ideals*, overflows into the ardently sought love object, making room for the *amorous passion* that, with the partner, idealizes the drives and their satisfactions" (15). Yes, behind these ravages of the self and disparagement of the failed other awaits a story of love, but the story is counterintuitive and battered about by resistance to the emotional situation of education, or what I am calling education as our human condition. Teachers and professors are not immune from the transference since their Eros and the drive to know force learning into places never meant to be education; their adolescent syndrome may take the form of splitting their students into good or bad, critical or stupid, and successful or failed. The ego's splitting of the outside world has a comparable internal process—that something is happening within the speaker when the world is torn into bits and pieces—and it is the professor or teacher that bears witness to a broken pedagogy. For the psychoanalyst, the dilemma is idealization of the object or the magical bestowal of impossible goodness that is then followed by a terrible fear of its loss. The adolescent, Kristeva maintains, is a believer in paradise and has given up her or his interest in research questions. And in Kristeva's view, the bare elements of ideals are also our liens.

Characters

We have already met a number of characters, and their study is the mainstay of contemporary psychoanalysis, literature, and clinical constructions and, in this book, a means to access, hold, handle, and use the human condition of education. But characters are elusive beings due to the fact that they are composite figures of objects in mind and because of their complexity allude to a world of others and the predicaments of knowing one's place. Joyce McDougall (1986) understands the theater of the mind as their stage and scenario: "We do not escape the roles that our unconscious selves intend us to play, frequently using people in our lives today as stand-ins to settle problems of the past" (7). Young-Bruehl (1991) turned to character studies after writing her biographies of Hannah Arendt and Anna Freud. She called this work creative characters, with a focus on individuals' processes and crisis in creativity, and her study provided a style for thinking about learning that can be announced, argued over, and enjoy further transformation. Kristeva's (1995) characters are emblems for "new maladies of the soul." Mothers, fathers, children, lost loves, writers and artists, and even the adolescent novel are agonized by the failure of modern existence, the diminishment of private life, displacement or exile, and perhaps in terms of the symptoms now dominating university life, such internal characters challenge our understanding of attention, attachment, depression, and inexplicable anxieties over appearance and disappearance that play out in technologies of virtual reality and the obsessionality for answers, updates, news crawl, replays, and self-advertisement.

Another way into the idea of character can be found in Christopher Bollas's (1992) discussion of "idiom" where desire for taking in objects in the world creates an intermediate space for inner play with self-expression. A great deal goes with psychical reality, and Bollas then asks, "However are we to describe the character of the internal world given its dense complexity?" (52). As for how density is transferred into learning, the character stumbles on one of the many paradoxes of education: industrial arrangements of education seem to settle for the generalizability of instruction, transmission, and progress, while the character's vulnerability remains particular and subject to accidents and what is not known. But it is with the transitional space of teaching and learning that the character's predicaments emerge. To write one's way into the abstract qualities of this other education requires picturing character through its evocative textures and as a rough draft that can somehow convey its own erasures. Such an approach opposes character education as found in curriculum efforts, national pressures, and a history of moral anxieties over the subject's formation. Peter Brooks's (2011) exploration of literature argues that character is a slippery notion that does and should defy attempts at systematicity. Still, he maintains that character does have to do with self-knowledge and the problem of identity. But something has to fail for identity to be an occupation.

Antonino Ferro (2011) writes extensively on his method of character study from the vantage of how he listens to "narrative derivatives" (71): urgent emotions involving the stories told and a quality of the patient and the setting often form character scenarios that remind him of novels. And this affects Ferro's impressionistic writing style: "I have always considered the writing of psychoanalysis (and the experience of being inside an analytic session) very similar to the activity of a painter, someone intent on making verbal pictures that undergo constant change, construction and deconstruction both in colours and forms" (94). For Ferro, characters populate the psychoanalytic field and are to be played with. He goes even further: "The way I listen to the presentation of a case history is to treat the story of the case as if it were preceded by the expression, 'I had a dream about this patient'" (122). It is his way into both the enigmas of communicating one's work and treating the case study as a story from its vanishing point.

And yet the idea of character has a stormy history in psychoanalysis[6] beginning with Freud's turn to the enigmatic characters that overpopulate dreams and then to their reduction into a trait such as "the anal character" that Freud (1916) proposed in his early essay "Some Character-Types Met with in Psycho-Analytic Work." We readily use the image of analretentiveness to describe those who hoard and those who obsessively insist on the maintenance of strict order. But we hardly ask why. Freud named three types that emerge from their particular situations: the exceptions, the guilty ones, and those "wrecked by success" (316). The latter type brought Freud to speculate on the frustrations of libido and, more surprisingly, with what can happen when one gets one's wish. Any of these serve as masks of unconscious conflict. The exceptional character will feel that she or he has somehow escaped the unconscious, the guilty character will have never committed an actual crime, and those wrecked by success will somehow be plagued by the wish to lose. More characters would be created; perhaps the most enduring is the character of the comic arriving in time for the last laugh. For the psychoanalyst, character is as much a composite figure as it is a resistance to or compensation for its own incomplete structure. All these "types" manage to surprise and Freud turns to a "long digression into literature" (331) to sketch the splits that conceal the character's "multiple motivations" (329).

As used throughout this book, the notion of "character study" draws from both the vocabulary of literary representation that pictures the emergence, shape, style, and contours of the subject's predicaments from the side of its phantasies and psychoanalytic discussions of object relation theory that picture the internal world as composed from impressions of love and hate associated with actual and unreal others in mind. From the disappearing vantage point of object relation theory, the boundaries between self and other and inside and outside are porous but also soft to the touch and so impressive by design. It is with the literary imagination, as Brooks (2011) so compellingly suggests, that one ponders "the original meaning of character as that which is engraved" (105) and has a tendency to fade with time and use.

Henry James's ([1897] 1987) preface to his novel of human predicament, *The Spoils of Poynton*, describes the invention of the author as following "little processions" of characters: "A character is interesting as it comes out, and by the process and duration of that emergence, just as a procession is effective by the way it unrolls, turning to a mere mob if all of it passes at once" (30). Just as well, *if* the idea of education is to become more than a clamorous mob of pushy needs and heavy-handed responses, an effort of writing within the delicacies of education can present symptoms of learning through their emergence. James's preface is instructive for our character studies in another sense. In ruminating over what pushes him into the desire to write a story, James tells his readers that he waits for a "germ . . . dropped unwitting by my neighbor, a mere floating particle in the stream of talk" (23). There is the matter of overhearing in order to auscultate the story's heart.

Germs of Learning

I follow James's literary advice and wait for what is dropped. Here are some examples, many of which are developed throughout this book. For now, consider their skeletal rattles:

Student "A" hands me a paper with narrow margins, long paragraphs, and sentences that lose their object and undo meaning. The ideas are precocious, thorny, and wise. They are defended yet insightful. Wild romps through poetic images overrun the ideas of others. And in reading this paper, I feel as if I am losing my place, just as her thoughts vie for a place. It is as if she is worried about getting a word in edgewise, that if her words do not cover all the space, someone else will steal them from her. And no room is left for my comments.

Student "B" complains he cannot do independent work just as he asked to have an independent study. He knows independent work is one hallmark of writing a dissertation. And he wanted to do things for himself and prove his worth. But each time he sits down to read, he finds something else to do. He is disappointed but worries he has disappointed me. He wants to be independent but worries whether he can sustain his desire. He wishes to meet more often with me but cannot say why. Sitting in my office, he will close the door and begin crying. He holds in his hands a key chain that he clips and unclips with each complaint. It is as if he is saying that his ideas unclasp even as he tries to fit them together. But it is the clicking sound—his swift doing and undoing of the key clasp—that mesmerizes me. I have the feeling I am caught listening to an urgent telegraph that neither of us can decode.

Then there is group life. An extremely organized, high-achieving group of women students design an unbearable presentation for the class that begins with what they hope will be an exciting warm-up exercise. They change the furniture in the room, put on atmospheric music, and ask each member of the class to go the chalkboard and draw a picture of what they feel. More confusion emerges as each student is given a meager prize. Finally, the group leaders ask the class to discuss the shared text we have all read, titled *Memory*, by Philippe Grimbert (2007). But the class is silent and the leaders become deflated and disillusioned. Their posture goes missing. They were only trying to illustrate transference but forgot they too would be affected. Two hours after the class has ended I receive an email from one member:

Hi Guys

So . . . I "forgot" my copy of memory at the front of the room today I think, along with some brightly coloured chalk that my kids are looking for . . .

I guess if I look at the sequence of events leading up to the time I forgot my book I would have to say that

one not-so-great presentation + one character sketch
given back = leaving behind the object I need
for my final paper . . .

if I were to take an psychoanalytical approach to this I would have to say that I needed something to "blame" the mark of my final exam on. I guess what I am trying to say is . . . if I don't have the book I need to write my paper, then it can't be my fault if I don't do well . . . how could I do well if I forgot my book at school? It's not my fault . . . etc . . . etc . . .

In any case, do you have it? If you do, can I come back to school and get it? If not, if anyone turns it in can someone let me know?

Thanks guys

Conditions

A psychoanalytic approach to character studies of the human condition then begins with a few subjective or psychological facts that entwine character with its study: the human is the only creature that needs education and this need transforms into desire; that as self-theorizing subjects we grow up in school and family life during our most impressible and vulnerable years; that emotional logic, or transference, made from love, hate, and ambivalence plays out in what becomes of our relation to knowledge and the other; and, the work of symbolizing education as our human condition involves interpretation of its aftereffects. I call these processes subjective or psychological facts because, while we do not know their destiny, we can learn more from their duration and emergence in present values and attitudes toward language, others, and knowledge. With psychoanalytic sensibility we can ask, what is disquieting imagination for and how do we come to anticipate asymmetry, tolerate frustration, and accept difference, separation, and incompleteness in learning and life?

The large problem for any education is that the world is subjectively felt before anything else can be known. I consider this transitional space between subject and object as an opening to thoughts on the human condition through a revision of Hannah Arendt's (1958) expansive claim that we are always in the human condition because whatever the human meets becomes its condition for existence (9). While Arendt was more interested in conscious life and the activities of world reality, and while she took great care in setting aside human nature, psychoanalysts would understand as the fact of psychological life the condition of being affected. With psychoanalysis we must add the additional factor of emotional experiences of being with others as affected by phantasies of what the other knows, by a tendency to idealize knowledge through the transference, and by defenses against symbolizing emotional pain.

Psychoanalytic theory has its beginnings in the question of our human condition. Its vocabulary is a place of departure and return, handling words as sometimes a shortcut and, at other times, as a means to symbolize the short circuits of thought. Kristeva (1995) maintains that one of the difficulties of depression is that questions suffer from meaninglessness and leave in their wake a persecutory "why" that leads to nothing. "Even if the patient sees the analyst as a 'subject-presumed-to know," writes Kristeva, "analysts know that they are nothing more than questioning and questioned subjects" (89). And in trying to sketch the emotional logic that carries the analyst to wait, Kristeva brings the question into desire:

> I want you to tell me.... Though analytic interpretation adopts neither the melodic patterns nor the syntactic features of a question, it *adopts the psychological profile of a question*. I think I know something, but I give up and allow you to speak. You are the one who must know, speak, lie, and think. (88–89)

The ethics of therapeutic action may only emerge from putting to words a subjective dilemma ("a psychological profile of a question"), which can bear the weight and anxiety of asymmetrical relations, dependency, and uneven development.

Clinical Characters: "The Dictator and the Scribe"

The human is always subject to the uncertainties of bios, logos, eros, ethos, ethnos, and to the ambiguity of having to interpret reality through the affected psychical body, composed and compromised by the urgency of becoming a subject with and for others. These are the grand intersubjective themes of clinical writing, dedicated to interpreting the latency of communication: what has been held back, forgotten, acted out, displaced, and unconsciously repeated. At the heart of the case study is the literary dilemma of putting to words the transference, thought here as the unconscious desire for the other's knowledge, authority, and love.

Joyce McDougall's (McDougall and Lebovici 1969) rich account of a child's analysis is unusual in the history of clinical writing in two regards. Much of it is written by the patient's demand for the analyst to write everything he says in her notebook, and the analyst's character is made into a scribe. It can be read as a commentary on education and dependency that emerges from the clash of words that peppers the social bond with an unconscious history of love, hate, and ambivalence. We find here our vulnerability to language and the other through an interest in the convolutions of psychical life and its affects: anxiety, splitting into good and bad, compliance, resistance, attacks on linking, and ideality. Yet from haphazard events made to fend off profound emotional pain, with the other there can emerge the containment of thinking and a renewed curiosity toward the ongoing work of creating emotional significance (e.g., Bion 1994; Britzman 2011; Joseph 2000; Kristeva 2010a, 2007).

Let's meet the characters. Sammy Y. was nine and a half years old when his parents moved from the United States to Paris and brought him to Joyce McDougall, a child analyst. McDougall's account is already a circus of language (McDougall and Lebovici 1969). The analysis was conducted in English, originally written in French, and later translated into English. It is the first published narrative of a child analysis.[7] The frame follows their eight-month work through 166 sessions, five days a week. Letters between Sammy and McDougall are exchanged during vacations. The analysis came to a sudden end when Sammy's parents sent him back to the United States to attend a residential school that specialized in the treatment of schizophrenia, a difficult diagnosis subject to a history of psychiatric debate and, for those suffering in its terrors, heartbreak (Leader 2011).

Sammy set the singular conditions for both the analysis and the book that would follow. He said, "Now write what I dictate, I am your dictator!" (1). McDougall was ordered to be the silent scribe, the ignorant analyst. And in the beginning Sammy dictated his bizarre world and McDougall was only allowed to read his exact words back to him. It was not until the seventy-eighth session that Sammy began to write alongside of McDougall. Before that McDougall accepted the position of the ignorant scribe and accompanied Sammy into a world of imprisoned words.

By the fourth session, McDougall writes a note to herself: "He gives the impression of being under the sway of a terrifying fantasy whose intensity disturbs his capacity to communicate" (24). In the fifth session, after Sammy dictates a violent story of a magic face that can do anything it wants, McDougall writes: "At times he is using words as objects rather than as a means for communication" (31). She also realizes that she, the analyst, is the magic face and must hold in her writing all of his bad feelings. Sammy, she believes, has given up on the external word. In the tenth session, McDougall gives an interpretation: "Sammy, I think you are telling me that you have many troubled thoughts in which everything is sad or breaking up and you are afraid I can't do a thing to help you" (39). His reply is to scream out numbers, list more chapters in his story, and order her to shut up.

The sessions are harrowing to read. Sammy refuses McDougall's thoughts and complains he is bored. He demands more toys. He screams when she makes the slightest movements and continually demands matches to light. He throws water at her and kicks over the furniture. Sometimes he strikes her. McDougall only asks Sammy to use words. But there is no meeting between Sammy's preoccupation with his body and the words he hurtles. His elaborate narratives are full of sexual violence, murder, and angry shit. Eating is the same as being murdered. Many of his stories end with desperate threats. Often when the session is over Sammy refuses to leave. McDougall has to carry him out. In the first five weeks of analysis, he bites her, blows on her cheeks, demands that she only take down his words, tries to see her breasts, and wishes her to be naked. By the twenty-fourth session, McDougall reflects on her helplessness and Sammy's mounting aggression. She changes her approach, brings into the room the toys Sammy has asked for, and takes his lead. In the next session Sammy destroys all of the new toys.

By the thirty-fifth session, Sammy wishes "Dougie" to read his story back to him yet warns her, "Don't read it as though you are in love with your husband!" (76). He becomes preoccupied with her other patients and wishes to be the only one. But he also begins to ask her to read her thoughts about his story and tell him what he is thinking. This is a delicate task; often his sessions are filled with a torrent of words that seem to destroy themselves. Months later, McDougall will give a name to such talk: this is Sammy's special language. In session 63, McDougall begins to think with Sammy's wish to contain meaning and his hopes that her pen will not fail.

Slowly hints of dialogue emerge. In session 106 Sammy tells Dougie that everything is terribly sad, even the buildings are giving him frowns. McDougall says, "Perhaps there are bits of your own feeling that you've put on to the buildings and things outside you." Sammy replies, "This worries me. Do other people have these ideas too? It's bad, isn't it?" And McDougall says, "You seem to think that to have feelings is bad." "Yes, I do. Is it all right to feel things? Does it happen to other people?" (178). McDougall writes in summary: "I tell him there are many ways of imagining things; that many people do it, and we call it 'day-dreaming' because we realize that these things are not true. Sammy is most interested and happy to hear this" (179).

A few sessions later Sammy asks McDougall why he talks in a funny way. McDougall responds: "Yes, sometimes you use a sort of 'special talking.' Can you tell me more about it yourself?" (183). It is not until session 112 that McDougall tells Sammy when he is involved in his "special talking" and that this talk has replaced the work of fantasy and play. Along with the special talking, McDougall gives other names to Sammy's speech. There are "thinking troubles" and "dream-feelings," and shorthand for times when he feels far away from the world.

The analysis has ups and downs and both are needed. Most steady is McDougall's capacity to be with Sammy. She learns from him how to share his sense of his inner world. She also records her own difficulties in controlling herself during Sammy's tantrums, insults, and hitting. Most notable is that McDougall is able to place her practice at stake in order to create a relationship founded on the transference to his words.

Near the end of their work, Sammy asks if one only has troubles to bring to the analyst. They are listening to Sammy's choice of a recording of the Brandenburg Concerto.

> J.M.—Everything that you talk about is interesting in analysis. It doesn't have to be a trouble. Today you have told me your ideas about all kinds of things as you thought you felt like having a friendly talk rather than being a patient with 'troubles,' and perhaps also it's a way of proving that you can be like this with me without feeling that you're in any danger.
>
> S.—Maybe I wanted to have music today so as not to be a patient! . . . I think the music helped me to talk. (222–223)

The calmness of the session is unusual, and in the last sessions before Sammy leaves, more terrors ensue and McDougall is in doubt about offering any interpretations, as Sammy may need to speak of these terrors in order to manage his sense of loss in a galaxy of warring words. McDougall is left wondering how people who have no troubles at all can ever meet Sammy's troubling thoughts.

Yet at times, Sammy begins to realize the difference between his terrors and the world and that he may need these terrors to even notice the world. He wants to know, does anyone else feel as he does? Only then may horrible thoughts lose their omnipotent insistence. Their last session is filled with sadness and comes to an abrupt end with McDougall acknowledging to Sammy that he feels abandoned by her. It is an extraordinary goodbye, and the next day Sammy left Paris for his new school.

A Path to Free Association?

Kristeva (2000) has proposed psychoanalysis as a treatment of thought and words, a needed exchange for the right to the symbolic that links our constitutive dependency with others to the fragilities of meaning. That there is the asymmetrical relation between suffering and significance, she insists, qualifies psychical life and its creative desire that there be meaning to suffering's war on words. In Kristeva's (2000) view:

> "There is meaning": this will be my universal. And "I" use words of the tribe to inscribe my singularity. Je est un autre ("I is another"): this will be my difference, and "I" will express my specificity by distorting the nevertheless necessary clichés of the codes of communication and by constantly deconstructing ideas/ concepts/ideologies/ philosophies that "I" has inherited. . . .
>
> Other eras have had this experience. Its radicalness, however, is unique in our century, one of education and information. (19)

Can we now say, amid the ideality of education and information, and despite the war against the freedom of the mind, there is another scene to respond to, another affecting question that communicates what is most fragile and sad about the disparities of inheritance? Can we give words to situations when the social bond signifies a psychic collapse, abandonment of the subject, and a war on language? And, can we represent broken bonds for our repair?

In writing about why we write, read, teach, and learn from our deep dilemmas, sufferings, and pleasures with both psychoanalysis and education, there remains the open question of how we come to symbolize being with others and whether we can see something new in the false start, in the ways the self repeats its conflicts, in the mistakes we make and disclaim, and in affects unleashed and contained. For the Freudian, the influence is unconscious. The Lacanian will stress the subject's odd relation between desire and lack. The Kleinian will stay close to phantasies of the inner world of object relations and the anxieties made from trying to know what cannot be seen, while the Winnicottian will stress environmental provisions as the "good enough" response that accompanies the freedom dedicated to the use of the object. As for falling between these lines of thought and clinical practice, the psychoanalyst in the classroom will borrow only bits and pieces from these perspectives and question why one view seems more useful than another. I take seriously the advice of Darian Leader (2000) made from his discussion on the choice of questions for psychoanalysis: "Whatever research you do, something is pushing (or preventing) you from doing it" (2).

In this opening chapter, I have suggested that what pushes or drives each of us is an unconscious education that has a hand in our writing upon knowledge, our choice and stumbles with words, our signature conflicts of love and hate, and our phantasies that play in the field of teaching and learning. If these are the bare elements of education as our human condition and, as I hope to show, affect how we get to know the ways we read, write, listen, and speak, then what is most elemental is the reception of the other. Winnicott's ([1952] 1992) explicit message to psychoanalysts and parents comes to mind: *"There is no such thing as a baby"* (99). And, "The center of gravity of the being does not start off with the individual" (99). So it is with the start of pedagogy. There is no such thing as pedagogy without the other. But beginnings are difficult and instruct my attempts to articulate an affectionate and forgiving theory of learning capable of containing the frustrations and the aggressions of drives made from love and hate that take their shape in conflicts, anxieties, defenses, and desires for an education yet to come. For me, there are two places where we are given a second chance to make up our minds: one is in the classroom, the other the clinic of psychoanalysis. I also believe that the future of education depends upon how we present the audacity of our work.

The chapters that follow have one foot in observations on teaching and learning in the university classroom and the other foot in discussions of clinical life. As a psychoanalyst, I continue learning to take things personally and question how I am affected and disaffected by working with others. The value of free association as a means of drawing together disparate events and recommending psychical life is always being learned. I extend psychoanalytic views to redraw my years of teaching in university classrooms into a new understanding of desire for pedagogy and to an affectionate theory of learning from the unconscious. Mainly, my interest is with ordinary problems of learning and teaching from the psychoanalytic field, literature, and pedagogical life with stops along the way to meet the characters that emerge from the emotional situations they hold in store and then suddenly release.

So what are the ordinary problems of teaching and learning? Complications are rooted in affect and the anxiety that begin object relations; we still want to keep an eye on the capacity for free association. Chapter by chapter, the problems concern: the handling of technique, the use of theory, regression to an earlier state, identity claims on the nature of gender, various reading and writing inhibitions, and last but not least, the teacher's mistakes. Winnicott's ([1963?] 1989) list of primal agonies suggests the internal dangers: falling forever, fragmentation, depersonalization, derealization, and isolation without any means of communication. All of these agonies lean on the subjective fact of failure to recognize dependency in educational relationships that is further complicated by the self's desire to be met by the other. Each chapter then proposes the workings of an emotional dilemma: aggression, destruction, inhibition, defense, and the transference, all situations that animate conflicted themes of loyalty, affiliation, investment, ideality, separation, and finding one's way.

Chapter 2 delivers Freud's technique papers on the problems of learning psychoanalysis to the university. His papers are read as an allegory for introducing university pedagogy and as a lesson in waiting. I speculate on why Freud wrote them, give a little history of how they were received, and ask what it is to think with them today and treat the clinic as a metaphor for classroom life. They are not so much teaching tools as they are warning devices made from character studies that, due to the pitfalls of intersubjective work and the psychoanalyst's subjective positions in the transference, may be linked to the difficulties the psychoanalyst creates and encounters. At the heart of each technical paper is Freud's advice on positive and negative transference. They are subjective facts of learning and present as obstacles to their knowing. Even then, or especially because of transference, a story emerges from the ways attachments are made and disclaimed and disquieting imagination takes hold. It seems the best Freud could do was to treat technical advice only as recommendations for beginning practice. The paradox is that rules are not easily followed and everyone knows this. That which does rule the relation, however, namely, the transference, becomes the heart of technique and its greatest obstacle. Freud stays with the problem of falling in love, and this brings us to ask, what is love in learning? How strange then that Freud advises us to notice through the portals of love the afterwardness of misunderstandings, pedagogical ambitions, and unintended events in both the clinic and the classroom. And yet, something resists their reading and love can hardly wait. The chapter works through a sequence of learning events that accompanied my introduction to Freud's papers on psychoanalytic techniques in a graduate seminar. Forgetting of techniques and being instructed by mistakes is also the topic of chapter 7.

Chapter 3 belongs to the studio of words in classroom life that begin with the well-worn question, what is the use of theory? The question is double-edged. It is asked when theory feels alien and when we wonder about the theory we bring to how we believe learning should unfold. Working from Winnicott's ([1968] 1989) discussion of the use of the object and the question of the fate of the transitional object, I consider theory's reception and ask why, in university classrooms, in professional organizations, in literature, and in times when trying to convey why theory is so difficult to grasp, theory becomes an emotionally fraught topic, subject to fear of theory, writing inhibitions, and worries over originality. These little theory wars are taken through their emotional character in order to ask, what is feared and desired when theory is feared and desired? Many of the themes return in chapter 6, where I discuss the writer's vast and unfinished theories of anxiety. Chapter 6 presents a variation on the question, what is the use of theory? We will ask, what is the use of words?

Chapter 4 turns on the question of regression in the professions through the problems that the concept and character of adolescence presents to education. By the way, the chapter is concerned with repetitions: déjà vu, the already communicated déjà raconté, and the uncanny. I ask how encounters with adolescence and its quest for truth, beauty, and thought can be used as a psychoanalytic frame for understanding the education of the helping professions. But a significant conflict resides in the state of professional knowledge toward psychical life that tends to be expressed in the fields of psychology and education as alienation between developmental theory and pedagogy. The heart of the chapter is a character study of my undergraduate teacher education course, The Adolescent and the Teacher, which readers will meet again in chapter 7. Chapter 4, however, explores why the nature of adolescence, while difficult to know, may be used as commentary on the impossible professions. The discussion leans on the psychoanalytic idea that adults working in schools are subject to their adolescence—elemental sets of internal conflicts, phantasies, and defenses—that return in professional knowledge as demands for certainty and as a belief that learning is a tonic to conflict as opposed to conflict's delegate. Working with Kristeva's (2007) formulation of "the adolescent syndrome of ideality," I speculate on psychical life as our most radical relation to the self and other. And yet, there is something uncanny in our theories of adolescence: we have all been through it before and may decide that it belongs to the birds.

Another scene of ideality is created when professors try to use the topic of gender as an instruction for how students should behave. It is a losing battle, and chapter 5 concerns both the anxieties and madness of gender lectures with two psychoanalytic views on the valence of aggression and its uses in psychical reality. Both views lean upon the idea that gender has an unconscious life. The chapter returns to the 1936 lectures on the emotional life of gender given by Melanie Klein and Joan Riviere to a public about to go to war (Klein and Riviere 1937). These psychoanalysts are known for representing "the mad side" of gender and consider femininity and masculinity as lending emotional weight to the body and as one source for phantasy material that propels gender's reach into symbolization, conflicts, and intersubjectivity. Their views are brought into tension with Winnicott's revision of aggression in gender development. While historical questions on the relation between psychoanalytic theories of gender and the context of World War II are raised, Winnicott turns to a little war in the emotional life of gender to analyze traces of mental pain that history leaves in its wake. He raises the new problem of the play between internal and external reality, and discusses how a one-sided take on gender as either masculine or feminine and as the entire experience and goal of embodiment forecloses attempts to understand the self's search for becoming a subject with other subjects. Loyalty to one side, or the defense of splitting into good and bad, itself the condition for war, has as one of its roots gender polarity. The madness of lecturing on gender resides in conveying this problem as well as something about our own gender madness. I lean upon a psychoanalytic allegory: that a return to historical discussion in psychoanalysis and the tensions within the psychoanalytic field on the problems of representations of gender can be used to reflect on our world and create elbow room needed to reconceptualize the currency, difficulties, and emotional obstacles repeated in contemporary pedagogical efforts and research into gendered subjectivity.

Chapter 6, "The Untold Story of the Writing Block," pursues the question of anxiety as a human condition and as a prominent affect in writing and in the so-called writing block. The untold story holds two paradoxes. One is that a great many professors and students come to the university to have their writing block and this brings the idea that the only people who care about and damn the writing block are those who desire to write. The other paradox belongs to the writing: one can be in the midst of a writing block and not quite know that. Our only clue is that a compliant text is written. Again, we must tarry with unconscious education. My interest is with the character of writing and that the writer must involve her or himself with the intermingling of phantasy and reality due to the double fact that the writer has to rely upon the self and that writing is also a means to create a self who writes. I begin with anxiety's delegates known as phantasy mentioned by writers, professors, and psychoanalysts. One never knows if one has created the writing block or has found it. This is the writer's paradox, and literature will be of use, as will discussions of writing anxiety in psychoanalytic publications and literature. Another term for the writing block is writing neurosis, and the neurosis opens to the destiny of love and loss in the desire to write. The problem in a nutshell is that one can be in the midst of a writing block while obsessing over the writing, and this turns out to be the never-ending story. But this paradox belongs to the latency of anxiety, that one can be in its throes and not know that. The writing of the chapter repeats that dilemma and something does resist its telling. Much will lean on the question of destruction, thought about in this chapter through D.W. Winnicott's ([1956] 1994) notion of the antisocial tendency.

The formulation of everyday psychopathologies in education gives permit to chapter 7, where I turn to the world of mistakes in pedagogy. It is a wild world, yet we tend to have more discussions on how to avoid it. In my view classrooms offer favorable conditions for so many mistakes, and this is due to the fact that so much is unknown while we attempt to get to know our work. Mistakes come without invitation, and the psychopathologies as symptomatic acts spin the subject out of control. Yet mistakes, just as dreams, may well be the royal road to knowledge of the unconscious. So the chapter may be read as in dialogue with chapter 2, where Freud's technical papers catalogue the ordinary mistakes of clinical practice. I open pedagogy to its fault lines: sleeping, dreaming, falling, forgetting, pretending to know, and transference neurosis. Readers are invited to consider a psychical configuration that has as its limit a narrative conundrum professors and psychoanalysts share when trying to depict the felt qualities of their work: a great deal is experienced before anything can be known and learning from the contingencies of the psychopathologies of everyday education are of a different order than our anticipation of how things should proceed. It is as if we wish for mistakes in order to even notice that our pedagogy also expresses the unconscious through puzzling symptomatic acts. Such excess founds literature, the classroom, and clinical writing and comes to compose *education as our human condition*. Once mistakes are made, they have to be noticed to affect our affection for and afflictions in teaching and learning. Then the stage is set for a character study of my pedagogy. Here, the adolescent teacher and the adolescent psychoanalyst may take a bow. The chapter does not instruct on how to make mistakes. We already know that. What can still be explored, however, after the fact, are their phantasy sequences. While mistakes may be typically brushed aside by the urgency to act as if they are meaningless, misstep by misstep, we stumble into our human condition that is created and waiting to be found.

2

"An Unexpected Novelty"

Freud's Technique Papers Go to the University

> Something seems to creep in which has not been taken into account in our sum . . . an unexpected novelty . . .
>
> —Sigmund Freud, *Introductory Lectures on Psycho-Analysis, Part 3*

Simple Things, or The Wish to Learn

Between 1911 and 1915 Freud wrote a series of six introductions on beginning techniques for those wishing to learn the practice of psychoanalysis. To give oneself over to the delicacies of psychoanalytic sensibility, Freud recommends simple things to hold in mind. For example: let the patient do the talking, try to establish rapport, sustain neutrality, invite free association, listen with free-floating attention, take the unconscious as guide, and move slowly. The psychoanalyst must learn to wait. But it is the surprising arts and crafts of psychical life—one's own and others—that instruct. And this cannot be planned as the unexpected leftover questions, forgotten demands, and well-worn desires baffle communication. Dreams, slips of the tongue, oxymoron, mishearing, and sighs, wishes, phantasies, and jokes, for instance, are tipoffs to the velocity of the unconscious. The techniques themselves awaken these passions as well as question what puts them to sleep. There is nothing quite like the frisson of psychical reality, and Freud's technique papers must bow to the work of that introduction.

So psychoanalytic techniques, Freud counsels, may appear simple, but they leave us feeling our way into impressive learning complications of the emotional kind. Taking the unconscious as a guide and trying to establish rapport with the other while entangled in the fascinations of free association makes moving slowly difficult. Judging the way of words with the need to take action before knowing in advance what has happened bothers neutrality. And permitting others their say interferes with the urgency of anticipating the point of their meaning. A great deal is unknown, much is disguised, one event substitutes for another, and stories seem to run backward. Freud expects communication to be in pieces. Throughout these technique papers Freud's pedagogical approach may feel counterintuitive. He places special emphasis on the analyst and analysand strains of resistance to his advice and then introduces the surprising form resistance will take.

The more one reads into these intricacies, the more one feels one's own reading matters and marvels over what carries the day: the techniques themselves or a residuum of desire repeated in the wish to learn? The pedagogical situation Freud encountered and now leaves us to present opens a learning paradox: any introduction to psychoanalysis steps in the middle of something already there. Every technique, including the simple things to keep in mind, effectuates the expansive, creeping, and unsettling psychoanalytic fact of the transference that Freud discovered close to home in his dreams, his clinic and case studies, his abundant archive of letters, and within the psychoanalytic movement's group psychology. In all these dramas the characters of learning present naked humanity: a scattering love and hate, a scurry of anxiety, and a tinge of ambivalence and guilt over what sort of knowledge may prevail. And this leads Freud to place into the center of communication the transference as our passionate affairs that somehow manage to express the aftereffects of education and our hopes for something new.

Titling some of his papers "Recommendations for Practice" carries no guarantee for how they will be read and written. And perhaps there is no help since the language of psychoanalysis is affected by the details of its theory of psychical life. Everything is grist for the mill. The theory is incredibly sticky and does affect its reading and writing. We are never quite sure whether we are greeted by recommendations to try out or rules that try us out. And the theory encourages these conflicted readings! Such ambiguity gives free play to our questions. As for Freud, his writing stays closest to the emotional situations of learning that magnify what divides the conflicted subject. It is an approach that does seem to animate and present the wish to learn as much as it serves to uncover that other wish: resistance to learning. More than a few analysts over the last century have voiced frustration with Freud's discourse on mistakes and his emphasis on what analysts must not do but perhaps cannot help but do. It is, after all, runaway meaning that bothers our good intentions and wrecks the security that we already know what we think. And there is something ironic about techniques that take the side of not knowing and that come with directions one can hardly believe. Yet there is no other way to present the unconscious except from the side of what we don't mean to do and say but must do and say anyway. What's left is to examine the burns and flare-ups of smoldering meaning. The unconscious, Freud maintains, fires the fuel of communication, investigation, and interpretation—and too affects the learning procedures that his (1914a) fifth technique paper named as "Remembering, Repeating, and Working Through."

As for the writing of these papers, stormy history plays its part. Freud's topic was influenced by addressing a young psychoanalytic movement under construction, splitting at the seams, and living with the terrors of World War I. His recommendations find their metaphors in battlefields and opponents, in objections and obstacles, in reconnaissance missions and retreats, and as the analyst's struggle on three fronts: the patient's resistance, the analyst's resistance, and the general public's resistance to psychoanalysis. Even as his discussion nestles into the cushion of "recommendations," the bite comes in his writing voice: authoritative, critical, and demanding. Years after the publication of his series, in a letter to Sándor Ferenczi, Freud expressed both regret over their negative tone and chagrin at their rigid reading (Rachman 1997).[1]

Yet the psychology of the fundamental rule of free association does something to sensate speech and to the way in which words are heard. The drift of thought is hardly cooperating. The analyst requests the analysand to say what is on one's mind without knowing its destiny, to fight against censoring thoughts or the tendency to disguise them through innuendo and forgetting, and mostly, to be courageous with honesty. The method of free association may only be encouraged since the request is to break all rules. One may feel, in speaking this way to another, as if it is the utterance and not the tongue that leaves words in tatters. And in stepping into the middle of something—for after all that is what speaking words must do—both the analyst and the analysand wrestle with what comes before free association and what each recommendation must bow to. Freud's (1913) paper "On Beginning the Treatment" introduces the psychoanalytic situation:

> I think I am well-advised, however, to call these rules 'recommendations' and not to claim any unconditional acceptance for them. The extraordinary diversity of the psychical constellations concerned, the plasticity of all mental processes and the wealth of determining factors oppose any mechanization of the technique;

and they bring it about that a course of action that is as a rule justified may at times prove ineffective, whilst one that is usually mistaken may once in a while lead to the desired end. (123)

Three years later when introducing the general public to psychoanalysis, Freud's (1916–1917) lecture on transference begins with his mistaken views:

> We believed, to be sure, that we had reckoned with all the motives concerned in the treatment, that we had completely rationalized the situation between us and the patients so that it could be looked over at a glance like a sum in arithmetic; yet in spite of all this, something seems to creep in which has not been taken into account in our sum . . . an unexpected novelty . . . (439)

And the unexpected novelty is, well, unexpected and utterly human. It is unconscious, unanticipated, a presence against all odds, hard to believe, and difficult to place. A few pages later Freud gives this unexpected novelty a middle name: "This new fact, which we thus recognize so unwillingly, is known by us as *transference*" (442; italics original). The novel transference that so affected Freud and the destiny of the talking cure that he will try to introduce is oddly familiar. It revolves around a surprising demand for the other's love and hate. Even more, psychoanalysis will call upon transference as the heart of technique. In the prism of transference the analyst appears in many familiar guises: interlocutor and baffler, friend and foe, lover and betrayer, container and sieve, mother and father, sister and brother, and investigator and nebbish. The analyst reminds the analysand of someone else. Playing these characters and freely associating to them requires great tact, the assumption of uncertainty, the delay of gratification, and an interest in the enfoldments of errors, accidents, phantasy, dreams, with life's contingencies.

Contemporary analysts focus on how much has changed since Freud wrote his recommendations (Seulin and Saragnano 2012). Yes there are, to quote Kristeva (1995), "new maladies of the soul." Educators too would say their students experience new maladies of virtual education. And, too, we can identify new maladies of the system that affect both education and psychoanalysis. With intensification of professionalization, the creep of diagnostic manuals, the happiness promised by pharmaceutical industries, and the immediacy of virtual technologies and instant answers come industries of self-help, an avalanche of teaching manuals, the ideality of neuroscience and biology, and campaigns for improving the brain. Self-diagnosis seems to be our fate and self-improvement our suffering. Today's analyst and analysand are affected by all this white noise even as they experience the long debates Freud's technique papers set into motion: making something more of the conflicts between significance and insignificance, surface and depth, infant and adult, reality and phantasy, and clinic and theory. Like those who came before, contemporary analysts advocate a greater presence for psychoanalysis in the world and a greater world presence in psychoanalysis. They too write to a wider public on matters of cultural suffering, modes of violence, wrongheaded social policy, poverty, social hatred, the failures of social contracts, and the miniature dramas played in the clinic. Indeed, particularly with the lay analysts, world events do affect the shape of techniques, the feel of the clinic, the intimacies of suffering, and our audacity to become an analyst and question what psychoanalysis means for us today.[2]

Dynamically speaking and regardless of one's school of thought, that unexpected novelty—the wiggles and impasses of transference to psychoanalysis—remains an abiding dilemma (Dean 2013; Esman 1990; Fromm 2012; Kristeva 2000; Leffert 2013; Oclsner 2013; Reeder 2008). André Green's (2011) discussion of his fifty years of clinical practice admits what barely changes and what is most unsatisfying or incomplete. His argument is that neither failure in psychoanalysis nor the process of disillusionment is well understood. His point is that psychoanalysis touches on the soft spot of our incompleteness. So no one can settle the course of life questions Freud's techniques open: why change is so difficult for the subject, why we remain loyal to things long gone, why we fall in love, why new knowledge is sometimes felt as a blow to the old, and why the confusion of time, place, event, and person transfers into present scenes of discontentment, suffering, and desire. From whatever psychoanalytic school of thought, the long reach of love and its history of painful loss is an abiding dilemma and the analytic couple still has the slow work of writing into a novel education. When leaving the consulting room for the privacy of his study, Green (2005b) thinks more about this work of writing from love and strife. He wishes for an affected reading and writing practice and treats symbolization as emerging from love that he describes as "(two broken halves which are joined together to form a *third*)" (11; italics original). To understand the evocative power of symbolization Green turns to the experience of reading mythology, literary work, and aesthetics, all unafraid of incompleteness and that call upon the reader's imagination and reverie. There too the transference plays and leads to Green's bare conclusion for how we may write of it: "in any case passion will be our model" (10).

Might passion also be our case for imagining education as the novelty for changing minds? Taking this question further, might passion for reading and writing become a way to imagine a destiny for psychoanalysis and education? The future of pedagogy, as much as the future of psychoanalysis, depends upon our capacity to symbolize and communicate lively experience and discussion on how we are affected by our work or what we do learn from trying to sustain our freedom and desire with others (Quinodoz et al. 2006). Freud's writing serves this model, and he insured that psychoanalysts would have to become clinicians, teachers, and writers who dream. He wrote a great deal to the general public and did so not only to clear the air of misconceptions about psychoanalysis. His passion involved free association and giving to words their story of love and hate. The technique papers are one such case. In this chapter Freud's simple things to keep in mind become an allegory for the educator's emotional world and our entry point for getting to know the attractions of the passionate fact of transference.

Knock, Knock. Who Is There?

The transference does not stop at the psychoanalyst's door. It knocks about in pedagogical relations, theories of learning, viewpoints, and arguments. It rattles our learning constructs, procedures, and curricular goals. It binds our misperceptions and confuses reality and phantasy. In the classroom, too, the teacher as character—her passion, knowledge, and authority, and her ignorance, mistakes, and indifference—is oddly familiar and so animates the student and teacher's transference of love and hate onto the presence of pedagogy. Yes, the transference has a different flavor in the classroom, though the problem of unwilling recognition—the emotional situation of not wanting to know anything about that—leaves indigestion, even as we try to relieve it with the antacid of pedagogy that we must also admit is hard to swallow. Pedagogy must gamble with new and old knowledge and the vulnerabilities, hardships, and hurt feelings that the transference conveys and that the emotional situation of teaching and learning also stirs. Skipping ahead to Freud's (1933) "New Introductory Lectures on Psycho-Analysis"—the late lectures written again to the general public—we meet the educator's dilemma: "Thus education has to find its way between the Scylla of non-interference and the Charybdis of frustration. Unless this problem is entirely insoluble, an optimum must be discovered which will enable education to achieve the most and damage the least" (149). The problem is that the passionate transference works on both sides.

We can think of the classroom as also containing Freud's (1912a) formulation that the psychoanalytic situation sets in motion a double predicament. On one side the patient and analyst and the student and teacher are involved in a psychological situation, one of difference or asymmetry and of emotional vulnerability and dependency that does call upon a forgotten childhood of learning and of having to interpret the force of the other's words. Aulagnier (2001) analyzes in her study of language and self the force of such a relation that she calls "the violence of interpretation." Aulagnier has argued that the young child meets the words of the mother, the word bearer, with sexual theories and secret thoughts. Creativity, Aulagnier supposes, supports the capacity for a space where "the I must come about" (71) and become another word bearer: a self that represents her or his passions. "We owe it to psychoanalysis," Aulagnier writes, "to have shown that the need for the presence of an Other is in no way reducible to the vital functions that it must carry out" (72). Might education know this as well? Yet the "violence" of having language at all and originally contained by the mother is double-edged: words demand something of us and may feel persecutory. In times of safety words may be permitted their aggression and destruction. Only later can the subject sublimate or transform the other's words into an intersubjective space. Our backdrop of learning is created from interest or attachment to the other. In viewing learning from the inside out, our attention is given over to the learner's susceptibility to both love's impressions and anxiety over its loss. These deeply rooted experiences are one quality of our psychological or emotional situation.

The other side of this double predicament involves us with the presence of new and old relationships; people in the room and the crowds of characters made present through words, shadow referrals, and phantasy life. The psychoanalytic relation, and I think we can include pedagogical relations as well, creates the predicament Freud (1914a) named "an artificial illness" (154)—transference neurosis, transference love, and transference resistance—special love that leans on the psychoanalytic frame, the comfort of the setting, and the analyst's dedication to the work. The transference presents in styles of loving and hating. There is libidinal excitement, ideality, a turn away from reality, and the thing that does not add up, namely, "an unexpected novelty" of falling in love with the analyst. Freud's (1915a) last technical paper, "Observations on Transference-Love," stays close to what is unbelievably splendid: "To a well-educated layman (for that is what the ideal civilized person is in regard to psycho-analysis) things that have to do with love are incommensurable with everything else; they are, as it were, written on a special page on which no other writing is tolerated" (160). I would only add that even our ideal person might write in invisible ink.

Freud's (1914a) fifth technique paper, "Remembering, Repeating, and Working Through," stands as his strongest theory of learning from the clamors of transference. There, pressing into the soft ground of analysis, Freud pictures the force of resistance to the destiny of one's own mental acts that sinks the buoyancy of symbolization. "We have learnt," Freud writes, "that the patient repeats instead of remembering, and repeats under the conditions of resistance" (151). What is repeated as resistance? For Freud the answer is global: "everything that has already made its way from the sources of the repressed into his manifest personality—his inhibitions and unserviceable attitudes and his pathological character-traits . . . all his symptoms in the course of the treatment. . . . not as an event of the past, but as a present-day force" (151). Freud is quite adamant that it is beside the point for the analyst to explain to the patient that she is caught in the compulsion to repeat and that the form it will take is the demand for the analyst's love. Warning the patient that this will happen is a little like burning down one's house to prevent an accidental fire. In his (1913) paper on beginning treatment, Freud writes that if it may be easy for the analyst to surmise "secret wishes between the lines of [the patient's] complaints and the story of his illness," the analyst mustn't hurry, lest she fall into the temptation of "lightening diagnosis and 'express' treatments" (140). Everything, Freud argued, hinges on giving transference its playground, and this unexpected novelty, however uninvited, surprises the story of teaching and learning we thought we already knew.

The Passion for Writing

If stepping into the middle of something already unfolding is the abiding problem for psychoanalysis, we should also admit that the nature of its material is divided, fragmented, dreamy, symptomatic, and overdetermined. And this affects both its reading and writing. Michel de Certeau (1986) proposes symbolization of conflict as the disturbing factor in the Freudian novel: "psychoanalysis takes up the definition given to fiction as being a knowledge jeopardized and wounded by its otherness (the affect, etc.). . . . In the analytic field, this discourse is effective because it is 'touched' or wounded by the affect" (27). How does this education fare? What of its stormy seas? We know that topsy-turvy events, or the unexpected novelty of transference, affected Freud's (Freud and Breuer 1893–1895) psychoanalytic education and softened its hard edge. He observed that his earliest case studies "read like short stories" (160) and tells his readers that his techniques for writing began with a dramatic impasse, fatigue, depression, and inhibition tied to his struggle to leave behind his earliest techniques of suggestion and hypnosis to surrender to the astounding epistemology of the hysterics. But there was also Freud's (1956) melancholia, and his anxieties and symptoms were painstakingly recounted in his self-analysis that took an early form in his letters to Fliess written between the years 1887 and 1902. Then came breathtaking books on dreams, mistakes, sexuality, and jokes, and the hilarity and pathos of psychoanalytic objects that arrive from that other scene of unmeant things. Late in his career (1939) he would push writing to its breaking point with his psychoanalytic novel, *Moses and Monotheism*. The last pages let readers know that his constructions had reached the limits of inquiry because of the nature of the material and the novelty of writing one's way into cultural absence, exile, survival, and reparation.

To write into emerging problems—and so to write against the self—burdens narratives, not only because research conventions and the apparatus of academic knowledge keep watch over the logic of explication. The writer risks and loses the self in words. It is an open question as to whether the loss occurs because one cannot tell everything or settle into what is most partial about the subject. Or, perhaps the act of writing reminds us of our incompleteness and missing those long since gone. The other risk is that words call these lost objects back, convey more than what we intend, and communication carries both our repetitions and wishes for love. Lyndsey Stonebridge's (2007) study of wartime writing in midcentury British culture coined the term "the writing of anxiety." And it is difficult to say what writes: anxiety or the writer. As I was writing and rewriting this chapter, moving words along and feeling their limits, I found myself creating two files: one called "the chapter," the other "discarded content." I leave it to your imagination as to which version saw the light of day.

Lest we worry about falling into psychologism, we can wonder why the excess of affect freely associates with the act of writing. Shoshana Felman (2003) pressures both reading and writing with her enigmatic term "the literary thing" that, for her, carries the interminable and often agonizing question, "What does it mean to know?" (13). Freud knew of this linguistic mire or the difficulty of freely associating with psychoanalytic objects: for instance, words with things, affects with ideation, drives with objects, and dreams with the day's residues. Free association is a way into the phantasies of knowledge and what is most abstract about psychical life. Between "the writing of anxiety" and the "literary thing" we find a way to link disparate words, offhand remarks, and cut off stories to the currency of what is too close for comfort. André Green (1986) understands his passion for symbolization as "private madness": to write, to advance theory without proof, to stimulate more associations, and to dwell with our incompatible questions, doubts, and with what remains incomplete.

Putting all this to words while commenting on one's efforts in language threatens the object of inquiry as much as it does the one who inquires. Freud's earliest attempts, found in his *Studies on Hysteria* (Freud and Breuer 1893–1895), comment on his emphatic writing style while anticipating his poor reception. For some reason Freud placed his thoughts in parenthesis:

> (I am making use here of a number of similes, all of which have only a very limited resemblance to my subject and which, moreover, are incompatible with one another. I am aware that this is so, and I am in no danger of over-estimating their value.

But my purpose in using them is to throw light from different directions on a highly complicated topic which has never yet been represented. I shall therefore venture to continue in the following pages to introduce similes in the same manner, though I know this is not free from objection.) (291)

It is hard to say whose objections matter the most, especially due to the fact that writing itself is an objection not only to others but also to the frustrations brought on by trying to squeeze objects into words. We know some trouble is being made when we cannot control how words are received.

Minding the Gap

What may gradually dawn on readers is that the techniques advise us to put our theory in parenthesis and that if we can manage to place knowledge on hold, a different conversation founded in the ethics of listening emerges. With a simple sentence, in Freud's (1913) paper "On Beginning the Treatment," the analyst introduces psychoanalytic time: "Before I can say anything to you I must know a great deal about you; please tell me what you know about yourself" (134). The invitation steps into the middle of something, including what becomes difficult to say to someone else while maintaining the belief that the analyst already knows. The shared rule is that judgment is to be suspended even if the thoughts are unpleasant. "You must never give into these criticisms, but must say it precisely because you feel an aversion to doing so. Later on you will find out and learn to understand the reason for this injunction, which is really the only one you have to follow. So say whatever goes through your mind" (135). Before, during, and after qualifies "whatever" and serves as introduction to "the fundamental rule of free association." As for trying to describe what then happens, eighty years later the analyst Christopher Bollas (1991) expresses the clinical conundrum: "It is next to impossible to account for what transpires in a psychoanalysis" (7). Bollas then adds, yes, there are interpretations, "but much of our work involves exploring issues that are not clear" (54).

And in the spirit of seeing what is not there Freud (1913) asks the patient to become a fellow traveler: "Act as though . . . you were a traveller sitting next to the window of a railway carriage and describing to someone inside the carriage the changing views which you see outside" (135). It is a savvy approach to the train of thought and narrating the vanishing point of the self's scenery. It takes quite a while to enjoy romps through the day's residues, ponder forgotten events one has known all along, experience loss of words and the agony of missed experience, and play in the field of the unavoidable transference. As for the traveler in the train and the "someone inside," both are characters for imagination. The patient is speaking to someone, but whom? And the analyst is listening to something, but what?

Many of the peppered warnings in Freud's recommendations pass education through the mask of tragicomedy. "Under present-day conditions," Freud (1912b) observes in his second paper to those practicing psychoanalysis, "the feeling that is most dangerous to a psycho-analyst is the therapeutic ambition to achieve by this novel and much disputed method something that will produce a convincing effect upon other people" (115). But just the opposite occurs when Freud gives his equation: "educative ambition is of as little use as therapeutic ambition" (119). The seductions of ambition come with excessive self-regard and overconfidence in one's knowledge. As another version of love, this piece of transference leads to misrecognition of who is in charge and who may take credit.

The educative ambition then is tied not to knowledge but to that which irks it on. Freud's (1915a) paper on transference love argues that the analyst "must recognize that the patient's falling in love is induced by the analytic situation and is not to be attributed to the charms of his own person" (160–161). He emphasizes two different points of view and their collision: "there can be no doubt that the outbreak of a passionate demand for love is largely the work of resistance" (162). The incredible demand for love, however, holds a great deal in store, including the analyst's weak spot of ambition, education, and faith in conversion. It is at this point in the transference love paper that Freud tells a crowded joke about an insurance agent and a man of God:

> The insurance agent, a free thinker, lay at the point of death and his relatives insisted on bringing in a man of God to convert him before he died. The interview lasted so long that those who were waiting outside began to have hopes. At last the door of the sick-chamber opened. The free thinker had not been converted; but the pastor went away insured. (165)

The beauty of the joke is that one is never quite sure what the laugh is about: the tickles of phantasies, the seductions of persuasion and belief, the dangers of the transference and its wish for insurance, the dashed hopes of relatives, the pleasures of winning and losing, or the resistance to the psychoanalytic situation. We don't really know who has the last laugh.

Given the complexity of group psychology, the surprising insistence is for simplicity, and what makes these papers an adventure in learning is Freud's (1912b) view that the technique itself and its mainstay "is a simple one . . . it rejects the use of any special expedient (even that of taking notes). It consists simply in not directing one's notice to anything in particular and in maintaining the same "'evenly suspended attention' (as I have called it) in the face of all that one hears" (111–112). The word "simple" appears throughout these papers and signifies a panorama of what is basic, radical, and uncluttered, along with what is ordinary, idiotic, and easy to dismiss. Because beginning techniques attempt to catch up to a process already underway, Freud takes the path of least resistance and emphasizes attunement to the unconscious: "He should simply listen, and not bother about whether he is keeping anything in mind" (112). But the reason for waiting concerns listening for the deferral of knowledge: "It must not be forgotten," Freud writes, "that the things one hears are for the most part things whose meaning is only recognized later on" (112).

Freud's (1911) first paper on handling dream interpretation even throws the dream of interpretation into question:

> I know that it is asking a great deal, not only of the patient but also of the doctor, to expect them to give up their conscious purposive aims during the treatment, and to abandon themselves to a guidance which, in spite of everything, still seems to us 'accidental.' But I can answer for it that one is rewarded every time one resolves to have faith in one's own theoretical principles, and prevails upon oneself not to dispute the guidance of the unconscious in establishing connecting links. (94)

We are left with the idea that techniques lean on our own fragile design and, just like us, are subject to crumbling reason, forgetting, wishes, accidents, and to the dreams of practice.

The Unwilling Arrival of Pedagogy

James Strachey's (1968b) introduction to the technique papers notes Freud's reluctance to write anything like "Aids to Young Analysts" (87). He also mentions Freud's skepticism of practicing psychoanalysis without one's own analysis. Yet by writing to the general public and sketching a novel education, Freud must have believed that beyond the clinic learning psychoanalysis is available to anyone (Britzman 2007). And nowhere was this insistence more clear than when Freud discussed the uses of psychoanalysis for teachers and students to ask whether human desire might open how we imagine pedagogical relations as instructed by the psychological predicaments that belong to learning.[3]

Freud's colleague August Aichhorn (1990) was one of the first to discuss the transference in the pedagogical situation:

> When we speak of the transference in connexion with social re-education, we mean the emotional response of the pupil toward the educator or counselor or therapist, as the case may be, without meaning that it takes place in exactly the same way as in an analysis. The "counter-transference" is the emotional attitude of the teacher toward the pupil . . . (94)

The transference, Aichhorn goes on to describe, "is more than a feeling out" (100). It goes both ways and has the immediacy of feeling the affect's tenacity to work for and against the certainty and completeness of one's impressions. Hard to believe that the transference is there just as one thinks one is right, just as one feels the need to act now, and just as one throws to the wind the question of what next. And, transference cannot be explained away through intellectual reasoning. One cannot tell the other to stop it and be unaffected. The transference cannot be a teaching device since it carries on its own instructions.[4] And yet, without the interested and invested transference there is no learning.

So what then happens if the pedagogical relation rests not in enlightenment but rather in the transference? We are entering the more uncertain question of how to learn from the urgencies of the emotional world and what happens to our education if we leave suggestion to welcome the epistemology of students. Might Freud's change of mind give us in education a new approach? In the middle of his work and due to the transference, Freud found a terrific problem with emphasizing rationality as the only pedagogy: merely explaining why knowledge is good did not solve the emotional dilemmas of the subject. Nor could a rationalist approach reach into the problem of why we suffer for love, wish for authority, and worry about dependency, separation, and loss. He turned his attention away from enlightenment to ordinary experiences of fear, anxiety, and desire in human relationships and wondered about resistance to change, the defense of perfection, and the ego's compromises. Freud was also writing in a world at war and saw for himself the violence, destruction, and hatred between and within nations. His big question then was not so much why we need knowledge but why we don't want it. In this refusal he saw transference between love and authority established within group psychology and in the Oedipal structure of families and schools. Rather than idealize education, he seemed to say, notice why learning carries resistance to knowledge of it. Notice the compulsion to repeat childhood conflicts in new situations. Ask why learning makes us nervous. Look into what happens when one feels the swipe of dependency, helplessness, and meaninglessness. Be curious about what misunderstanding holds in store.

The new psychoanalytic techniques emerged from the question of transference and whether one may learn the courage to invent from the shreds of meaning something more than what has already happened. A century later, Kristeva (1995) would go as far as defining psychoanalysis as a symbolic antidepressant for the treatment of thought and language, and the therapist would be a speech therapist of desire. For Jonathan Lear (2009) psychoanalysis's final cause would be more freedom. Following from Kristeva and Lear, I think we may ask if education too can be a metaphorical antidepressant, a treatment for language and thought and a quest for narrative freedom.

Freud continued to pressure knowledge of pedagogy with the passions of learning in two companion essays written to the general public: "A Difficulty in the Path of Psycho-Analysis" (1917) and "On the Teaching of Psycho-Analysis in Universities" (1919c). The essay on difficulties is a stringent critique of academic psychology and psychiatry and their eschewals of libido theory for the cover of behaviorism. It carries a number of well-quoted sentences; perhaps most memorable yet easily forgotten is this one: "*The ego is not master in its own house*" (1917, 143; italics original). And in the difficulties essay Freud mentions education as playing a part in the destruction of narcissistic illusions, yet if it must address the ego in such work, it can only mean that education cannot be complete. The optimal balance Freud (1933) would put forward later tips education to the side of frustration and the delay of immediate satisfaction.

Freud's (1919c) essay on teaching psychoanalysis has two points of view: one of psychoanalysis and the other of the university. The university, he thought, had the most to gain, though today I believe that psychoanalysis needs the university, not for certification but for enlivenment. Freud's paper is not elegant. It has the feel of being dashed off. And perhaps it was, as he wrote it to support his colleague Sándor Ferenczi's bid for the first university chair in psychoanalysis in Hungary (Erős et al. 2013). At the time, psychoanalysis was not in the university and no one could say what would happen. Freud's essay carries one deeply affecting sentence that comes with both a disclaimer for pedagogy and a wish for pedagogy to arrive: "it will be enough if [one] learns something *about* psychoanalysis and something *from* it" (173). As for introducing psychoanalysis to today's university and as for tying its introduction to the middle of something already occurring, Freud's techniques may help us remember a triple challenge: study what does go wrong, what feels uncertain, and what obstacles stand in the way; use these obstacles and resistances with creativity, imagination, free-floating attention, neutrality; and, write more (Britzman 2009 and 2013).

Knock, Knock. Who Is There? The Wish to Learn

Now one of the big surprises in Freud's (1913) paper "On Beginning the Treatment" concerns the status of the analyst's beloved knowledge. Freud advises against thinking that we are only addressing intellectual ideas, an unusual challenge to the ideality of knowledge in the university. Recall that Freud left the theory of education as enlightenment for the more stormy waters of anxieties and desires in learning. It is not only that new ideas affect the ideas one already holds. Rather, the affect involved with ideas we already hold transfers into the reception of new ideas and to the figure of the teacher. Our libidinal attachment to old ideas renders any change of mind as a conflict between loyalty to the known and anxieties over the loss of love. A whole imaginary of what pedagogy may now entail is at stake, including the working through of the anxiety that everything one already knows without knowing why must be destroyed.

To write a narrative after the effusions of pedagogical relations presents a number of dilemmas. First, to return to Bollas's (1991) view, classroom events are notoriously difficult to describe due to the fact that much of what we encounter is not clear and a latency or repression closes off the chaos of learning from our feelings of it. Second, the imaginative reconstruction of unclear events—that "literary thing"—involves the writer's anxieties and liberties with transference to words. The time of the event is different from its writing, and both are partial in the sense of being fragmented from their source. Third, there is the danger of making cohesive what cannot cohere. Only by noting dilemmas—what Freud saw as obstacles or resistance—do we create our case as its study. With these caveats in mind as associating between "the writing of anxiety" and the "literary thing," I present two cases of teaching psychoanalysis in the university and the unexpected novelty of working from Freud's papers on techniques.

Anxiety

In an undergraduate lecture I introduce the writing of Anna Freud. Her work and interest was in communicating with teachers while introducing psychoanalysis to them. I described her little essay (1952) entitled "Answering Teachers' Questions," where she presents three dangers that threaten the teacher, along with their questions. Before turning to her discussion, I asked the students, "What dangers do you think today's teachers face?" Many felt the greatest danger was losing control of the class. I then asked, "But why is that dangerous?" It was here that we made our way into the teacher's vulnerability to anxieties over her or his loss of authority, love, and competence before anything could even be established. Everyone had reasons for why the teacher crumbles, perhaps drawn from their avalanche of student school experience. We could joke about the student's desire to drive teachers crazy, get them off task, make them cry or laugh, and ask ridiculous questions. This particular class had just read Sophocles's play *Oedipus Rex* and there we asked about the differences among what we may control, what others control, and what is beyond anyone's control. I brought this idea back to them. We slowly worked our way into the unanticipated idea of what the teacher cannot control but may handle with care and questions.

Miss Freud's three dangers referenced control, but through it all the great danger played in the teacher's transference to some mythic authority and directed a one-way belief about the relationships between children and adults. In knocking on the door of beliefs to ask what's behind them, Miss Freud delivered the surprising question, how well does the teacher know herself/himself?

The three dangers really add up to one: forgetting the difference between the child and adult through rescue fantasy. The dangers have to do with making contact, with thinking one is only helping, and with repeating one's childhood anxieties of losing love in the guise of teaching. Miss Freud's audience seemed to be in transference with the teachers' dangers. Someone asked, "If we adapt this point of view, don't we become impersonal in our relation with children?" Another question: "But should the teacher help the child?" Miss Freud's reply was simple: the teacher helps the child by varying her or his expectations, anxieties, and demands. That is, relax and tolerate the delay of learning. And teachers may take delay as pedagogy's remainder. Learning is delayed because we feel before we know and learn before we understand, akin to Freud's (1914a) notion of "remembering, repeating, and working through." The delay of learning also involves an empty space and deferral of immediate satisfaction. It turns out that Sigmund Freud's (1933) optimal balance between noninterference and frustration depends on the teacher who accepts frustration and still manages to relax. We could only inch our way into this transitional space.

Transference Neurosis

Nervous themes of helplessness and vulnerability arrived with great fanfare in my graduate seminar in psychoanalytic theory and pedagogy. My surprise was that both topics required the problem of introducing what goes without saying. Only after the seminar was over could I begin to think more about my odd experience of waiting and wanting to begin while things I knew nothing about were already underway.

I noticed that in the beginning of the course the students already had strong ideas about both psychoanalysis and education, and I had the strong feeling of stepping into the middle of something. The students may have been a little worried about their professor and whether they could just speak their minds. Would I love the material more than them? Could they wreck my pedagogy? Would I survive? The regular parameters for transference were in place: weekly meetings, some reading and writing assignments, and the dreaded accrual of grades. Each week I asked them to come to the seminar with their questions on the readings. The seminar frame invited psychoanalytic predicaments.

I began by showing, over a number of weeks, portions of a short film titled *Encounters Through Generations* composed from interviews of very old psychoanalysts who were asked to look back on learning their profession (British Psychoanalytical Society 2012). On the first viewing, I asked, "What did you notice?" Many students were critical of the analysts. They were bourgeois and out of step. When I asked how they knew this, they began to discuss why psychoanalysis bothered them. As they watched each section of the film, I kept asking what they noticed. It took a few viewings to notice very old people looking back on their mistakes, disappointments, and excitement in learning a profession.

I can now say that our transference neurosis in the first few weeks of the seminar ran with the familiar question of who would influence whom. What it means to be influenced, however, was late to arrive. Many students expressed their worries through the judgment that the psychoanalyst imposed viewpoints on others and so was ethically suspect. Not everything, they continued to remind me, had to do with feelings! In thinking about the transference with me, I took their criticisms as information about their worries of what I would do. Taking a general remark personally, considering the utterance as an association to what has occurred somewhere else is one way to think within the transference. What is transferred is the affective force of the relationship as runaway meaning. Who, they seemed to imply, would be the authority in this seminar? Was I secretly psychoanalyzing the students? Would I be like a bad mother and force-feed them with food that only I liked? Would I be the authoritarian father who imposed the law? They did not want to be brainwashed.

I wondered what ideas meant that they should be so dangerous and what the students believed they would lose if they entertained the ideas of the unconscious, transference, and resistance. Now the difficulty is that any imposition of what we faced would ruin their exploration and mine. So I had to wait, tolerate my frustration, move slowly to learn more from what students thought, and notice when we could make contact. My manifest question was how to help unfold a process that was already taking place. The latent question was whether I could tolerate what was beyond my control.

Two accidents, or perhaps one big one that came in two acts, opened us to noticing our emotional situation. We were having an unplanned discussion on pedagogy in the university. Many of the graduate students served as teaching assistants and were practicing their pedagogy in small groups of undergraduate tutorials. One member of the seminar admitted that she had a difficult undergraduate student in her class and did not like this person at all. They seemed to fight with one another, and the undergraduate complained that the class was useless. Each encounter felt more frustrating than the previous one. The graduate student realized that when grading this angry student's paper, she found herself wishing the useless student would fail. The seminar members seemed shaken as they tried to find a link between the undergraduate's complaint about the useless teacher and the teacher's wish to fail the student. Perhaps this phantasy was too much to bear, and the discussion suddenly turned into an advice session: others in the seminar began to suggest teaching tips. They tried to take away the problem and thought, perhaps, that proper techniques would shield them all from their bad feelings. So much was going on in the room that I found myself exhausted. It was difficult to decide who was doing what to whom. The best I could do was end the session, I mean, the seminar, perhaps an indication of my revenge, or countertransference. I left feeling rather useless, though at the time I did not give this feeling its air. Much later I understood that listening to feelings of hatred left me in tatters, oddly repeating hated feelings.

Hate is a difficult feeling to endure let alone discuss its unconscious links to love. Hate may lead us into our aggression, to the teacher's schadenfreude, enjoyment at the student's downfall. Later, feeling hate may turn into the guilt and pain of finding oneself helpless and still in charge. In one of his bravest papers, Winnicott ([1947] 1992) wrote of his own hate in the countertransference and made the observation that unless we understand the depth of our hate, we cannot really feel the power of love. He was discussing "the nature of the emotional burden" of practice (194) and gave the rule that can be extended into teaching: "However much he loves his patients he cannot avoid hating them and fearing them, and the better he knows this the less the hate and fear be the motives determining what he does to his patients" (195). In perhaps a more subtle way, Anna Freud made a similar point when she opened the dangers of teaching to the teacher's emotional world with the experiences of dependency, frustration, and anxiety that go hand in hand with the wish to only be helpful and in control.

A week later the second accident occurred. Feelings of hatred returned as the seminar broke out into writing anxiety. The form it took was with worries over grading their students' papers; perhaps a consequence of the unbearable wish to fail the student that was expressed the week before. Many stated they hated giving grades and were in agony. No one could give any advice and the feelings of hatred were freely expressed, as if it is more acceptable to hate a structural constraint or have to comply than it is to hate a student and have to change one's mind. Perhaps in the back of everyone's mind was the wish for the teacher's revenge, though on a conscious level, everyone only wanted to be helpful, provided that one receive a good, interesting paper and rewarded it with a good grade. On the manifest level receiving good papers was equated to being a wonderful teacher. The latency returns while grading papers, and there feelings are hated. The teacher may notice her or his difference from the student but also her or his transference to fantastic expectations that push one to ignore the student's paper, grade it harshly, hate bad grammar, feel guilty, or give up on ever helping anyone. The hopeless is passed around but where does it land? We can be sure that no one complains about receiving a great paper. Or maybe that complaint is too unbearable to note. And there is also the giving of the thorny grade and the teacher's transference history of receiving them.

An accidental remark could bear the weight of the dangers or anxiety—what I have been naming as the emotional situation of learning. Someone blurted out: "I always feel worried when handing back student feelings." The sentence slipped between "the writing of anxiety" and that "literary thing" and cracked us up. The student may have meant to say, "I always feel bad when handing back the graded student papers, for I know they will take the grade harshly and ignore my helpful comments." Or, perhaps: "Yes, I hate grading papers and worry that this hatred will worm its way into my response and their feelings." Or, perhaps this was a communication to me, something along the lines of "I will hate you when you grade my paper because I love you and you hate me with grades." The odd part was the ways transference instructs and that if we did not know what the slip slid into, for after all, a great deal of passion near and far is involved, we did grasp the comedy, urgency, and poignancy of transference, something that we also understood could not be taught but when felt becomes the material for the heart of learning. Yes, we try to exchange knowledge while in the transference we express what bothers our clarity.

Transference Postscript

I presented an earlier version of this chapter to a conference in Toronto. And in that audience sat many of the students in my seminar in psychoanalysis whom I thought had survived it. In stepping into the middle of something, I felt my writing anxiety transformed into reading anxiety. Was my theory too sticky? Had I blown my cover? Was I about to present my neurosis or theirs? Were my words ruining their story? Would they then ruin mine? After that presentation, one of the students in the audience who had been in the seminar said to me, "I didn't realize I was being so mean to you!" Was that the student's experience or mine? Or, perhaps we gave another turn to the transference?

In old age, the psychoanalyst J.-B. Pontalis (1993) wrote a little memoir titled *Love of Beginnings*. His writing admitted the struggle over where to place his book: autobiography, philosophy, literature, or short story? He wished to say more about how he came to his profession but beyond noting his youthful disenchantment and a strong dose of chance, refused a tidy conclusion. There is always more than one beginning, or we are always beginning, always introducing. As I wrote this chapter, Pontalis's title kept pressing on my thoughts. Can we really love beginnings and beginners? What about having to begin over and over? Pontalis comments on words and his passion for the torment of learning:

> I must begin with the H school. That is because it is there that I see the starting-point of my torments, at least of the one that will be my subject here: the love and hatred of language. I don't know if it's hatred or love that wins out; I am undertaking this book only in order to grasp and recover . . . the nature of this passion that (I sometimes imagine) rules my every suffering, however apparently unconnected with it: anxieties of love, for example, grief, distress of mind or sudden animation—in short, everything that presents itself as a change of state. (1)

So here it is again: both psychoanalysis and pedagogy involve a changing of state, passions thought about here through the maddening embrace of transference to words. What then is it that is held in thrall, or captivation? Perhaps only the touch of something we know nothing about. We can never be sure of the destiny of that thorny unconscious utterance: "I don't know if it is hatred or love . . ."

3

What Is the Use of Theory?

> It is *the delicacy of the speaking being* that the analyst listens for today.... The Freudian journey into the *night of desire* was followed by attention to the *capacity to think*: never one without the other.
>
> —Julia Kristeva, "Liberty, Equality, Fraternity and . . . Vulnerability"

A School of Transference

Should psychoanalysis be taught in the university? And can the university give psychoanalysis its due? These questions opened Freud's (1919c) essay, "On the Teaching of Psycho-Analysis in Universities." They still need asking for a compelling, speculative story of education that involves teaching and learning with the creation, conveyance, and reception of the character of theory. Should we then teach psychoanalysis in the university, would we be willing to question our hopes for its knowledge with the quarrels of our psychical life? Would we remember the theory we already hold—the wild, forgotten one forged in a childhood of passionate sexual research? What are the difficulties in narrating these forgotten affairs that return to the university as resistance to theory? Is this resistance a quality of psychical life and its affected belief, or is resistance a quality of theory? Freud leaves us to ponder these questions when he wonders whether psychoanalysis can be taught by asking whether it can be learned. He (1919c) tucks his consolation inside a lesson plan: it would be enough to learn "something *about* psychoanalysis and something *from* it" (173; italics original).

How strange to bring to the university a soft theory, tender to the touch of our affected beliefs and to the styles of teaching and learning that invite emotional situations as a resource of inquiry. One may argue that it is a bad idea to present a theory that freely associates the conflicts we have with the theory we already hold. And what can we make of Freud's claim that psychoanalysis is affected theory that wavers between lifting repression and, through the transference, repeats what has not been remembered? His (1919c) two parameters—that the curriculum be open to anyone interested and that it should not be sequestered in the medical school—lead to a third unusual, I almost wrote *impractical*, insistence. To think about our theory of theory the best material is the most unbelievable and takes us into the fictions of life. Freud recommends imaginative works such as novels, plays, and short stories. One hundred years later, Kristeva (2010b) advises us to keep reading; or rather, she tells doctors that if they are to enter into relations of suffering, they must read very long novels.

These literary affairs may remind us that while there is something inconceivable about the destiny of affected beliefs, we can still imagine how the human manages both to be obdurate in views and impressionable by design. Imaginative works freely admit the difficulties of the speaking subject: for instance, the phantasies made when our motives forget their objects or hold them too close; or when, for example, our words mean more than we want and carry wishes for things we cannot have. Literature, or the affecting world of words, permits free association to the drama and reverie of language and invites us to wonder about our own magical thinking and the shock of its disclosure. Readers become like the characters they meet, entangled in impressive ties of desire for transference. There, too, we lend to literature our aesthetic conflicts to be reacquainted with quests for beauty, truth, and love (Meltzer and Williams 1988). But to take notice from all of this life—where passion turns against its best-made plans, where accidents devise meaning, where words defy and are deceived by the gravitational pull of the mind's lost objects, and where there comes deferral—to notice what else communication carries requires learning a theory of reading. Psychoanalysis proposes that we learn to read between the lines; study what we dismiss; read for the gaps, mishaps, and misrecognition; and read for where the text resists our meaning. We are invited to join a school of transference to see for ourselves how the conveyance to the other of our wishes for authority, love, and even revenge are resplendent in our earliest play and then a second chance occurs in the transference to theory.

In this chapter Freud's doubts over what may happen in teaching and learning psychoanalysis in the university become an occasion for asking, *what is the use of theory?* The question is familiar and estranging in classrooms and life; it carries consternation and frustration and, given time, can sway into creativity and transform conditions for learning. Yet theory, or questions posed to problems in life, side by side with its "uses," is notoriously difficult to define, partly because we are self-theorizing creatures and that theory is like the air we breathe. The other conundrum is that even if often dismissed as "only theory," we cannot help ourselves from asking the question why. Since the audacity of theory contains a kernel of aggression and seeks to either destroy old views or protect them from changing, theory is not benign. On these matters, the use of theory may take on the fury of revenge: the best belongs to the theorist's desire to write theory and the worst, in theory, is falling into writing inhibitions.

Everything hinges on how we understand the use of the object of theory. With the work of D. W. Winnicott ([1968]1989) we enter the backdrop of subjective experience from the perspective of the baby that he named "object relating" and "object use." His terms are counterintuitive. In object relating, the experience is ruthless and the subject, Winnicott proposes, "is an isolate" (221). Winnicott simply states the gap: "Here is the subject and there is the object, but in the experience of the subject there can be no use of the object" (234). There is not yet the other. As a step toward bumping into the world while becoming a self, object relating involves mainly ego processes. Object usage has to do with the object itself, beyond the subject's projections. In both procedures Winnicott suggests a paradox to be accepted in learning: "The baby creates the object, but the object was there waiting to be created and to become a cathected object.... we all know that we will never challenge the baby to elicit an answer to the question: did you create that or did you find it?" (221). The paradox involves an implicit destruction of the object, and if the object survives without retaliation, the object becomes real and as a shared reality can be created. Theory may open transitional areas of illusion, disillusion, and re-illusion, and, yet, a great deal depends upon whether our use of theory can tolerate the paradox of trying to learn from abstracting subjective experiences into a shared experience of thought. Winnicott suggests that from a very early age, we are always playing with reality and the consequence of this play rests in a good-enough response from the other. He ([1968] 1989) notes the fragility of sequence: "(1) Subject *relates* to object. (2) Object is in process of being found instead of placed by the subject in the world. (3) Subject destroys object. (4) Object survives the destruction. (5) Subject can use object" (227). My sense is that the crucial moment is opened with Winnicott's third sequence: "Subject destroys object." However imaginary the destruction may be, that is, the subject in theory destroys the object, the subject also questions whether the theory or the self will fail or survive. And then the problem becomes, what is felt in theory?

At first there is the subject's experience of relating to the object. What is felt in theory is anxiety, understood as a warning for what has already happened before but carried forward to new learning events. The anxiety is that one's own theory of what might happen in teaching and learning is in danger of exposure and defamiliarization. We are vulnerable to something unknown and something might happen to us. Anxiety anticipates that a great deal will be lost should more be thought and animates, through phantasies of learning and teaching, the emotional logic of resistance to theory. Anxiety is our most incredible or unbelievable material—and deeply theoretical. In the university, where we may both suffer words and make words suffer, we also find new symptoms of defending against anxiety that are difficult to understand: resistance to theory, hostility to reading, hatred of language through worries over jargon, writing inhibitions, and fear of theory. I look into these situations of loss in order to suggest something new about the emotional use of theory. The psychoanalytic ethic in this work is built by the idea that to tolerate the opening of the mind requires listening with a difference to the conflicts of meanings audible and inaudible just at the point that they reach defensive mechanisms of closure.

The analysis draws from the clinics of literary theory, novels, psychoanalysis, and pedagogy. I call these clinics *studios of words* for both the problems they propose and the means by which they create new narratives that welcome the mind's freedom to use the object and imagine the ways we are affected by the words of others. As clinics, they contain symptomatic acts and involve thinking about our theory of theory by questioning how significance occurs, by asking what is important, and through conveying an interest in the loss and restoration of meaning. In these precarious matters, Kristeva (2010a) risks her tipping point and gestures to ours: "Twenty-five years of analytic practice has convinced me that listening to the unconscious reveals the *vulnerability of the speaking being*, at the borders of biology and meaning, a permanent imbalance, a source of anxiety but also creativity" (41; italics original). Let us turn then to problems of theory internal to the pedagogical dilemmas of the literary clinic.

Literary Life

More than forty years ago, the Modern Language Association asked Paul de Man (1989) to write a chapter on literary theory. They may as well have asked, should we teach theory in the university? The association wanted de Man to tame the beast he had already set free and prove to them that even his own naughty literary theory can behave. But it won't, and this refusal ushers in a theory of theory. The story is familiar: officials instructed him to anchor theory to the practice of teaching and, with clear language devoid of ambiguity, demonstrate the utility of application. Instead, de Man acknowledged his resistance to their school essay by arguing for the impossibility of theory. The association rejected this wager, and de Man published his essay in his last book, *The Resistance to Theory*. There, he wrote: "A general statement about literary theory should not, in theory, start from pragmatic considerations" (1989, 4). It should begin with reading for our affective blindness, and his remarks moved him quickly into the problems with what is disavowed. It is almost as if de Man argued for the right to be impractical and to encounter the things not known.

De Man's (1989) defense of theory stayed within theory's own uncertain terms as he worked his way into the heart of the matter: "The resistance to theory is a resistance to the use of language about language. It is therefore a resistance to language itself or to the possibility that language contains factors or functions that cannot be reduced to intuition" (12–13). Language is theory and if theory can only be about more theory, if this relation can never end, such a revelation may leave our knowledge in tatters. The theoretical, it turns out, is to be taken personally—as a sign of force—and for de Man the resistance to theory, now in the form of an association's demand for a language manual, signifies resistance to the divided subject and to the arbitrary relation between words and the things to which they refer. From a Winnicottian perspective, the association is caught in object relating and answers the paradox with its insistence that theory is to be found and not created.

De Man's critique of the Modern Language Association's insistence on the professionalization of theory brings another narcissistic blow, since language comes with a rejoinder. He moves inside the professionalization of theory, finding its illusion of objectivity, and with irony tells us that the Modern Language Association can neither stand language nor associate with it. For de Man, language is a sliding chain of signifiers that propels the desire to determine and confuse our boundaries (29). His idea is that to address and be addressed by literary theory one must pass through the anxiety made from having to treat words as the subject of alienation. This literary theory—and for de Man, we are speaking of deconstruction—unsettles the meaning we may want and need and in turn confronts us with something that cannot be read, namely, our resistance to reading. De Man however, makes one more turn: "Nothing can overcome the resistance to theory since theory is itself this resistance" (19). Here we may hear a variation of Freud's questions, that is, whether theory can be taught by asking whether it can be learned. What then can be said about this theory, the one we do not know we have?

Shoshana Felman (1987) places resistance to theory into the heart of the crisis of teaching and learning. She then asks, from where does authority come? While a graduate student, Felman accidently found a book by Jacques Lacan and her supervisor warned her away from it. Not only did she read Lacan, she wrote a book about her adventure in reading and posed a new question: How does the teacher's transference to knowledge, implicate the teacher's pedagogy? Transference is part of the teacher's crisis and one form the crisis takes is the teacher's resistance to the uses of pedagogy. Felman also supposes that the teacher's resistance to pedagogy will take a familiar, even maddening dynamic. If the teacher names resistance as belonging only to the other, she steps into the position of what Lacan (1998b) called "the subject presumed to know" (267). If the teacher ignores this omnipotence and narcissistic gratification, she is likely to fall into Lacan's (1998a) other trap, "the passion for ignorance" (121). Symbolizing the teacher's resistance provides a fresh approach. Again, thinking with literary theory helps. For instance, in his lectures titled *The Preparation of the Novel*, Roland Barthes (2011) creates a pedagogical phantasy: "The principle is a general one: the subject is not to be repressed—whatever the risks of subjectivity. . . . Better the illusions of subjectivity than the impostures of objectivity. Better the Imaginary of the subject than its censorship" (3). We can recall Winnicott's forbidden question of whether we find theory or create it. Better to allow for experiences of object relating and object use than to reduce our efforts to a set of instructions to follow.

One might notice that subjectivity is our greatest risk, a vulnerability to repression and disaffection that occurs whenever one faces the freedom to change the mind, leave the prohibition not to, and destroy that nagging thought that something might happen. Yet, when the subject represses, things have already happened. With Kleinian flair, Eve Sedgwick (1997) turns to the question of teaching literature, where the theory we bring to texts wavers between the hard paranoid/schizoid and the soft depressive positions. Sedgwick asks: "To change one's understanding of the reasons for one's practice, or the meanings of one's practice—is it not, under this understanding of theory, to change one's practice?" (23). Her view led me to wonder if we are always in theory kindergarten and, along with the thought, what would it take to enjoy (again) our rough-and-tumble play (Britzman 2002)? Like Freud, de Man, and Felman, Sedgwick turns to the emotional uses of theory.

What changes the mind? This is very hard to say. Yet to change one's mind does require a willingness to question what is already thought with the affected idea that reason is not an alibi. Jacqueline Rose (1993) identified this dilemma when she pointed out that no one could give reasons to reasons and that no one reason can serve as the cause for every cause. Rose was grappling with the question of the limits of knowledge and whether the limits are things to be overcome or whether such limits are a quality of the necessary failure of knowledge. Theory inherits this dilemma and emerges when something is unreasonable: anxiety over knowing what it is we do not know. Melanie Klein ([1946] 1975) simply called this unreasonable theory "phantasy." Klein identified the importance of phantasy to the life of the infant's mind as phantasy animates imagination and a desire for symbolization. Marcia Cavell (1993) emphasizes the social bond as ties to dependency on others and on symbolization and as indicating both the human condition of neurosis and education.

Perhaps it takes a novel to understand what is unreasonable about the frailty of this social bond, vulnerable as it is to misunderstanding, compliance, and repression. Resistance to being affected by our dependence on words may be our best way to lose our mind. What may bother us is that language gives us a foothold into meaning until it slips and we must take the fall. Jennifer Egan's (2011) novel, *A Visit from the Goon Squad*, gives a few pages to a minor character, Rebecca, a university professor, a rising academic star, and a mother. She wrote a book on "the phenomenon of word casings,"

> a term she'd invented for words that no longer had meaning outside of quotation marks. English was full of these empty words—"friend" and "real" and "story" and "change"—words that had been shucked of their meanings and reduced to husks. Some, like "identity," "search," and "cloud," had been drained of life by their Web usage. With others, the reasons were more complex; how had "American" become an ironic term? How had "democracy" come to be used in an arch, mocking way? (262)

Yet, the professor's sublime theory of the loss of theory can neither give protection from what does not happen in language nor can it prepare her for the return of the repressed. Rebecca is waiting for a concert that may never begin and has lost her husband and baby in the restless crowd. Then comes his text message. It has the remarkable appearance of abandoned letters, lost vowels, and chewed-up words. Mouthing them sounds like the garbles of baby talk, perhaps an attack on inner speech. In our drive for attachment, have we lost touch? There is a baby, now encased in an argument with her husband, who, in spite of promising not to, gave their two-year-old daughter a "lollipop," the baby's word for the smart phone. The baby keeps calling for her lollipop, a word that sweetens the baby's revenge. Readers may wonder, so who is encased in what?

Egan's novel gives notice to the situation of language with the comedy of communication: that we cannot really quote ourselves as we speak even if language and the wild gesture of wiggly fingers performing scare quotes gives us this illusion. As we try to encase the meaning of words, what the other does with them discloses the unspeakable. Then, too, the wish to capture the other in a perfect language that goes without saying is always being ruined by unexpected events and deferrals such as broken promises, missed encounters, parental anxiety, baby talk, demands for lollipops, and the elusions created when others pretend to carry out our wishes. But this means that no one may possess the last theory, or the theory that ends all theory. It also means that theory is not behavior.

To Listen for the Subject of Theory

Problems internal to the classroom seem to repeat, with variation, the question, *what is the use of theory*? In beginning this chapter I asked, if psychoanalysis were taught in the university would the teacher be willing to go behind the scenes of her beloved knowledge and handle the quarrels of psychical life? The teacher's dual dependency on symbolization and on others is the crisis, and pedagogy emerges from anxiety over losing the topic and being left only with what is impossible for the students. Then, the teacher may teach in spite of the students and even to spite the students. We have an example here of pedagogy as object relating and may ask, can the teacher then listen to the student's revenge and destruction of the object and survive without retaliating?

When my undergraduate education class tried to explain to me why they did not like reading a psychoanalytic text on adolescent development that I assigned—and indeed, some students decided they hated the book without having read it—they began by expressing feelings of persecution that quickly dissipated into phantasmal evasions. The classroom became a madhouse. Many felt the book was driving them crazy. "It" was hard to understand and made too much of things. Sounding a bit like the Modern Language Association, they argued that the book was needlessly complicated, too theoretical. The author used unfamiliar words and had the audacity to change the meanings of the words the students felt they already knew. Some students argued that the author was only making up difficult things. More than a few students felt the examples the author gave were crazy (or unbelievable). From there, they drew two more conclusions. If the author was driving them crazy, it must only mean that she herself was insane to write such a book and, by association, as I was the professor who assigned the text, I must be the craziest of all. Now beyond the first question of who is doing what to whom, and knowing full well I am bothering my students, their objections are a splendid indication of theory as emerging from our aesthetic conflicts, or anxiety over the nature of beauty, truth, and love.

Aesthetic conflicts involve a homemade story of runaway theory, where students manage, against all odds, to project what they fear into the new theory that then returns as persecution and justifies their hostility. It is a rather vicious circle. Their reasons form the resistance; should students consider their use of theory, would they too have to lose their bearings and go crazy? The emotional logic of resisting theory is dazzling. We are beholden to a theory we do not know we have and experience this not knowing as resistance to theory. And when we encounter a theory we do not know we have, we experience a theory we don't know we hold. We actually involve ourselves in the crush of two theories: the forgotten one already held and the one experienced but incapable of being remembered. Which theory can teachers and students destroy when the fight is between belonging and separation, judgments of good and bad, and the defenses of identification and splitting? It is as if the subject of theory is caught in the middle and the only way around the conflict is through negation: *it is not my theory*.

Freud (1925c) presents the idea that thinking is a form of judgment that involves negating thoughts. His theory of negation is contingent on his discovery that "perception is not a purely passive process" (238) and carries forward into the world our earliest wishes to refind the lost object that gave the mind its first satisfaction. Thinking, or the capacity for thought experiments to delay bodily action, involves not only ideas but also an interest in how and why we feel them. When listening to negations in the analytic setting, Freud (1925a) advises the analyst to take away the "no." His essay begins:

> The manner in which our patients bring forward their associations during the work of analysis gives us an opportunity for making some interesting observations. 'Now you'll think I mean to say something insulting, but really I've no such intention.' We realize that this is a rejection, by projection, of an idea that has just come up. Or: 'You ask who this person in the dream can be. It's *not* my mother.' We emend this to: 'So it *is* his mother.' In our interpretation, we take the liberty of disregarding the negation and of picking out the subject-matter alone of the association. It is as though the patient had said: 'It's true that my mother came into my mind as I thought of this person, but I don't feel inclined to let the association count.' (235)

Psychical events feel like more than consciousness of them and with every new thought, now as a feeling about feelings, an old theory is affectively insulted. It is not so much that we do not mean what we say, but rather that we say more than we consciously mean to feel. This orientation to listening to the speaking subject places the psychoanalyst in an estranging position since the analyst does not know what the patient means and, by asking for free association, invites what neither expects. Just as the psychoanalytic curriculum assumes the best material is the most unbelievable, Freud acknowledged that psychoanalytic theory is unbelievable, although he maintained that is no reason to abandon its ideas. The concept of negation allows for this experiment in unbelievable meaning. In mentioning, "No, I would have never thought of that," one can face what is furthest from the mind and learn from what is most vulnerable about having to speak to the other of meaningless things.

One consequence of this linguistic treatment, of treating words as theory, is that what opposes theory is neither practice nor experience. Its great opponent is mental inhibition, attacks on the mind, and a destruction of our chance to freely associate with new ideas and the emotional experience we dream. It is here that we can ask whether theory, our most ineffable project, can be defended, perhaps in the way in which Shelley (1921) long ago defended poetry: as the capacity for narrative revolt that includes curiosity with what stops it short. However, because theory holds no guarantee, because it does not come with a stamp of approval, because theory resides with problems, and because theory is resistance, we are sent to work. Theory, both the one we hold and the one met, is an adventure with vulnerable meaning and involves playing with reality.

Writing Inhibitions

Writing inhibitions are particularly painful in university life. There is an inhibition with committing words to a blank page, but also there may be endless rewriting without reasons and a refusal to throw away what already feels useless, just in case a use can be found. The writer cannot decide what is important and unimportant. The judgments on the matter on the page are harsh, self-berating, and terribly premature. It is as if the writer's compromise is self-erasure. The writer's impossible theory for how to write seems to begin with the wish to possess the ideal conditions that must exist before one can write so that words too can be perfect. This rule that cannot be followed ends up in the service of blame, a feature of melancholic suffering. Words seem to turn against the self. This is what the symptom of writing inhibitions feels like. We struggle with finding the right word while nothing comes due; depression sinks words into disappointing things (Kristeva 1989).

One of the paradoxes of literature is that an author may write a novel whose character suffers from writing inhibitions. The narrator in Italo Svevo's (2003) absurd novel *Zeno's Conscience* tries to take the advice of his psychoanalyst and write the story of his entire life. We can notice some bad advice or perhaps a psychoanalytic joke that forgot its punch line. Svevo's psychoanalytic parody runs for 437 pages. Much of the novel is about not being able to write. Zeno manages to hold a pencil, immediately falls asleep, wakes up, goes out for a coffee, looks for a cigarette in an attempt to stop smoking, and congratulates himself on his efforts. It is as if Zeno wishes to kill time. He finished neither his story nor his analysis. Neurosis wins the day, though the irony of the novel opens with the words of Doctor S., Zeno's analyst, who writes in the preface, "I am publishing them in revenge, and I hope he is displeased" (3). Dr. S. offers to share the profits from publication, though he is sure no one will read the book.

A great deal happens in not being able to write. Two clinical fragments from the psychoanalysts Hans Loewald and Ernst Kris give a feel for what describing the writing block is up against. Both propose a constellation of thorny conflicts that wreck the desire for authorial responsibility. One of the surprises in clinical writing is just how often the neurosis hitches its fate to failing to meet the demands of teachers, who are treated like angry parents. It is in school where the child's repressed wish for originality and the authority this brings returns and fuses with the institutional demand to produce original work. In such emotional logic, originality becomes symbolically equated with compliance and compliance turns us into copycats. But the agony of giving birth to oneself does get caught in what Alice Pitt (2003) describes as matricide. Must something be killed off in order to write?

Let us meet a graduate student in Hans Loewald's (2000b) paper "The Waning of the Oedipal Complex":

> A student, working for a degree in the same field as his father's, had trouble in completing his thesis. He was brilliant: the thesis so far had progressed well. His father had died a year earlier. The patient began to procrastinate; he felt strongly that he needed support and advice from his thesis advisor. But he knew quite well that he was perfectly capable of finishing the work on his thesis without help. He chided himself for his delaying techniques. In part, these took the form of paralyzing doubts about the originality of his work which at other times and for good reasons he had no doubts. He also wanted encouragement and support from me, but he kept telling me that it was wholly his responsibility, not the advisor's or mine. . . . [Several sessions later] it dawned on me that he might be speaking of responsibility also in a sense not consciously intended by him. . . . Perhaps he was talking about being responsible for a crime. (388)

How, without falling into the trap of repeating the crime, would Loewald communicate this thought of what the patient did not intend when the patient feels certain that responsibility to interpret one's doubts is akin to listing one's faults and taking the blame? The dilemma they both share depends on symbolizing the phantasies of crime, where guilt over the desire to imitate the father, the thesis advisor, and the analyst originate a self that languishes in the punishing writing inhibition.

Kris's (1951) discussion of the ways in which psychoanalytic technique affects theoretical formulations contains a fragment of an analysis with another academic who suffers from a writing inhibition. Kris tells his readers that this is the professor's second analysis. While his first one helped him overcome some of his inhibitions, upon receiving an academic post new editions of his old conflicts returned and the professor sought another analyst and came to Kris. The patient complained he could not advance through the academic ranks because he could not do research. And if he did research, he might plagiarize ideas already written. The patient described his situation as feeling an impulse to steal the ideas of others. Kris notes his patient's dream of "a battle in which books were weapons and conquered books were swallowed during combat" (22). The patient then recalled going on a fishing trip as a young boy with his father and grandfather and watching the men compare the size of their catch. Kris summarizes his interpretation and the patient's association to it:

> The tendency to take, to bite, to steal was traced through many ramifications and disguises during latency and adolescence until it could be pointed out one day that the decisive displacement was to ideas. Only the ideas of others were truly interesting, only ideas one could take; hence the taking had to be engineered. . . . The patient was silent. . . . Then, as if reporting a sudden insight, he said: 'Every noon, when I leave here, before luncheon, and before returning to my office, I walk through X Street . . . and I look at the menus in the windows. In one of the restaurants I usually find my preferred dish—fresh brains.' (22)

Kris concludes: "The problem was to establish how the feeling, 'I am in danger of plagiarizing,' comes about" (23).

Feeling like plagiarizing takes us into the steam room of phantasy. And there, everyone sweats words. Kris writes that the patient's colleague actually stole the patient's own ideas—that the patient himself was the victim of a plagiarizer. Emotional logic turned the tables: left without brains, the patient may have felt like the copy, worried about repeating himself. So the analytic dilemma may also concern what else this patient communicated when he dreamt he was eating (or hording) words, left his analytic session in hunger, found a restaurant that served fresh brains, and had an insightful lunch. In my view, the professor's aesthetic conflict is caught between originality and influence, itself a permanent imbalance rather than a terrible choice. Can our use of words be both stylistically original and dependent on the influence of others at the same time? And yet writing does require that the writer steal words, take them off the hook, chew on ideas, spit them out, and then set them free. Writing, after all, is a turn toward the use of the object and does entail some benign destruction as well as the writer's survival.

In his last unfinished paper, "Some Elementary Lessons in Psycho-Analysis," Freud (1940) again sends readers back to school. We need to remember this small detail for when we are sent back to school, we return to an emotional world of learning theory, though rarely are we asked about these lessons. Freud draws the reader's attention to the verisimilitude of affect; how our feelings, made from the earliest infantile theories, carry into the present the child's conviction that no one can help. Changing that theory into a new approach to its old ideas is a delicate task. New theory, Freud (1940 [1938]) believes, is built with others, word by word:

> In this way one can get [the analysand] to take a part in building up a new theory about the subject and one can deal with his objections to it during the actual course of the joint work. . . . It follows the path along which the investigator himself has travelled earlier. In spite of all its advantages, it has the defect of not making a sufficiently striking effect upon the learner. (281)

So there is a problem with beginning with what is familiar or original about our theories. What we know too well is of no use. If the analyst stays with what the patient already knows, the patient's revenge is negation, "No news there," or "It goes without saying." On such occasions, everyone is encased in useless theory, repeating his or her sickness of words. The only way out is for the patient to be surprised by the analyst's capacity to listen differently to the negation, as if the patient said, "Yes, there is news. But what can that mean to what I thought I already knew?"

Writing inhibitions are also called "writing blocks." While I devote chapter 6 to its vast unfinished affairs, for now this term without a subject and an object that cannot be used should give us a clue that some forgotten thing objects to associating freely with words. It could be the fishing trip that Kris's patient remembered when he was only a small fry. Or it could be with the problem of what responsibility means that Loewald asked when his patient felt the loneliness of writing. Finding a better technique for writing or being given the instructions of time management does not solve the conflict since it is words that feel wasted. The inhibition belongs to the writer's theory of losing something that is not writing: old forgotten feelings of resentment, hostility, and helplessness displaced onto words. Cognitive instruction and time management may feel like "old news." A different use of theory is called for to face a decision to free oneself from the weight of the compulsion to repeat what has not been remembered. This would be where originality and influence can have their play. In a short paper on constructions in analysis, Freud (1937b) described the work as "liberating the fragment of historical truth from its distortions and its attachments to the actual present day and in leading it back to the point in the past to which it belongs" (268). And yet, the liberation involves mourning the loss and both occur side by side. What is liberated is not an idea but a piece of melancholia. The person can become curious, use the object, and so enlarge psychical affairs beyond what has already happened.

Fear of Theory

Roger Simon's (1992b) "The Fear of Theory" proposed that learning theory disrupts the immediacy of the graduate student's wishes to repeat past experiences in the presence of the teacher. Most disturbed are the idealizations of knowledge that can never fail and are now equated with stepping stones to a successful career. But the stones have crumbled with time and the new and old theory meet our doubts over value. These doubts are also a feature of theory, and for something like learning to be possible we have to involve ourselves with something not yet known. Simon's advice on teaching suggests attending to the uncertainties of possibility: "This is the first task of everyone who regrets the obscuring of eternity" (97). I want to link the worry that nothing can change, a feeling that also plagues anyone who suffers from writing inhibitions, to the attraction to the unconscious and the urgency of the pleasure principle.

To understand what we are up against, it is useful to put ourselves up against it. Freud's (1937a) late advice to psychoanalysts, found in his paper "Analysis Terminable and Interminable," does such work. He thinks through the thickets of the analyst's therapeutic ambitions and considers the wish to cure as the analyst's defense against the complaint that psychoanalysis takes too long and is too much trouble. If the objection is that psychoanalysis is only words, only words can meet this objection. Freud admits that analysis does take too long and is much trouble, though the same can be said of education. The shift he makes, however, is with an attention to analytic failure: "Instead of an enquiry into how a cure by analysis comes about (a matter which I think has been sufficiently elucidated) the question should be asked about what the obstacles are that stand in the way of such a cure" (221). The obstacles come in many forms, including unspeakable phantasies of what happens in theory.

The same year Freud wrote his paper on teaching in the university, he (1919b) published "A Child Is Being Beaten," an essay on the formation of phantasy, a fantastic theory of obscure, unbelievable impressions, leftover from the vagaries of infantile research. Freud wondered about the dreamlike sentence—"a child is being beaten"—that his patients often uttered when trying to remember the disappointments and pleasures of childhood love. Why does the speaker fall into this passive construction? Is the speaker watching others take their punishment, escaping the punishment she or he was supposed to have, or whispering the wish to beat and be beaten? Notably, Freud mentions school, where, amid the class of onlookers, teachers dole out public punishments. *Is a theory being written?* With the allowance of phantasy more sentences can be formulated, such as *a student is being educated*, with the qualification: *My teacher loves me and so must punish me with theory*. Could it be that the fear of theory contains an unconscious phantasy of the teacher's sadism and a student's wish to be beaten?

If theory is felt as if one needs to be taught a lesson that everyone already knows, for the student, not understanding the teacher's knowledge can be felt as losing the teacher's love. I place Simon's (1992b) formulation of "fear of theory" into this constellation of phantasy. Simon was writing of the agony of learning theory in the university with what happens for adults who are competent and successful when they enter graduate school and then begin to feel the pain of exposure when they cannot get their head around ideas they do not have. He rehearses the worn-down complaints: something might happen to the knowledge I already have; my family will laugh at me; my partner will leave me; things will be different, and I will confront my own disappointed wishes for love. But there is also a loss for the teacher, what Felman (1987) formulated as the crisis of teaching, or the teacher's resistance to symbolizing the affective ties of the pedagogical relation. If the teacher too feels theory is lost when the students seem to wreck it in learning, when they bring the revenge of misunderstanding, when the teacher mistakes her own education for the student's desire, or even when the teacher demands both originality and compliance, might we then express the teacher's phantasy—*a teacher is being beaten*—with the qualification: *my students love me and punish me with my hated theory*. Might we then begin to wonder about the phantasy of theory, however vengeful and beaten?

Fear of theory can be approached as a constellation of anxiety that binds teachers and students into a sadomasochistic transference. This imaginary relationship involves defenses and inhibitions made from phantasies of what else might happen as one confronts the gap or imbalance between how others disclose the world and our unspeakable wish to both become the sole author of meaning and the tablet the teacher writes upon. Theory, after all, may remind us of something we cannot remember: the passionate inexperience of having to learn before we understand while feeling the force of wishing to know without having to learn (Britzman 2002, 2009, 2013). To push a bit further, fear of theory operates with phantasy and involves a dash of hostility fueled by the aggression of narcissistic defenses. The anxiety expresses a combustible mixture of learning for the teacher or student's love while fearing that love will be lost. The phantasy defends against one of the most agonizing problems of learning and teaching: that the work of putting words to lost things provokes the pain of mourning. Something quite personal must be destroyed in order to play with new theory.

Working Through

Freud's (1914a) third model of psychoanalysis, "Remembering, Repeating, and Working Through," strikes a discordant note. This process converses with and destroys timeless libidinal associations or drive pressures for immediate satisfaction that merge with institutional ideals of expertise, functionalism, and reason (Britzman 2011). Such idealizations require terrible splitting: influence or originality, answers or questions, authorship or plagiarism, compliance or inhibition. As we saw in de Man's reply to the Modern Language Association's object relating to theory, in the two clinical discussions on writing inhibition in the work of Loewald and Kris, and in the homemade theories of students that add up to fear of theory, all these symptoms merge with professional and institutional ideality and disavowal of the uncertainty that theory must be used to be theory at all. Such difficulties may also give us a clue why Freud asked, can the university give psychoanalysis its due? If as de Man posited that theory is resistance, this too is a part of our earliest theory forged in object relating, when there was no word for what we did with our fragile inexperience. Working through is the means for questioning the attractions of the unconscious, what Freud once described as an empire of omnipotence. In Loewald's (2000a) view, the psychoanalytic movement is from passivity, to a creative activity: "The patient is not merely to be made aware of the existence of such contents in his psyche, but he is asked, implicitly if not explicitly, to own up to them as his wishes and conflicts and defenses to re-experience them as psychic activity of a nonautomatic nature" (93). Essentially, theory cannot be on automatic pilot or it will run on empty speech.

The problem is that if one cannot stand the mental pain of thinking, and there is no one to lend a hand to contain the anxiety, one gives away the mind. Paradoxically, psychical activity is both the transfer point for theory and the obstacle to understanding why we have theory at all. Freud's (1914a) technical paper, "Remembering, Repeating, and Working Through," stays with these difficulties: "The patient does not remember anything of what he has forgotten and repressed, but acts it out. He reproduces it not as a memory but as an action; he repeats it, without, of course, knowing that he is repeating it" (150). Freud is on the cusp of his new theory, the compulsion to repeat, when he writes: "We have learned that the patient repeats instead of remembering and repeats under the conditions of resistance . . . we must treat his illness, not as an event of the past but as a present day force" (151). The same may be said of education: we must treat our education not as an event that has passed but as a present-day force.

Encore!

When psychoanalysts are asked about their world, they too grapple with the question, what is the use of our theory? They take the wobbly work of resistance to psychoanalysis as a condition of their practice. The British Psychoanalytic Society (2012) made a short film, *Encounters Through Generations*. It is composed of interviews with the third generation of psychoanalysts. Most are women, between the ages of seventy to ninety years old, and at the time of the film, still working, writing, and teaching. Their analysts were Melanie Klein, Donald Winnicott, Wilfred Bion, and Anna Freud. In one segment, Hannah Segal (1918–2011), of the Kleinian school, was asked about the future of psychoanalysis in the United Kingdom. With her strong German accent she said:

> Speak of the world. I have a rather pessimistic view. In old age, people become more pessimistic. They know they are going to die and so they see the world in pieces. But beside that, actually, our culture is so anti-mind, violent attacks on the mind because our minds might not go along with the policies of the rich, mighty, and imperialistic ones. . . . The analytic ethos is very much in danger.

Segal may also be saying that to speak of the world is to speak of the mind.

Another analyst, Edna O'Shaughnessy, also urges psychoanalysis along. While objections are to be expected, she believes the key difficulty in psychoanalysis belongs to the question of *working through* understood as trying to know the self. Yet emotional knowledge is elusive, resistant, and subject to defense and inhibition. "We analysts," she tells her audience, "have the responsibility to have to know ourselves." She continued: "but we cannot know ourselves."

In her essay "Words and Working Through," O'Shaughnessy (1996) wrote, "A patient's talk is not simple" (138). Communication, she suggests, passes through a history of love and its impressive losses. While the worlds of others affect the self, something that is not the world affects the self as well: phantasies for a perfect communication without the noise of words, a wish for a world without uncertain theory. O'Shaughnessy asks, "Why do words have a special importance for working through?" (149). Her reply is elegant. "Words," she writes, "break omnipotence.... [And] Omnipotence is always hostile to verbalizations" (149).

Resistance comes in many forms: as theory, as language, as transference, as desire for authority and love, as anxiety over loss, as revenge, as negation, as the compulsion to repeat what has not been remembered, as repression, and as a wish for a perfect (omnipotent) theory (Kristeva 2009). All of this is unbelievable. Yet the idea that theory is resistance and that theory can resist the censorship of what goes without saying risks language as much as it does subjectivity. Putting this permanent imbalance of invention and influence into words is also to permit the paradox as to whether theory is found or created. Words may be our greatest learning challenge and where we may give the uses of theory its due. To notice these events as also risking the intersubjectivity of teaching and learning takes us beyond the phantasies of omnipotent control and the super-ego tyranny of professionalization. At the very least, teachers and students would have to imagine what education could become by asking what has happened in their education. But we may still have to stop at a restaurant to eat fresh brains.

4

The Adolescent Teacher

> The phenomenon presented by the patient in cases like this deserves to be called a '*fausse reconnaissance*,' and is completely analogous to what occurs in certain other cases and has been described as a '*déjà vu*.' In these other cases the subject has a spontaneous feeling such as 'I've been in this situation before,' or 'I've been through all this already,' without ever being in a position to confirm his conviction by discovering an actual recollection of the previous occasion.
>
> —Sigmund Freud, "Fausse Reconnaissance (Déjà raconté) in Psycho-Analytic Treatment"

Always Again

Sensations of déjà vu return us to where we felt we had already been. Something happened before and without volition we believe it is happening again. The aftertaste of déjà raconté belongs to the mouth and to echolalia, a rather strange mix of hearing and speaking. We have already said that or intended to say that. It is however, the feeling that is hard to shake off. Such subjective affairs suggest affective and intellectual uncertainty and a confusion of time, place, person, and situation. But trying to convey what these feelings feel like may leave communication in shambles. We can see in the epigraph to this chapter that as Freud (1914c) describes an uncertainty of perception, he does so with recourse to markers of certainty: *deserves*, *completely*, *conviction*, and *the actual*. In the psychoanalytic situation these spillovers of anxiety and insistent repetitions are beholden to unconscious thoughts, the ego's regression to childhood, some excess of leftover meaning, and a defended conviction that indeed, something inexplicably known but hard to place is happening again.

Freud's essay (1914c) begins with familiar events. He gives two examples of missed encounters or mistaken perceptions. The first one takes readers into the edges of an argument between the patient and the analyst. The patient says to the analyst, "I told you that before!" and the analyst has no recollection. Or, the patient asks, "But haven't I already told you? Or, did I tell someone else?" Both people in the room carry their convictions as to what is being said, unsaid, denied, unheard, or better, hidden away. It doesn't really matter who is right or wrong. The matter is with what to make of not knowing what is being said and heard. Most interesting is the affect that rushes conviction to its brink: a feeling that one is repeating oneself with an earlier scene that muscles its way into the present. Such exchanges that seem to have a life of their own bring Freud to think more about the compulsion to repeat both wishes and their disavowal. We have been there before and wish to return there again, but now as space travelers and mind readers. Much of this, as I will go on to discuss, involves separation anxiety, worries over what has been missed, lost, taken away, and yet may magically return. It is all so paradoxical, though a welcome one in the psychoanalytic situation since it is our wishes and phantasies that can be stretched back to the absurdities that called them forth and seem to carry them on.

Freud's (1914c) second example comes in the form of a letter he received from a reader of his work. It concludes his essay, and readers are left to wonder what the first part of the essay, and its staged near argument of separation anxiety, has to do with sexuality. The writer began his letter by disputing Freud's views of infantile sexuality. But as the letter continued, the writer suddenly felt "an amazement" and brought forth two memories that he then felt confirm Freud's view of psychical life. The first memory recollects his infantile theory that girls, just like boys, have a penis. But the second memory disrupts the first:

> I remember seeing my mother standing in front of the washing-stand and cleaning the glasses and washing-basin while I was playing in the same room and committing some misdemeanor. As a punishment my hand was soundly slapped. Then to my great terror I saw my little finger fall off; and in fact it fell into the pail. Knowing my mother was angry, I did not venture to say anything; but my terror grew still more intense when I saw the pail carried off soon afterwards. . . . For a long time I was

convinced that I had lost a finger—up to the time, I believe, at which I learnt to count. (27)

There is quite a bit of material here, and we can imagine the boy's misdemeanor pertained to sexual research that made his mother angry. That was his first failed secret and the letter admits it. If we think that at the same time as the slap sounded, the boy had a prior thought that the girl's penis went missing we have his second secret. He may have surmised, given the law of unconscious equation, that the same punishment may happen to him since it must have happened to her. But here the boy has no words for the missing finger that mother throws away. Conviction stands in but now as déjà vu. The boy had to learn to count on (sexual) difference as a solution to separation anxiety or what is commonly called "castration": a series of important losses that rather unwittingly usher in symbolization.

The compulsion to repeat in education, however, crosses the thin line between the "ah oh" of déjà vu and the always already "oh no" frustrations of déjà raconté. A typical example is when the professor walks into the new class and has the oddest feeling that she has been there before. The feeling seems to be confirmed as a student blurts out, "But we have already read these texts." Or, the professor repeats herself when she asks the class, "Have I already covered this? Have I discussed this before?" The room becomes restless again. "No matter, let's review." More than once have I made the mistake of picking up a lecture from the week before, presenting it to the class again, and feeling I had fallen behind. Each time the class stared at me in amazement, yet no one corrected me. In rehearsing what Freud (1901) called an "everyday psychopathology," and he lists quite a few—forgetting, slips of the tongue, bungled actions, superstitions, and errors—I am unsure whether I am repeating a wish or reporting on a fact. The letter to Freud had that same unease.

Another case not often discussed through the veil of déjà vu and déjà raconté revolves in the spinning phenomenon of the character of adolescence. We have already been there before; I have been through that before, and the perception is replaced by a conviction: I have been through it all before. No wonder then that the insistence *I have already told you that before* is so familiar and estranging. It has been said to us countless times by parents and teachers: "I told you that before!" usually followed by a threat of punishment: "And never do that again!" Even so, we do it again. It is adolescence's license that reminds adults of some forgotten thing they have already done but wish to forget. Not only are there memory problems; current spontaneous feelings seem to work against remembering what actually occurred during adolescence. And yet, if our theories of adolescence seem certain as to when it begins, we lose our momentum from doubts as to whether, or even how, it can end. Some feel we have two tries with adolescence: one as a teenager, the other as middle-age crisis. For those in its thrall the shock of the adolescent body is repeated in their theory of how adolescence ends and has the uncanny feel of a finger being cut off, dropped into the mother/teacher's pail, and thrown into the trash. There are rough drafts of this phantasy.

A graduate student working with me reported that in his tutorials, many young undergraduates agree that adolescence ends with some sort of terrible accident, punishment, and loss: a car crash, a death of the parent, a police arrest, for example. As an abject lesson for taking responsibility, castration immediately turns the naïve adolescent into a full-blown law-abiding adult. What becomes of the lost part, or of the adolescent, seems to stop there. However, we can take the theory backward: the sexuality of adolescence feels either so pleasurable that a trauma is required or one must get kicked out of it. In school life, those who do the kicking happen to be teachers who resemble earlier figures that the adolescent has already doubted.

Can the adolescent and the teacher meet, *even if they have met before?* I posed the first part of this question to one hundred undergraduate students in a teacher education course officially titled The Adolescent and the Teacher, and in this chapter I use some of the events in this course as a lens from which to view unconscious dimensions in learning a profession that is subject to phantasies of becoming someone else. In handling the question of whether these characters can meet, I am uncertain if emotional contact is beholden to the unreal realm of the frightening uncanny or to the repetition of time and speech made from déjà vu and déjà raconté.[1] Freud (1919a) we know, had a great deal to say about both and related such paranormal phenomena to the figuration of the double, or what he first calls, in his essay on the uncanny, "a special agency." A few years later, Freud will see this character as the super-ego, our greatest force for self-criticism, for the recommendation of guilt, for ideality, and for answering the question, friend or foe.[2] In "The Uncanny" Freud (1919a) writes, "There is a doubling, dividing and interchanging of the self. And finally there is a constant recurrence of the same thing—the repetition of the same features or character-traits or vicissitudes, of the same crimes, or even the same names through several consecutive generations" (234). Something is compulsively repeating. It all teeters between aesthetics and anxiety and some rather fantastic wishes not quite subject to infantile amnesia but to its remainder: omnipotent thoughts. "What is left over, however, and rejected as false," Freud (1918 [1914]) writes in his case study of Wolf Man, "is what is new in psycho-analysis and peculiar to it" (33).

Within the pedagogical encounter, something strangely estranged and terribly familiar compels the feeling that teaching has already happened and

I must make it happen again. What may surprise is that these psychical features obsessively repeat in professional fields of knowledge. One consequence for the fields of education and psychology is that of an exemplary alienation due to splitting into good and bad the anxious relations between psychological theories of development as taught in psychology departments and theories of pedagogy in faculties of education. Variations on this alienation find their way into the well-worn conflicts between education and psychology and teaching and learning and reach climax in the discord between theory and practice. In all these conflicts the transference object of human learning creates more dissonance since intersubjectivity leans upon what is unknown in self-other relations and brings into the present old conflicts between pleasure and reality. However, if pedagogy and developmental theory carry on urgent claims as to the nature, registration, and obduracy of adolescence, and if each proffers ready-made instructions on how the actual adolescent should express the quest for thought, beauty, and truth, neither the adolescent nor the professor can follow such directives. I observe this confusion in my course The Adolescent and the Teacher. Everyone in the room was once (or thought they were once) an adolescent and each of us has managed to repress intolerable thoughts by projecting them into our future students who come to us as threatening our pedagogy. And for this reason, teaching and learning feel both familiar and terribly estranging.

The psychoanalyst in the classroom can ask what else is met and missed when the adolescent and teacher try to meet. My claim is that encounters with adolescence take us to the heart of phantasies of learning to teach with others and the super-ego ideals that pressure the teacher's responses to both the profession and the students they meet. At first, the students learning to teach need to believe that only the adolescent has psychology and the teacher must manage that. They want techniques that promise successful pedagogy and imagine psychology as a last resort to explain a student's failure. They think of the school psychologist as only there to provide an office to send the student to for further testing. It is as if the backward glance of developmental theory is meant to destroy the presence of pedagogy by bringing disruptions best left at the classroom door: the messy lives of teachers and adolescents, the teacher's depression, the adolescent revolts needed for becoming, and the murky underworld of intersubjectivity. The students in my course are not the originators of this phantasy, although they do live inside its anxiety. Indeed, their identifications with the ideal object of knowledge and the heroic selfless professional are already rooted in the profession they hope to join. Such phantasies are urged along by daily routines, by the charts of learning objectives, and by the rules of the institution they know so well, since they grew up there. And yet, due to the ambivalence of projective identification, due to their emotional world, they also worry. Must they take in the lives of others and become emotionally involved with their students to learn as teachers? Must they, too, become the adolescent again? Why is this learning so uncanny, and how may it transform into a theory of pedagogy capable of withstanding the psychopathologies of everyday life that must include the teacher's regression?

I accidently renamed The Adolescent and the Teacher in two ways: The Adolescent and the Teacher, Can They Meet? and The Adolescent Teacher. It took time to notice these slips. They became apparent when I received assignments that carried one slip or the other, or when I received an email that began: "Hi Professor, I am an adolescent teacher in your class." And yet what is surprising is that we cannot really study adolescence without becoming one and feeling subject to what Bion (2000) calls "emotional storms" (321), or the atmosphere created when people meet.

I invite the students to speak in the language of psychoanalysis. Looking back, I invite uncanny education. They read Sophocles's play *Oedipus Rex* and are asked, why can't the adolescent or teacher be king? With Margot Waddell's (2002) *Inside Lives: Psychoanalysis and the Growth of the Personality*, I introduce the clinical writing of the British Object Relation school and its words: the thinking breast, projective identification, internalization, anxiety, K (knowledge) and minus K, love and hate, and the paranoid/schizoid and depressive positions. With Ishiguro's (2005) novel *Never Let Me Go*, they enter the lives of oddly formed characters, doubles or doppelgängers, that are given an education before they become organ donors for the "normals." The characters have been told and not told of their fate and so as an operation of language from the side of deception, we grapple with the question, what is reading all about? They also are asked to think what may happen when the adolescent and teacher meet as they watch Cantet's (2008) film *The Class*. The film became another occasion for uncanny feelings. It was as if the class that watched the film became its actors under the director. The reading road is bumpy, littered with objections, obstacles, and painful plaints. They want to know what clinical writing, novels, and plays have to do with education. They want to know what the breast has to do with pedagogy. I take all of their questions and doubts as our material and clinic.

My Freudian slip, *the adolescent teacher*, brings me to analyze my association and wander into the thickets of the dynamic unconscious, scenes of psychical continuity and disunity that gain momentum with the passing of each second. Furthermore, can the psychoanalyst and the teacher meet? This, too, carries on a number of pedagogical difficulties since the psychoanalytic request invites the linking together of disparate things with an interest in the unknown, a curiosity toward the circuitous route of transference of feelings between people and, from the meandering words of free association, care for the detours and fragility of the symbolization. To stretch this invitation further and, perhaps, to welcome what is most unwelcome about psychoanalysis, one more turn is made: just as the human can be characterized through conflicts of maturation, points of fixation and regression, areas of fusion and confusion, and profound phantasies of education, so, too, can the professions. Freud (1930 [1929]) posed this radical relationality in his study of unhappiness when he asked: Can the neurosis of culture be psychoanalyzed? And what would be its use?

In this chapter I treat my course The Adolescent and the Teacher as both a commentary on the ordinary learning quests for thought, beauty, and truth that a study of both adolescence and the teacher holds in store and as an extraordinary allegory used to analyze emotional life through the uncanny education of the helping professions. I consider the psychology of this alienation through the lens of a particular transference configuration that anticipates developing education. In a nutshell yet to be cracked, the adolescent with the teacher proposes the conflicts of their respective education and the soft ground of relationality that sinks under pressures for compliance, something the adolescent justifiably hates and the teacher feels she or he must demand and then receive back what is known to be hated. Helene Deutsch's (1967) insight into the adolescent world may be stretched into our time of pedagogy: "The adolescent lives his life, after all, between two worlds: one that has thus far complied with his demands and one that now demands his compliance" (34). Later, I link these tensions of authority, super-ego demands, and psychical history to Kristeva's (2007) formulation of the adolescent syndrome of ideality, an ego defense against the loss of the ideal object or the ideal ego. This doubling proposes a depth psychology that involves both the adolescent and teacher's struggle to reassemble phantasies of education, to what at first feels already set and carried forward with the weird command, "Repeat after me."

My discussion leans on the psychoanalytic idea that adults working in schools and professors teaching in the university are subject to their adolescence, and these elemental entanglements of internal conflicts, phantasies, and defenses that return in professional knowledge as demands for certainty and as a belief that learning is a tonic to conflict as opposed to conflict's delegate. These are also the gambles of psychical life as our most radical relation to the self and other. When people meet, so too do their internal worlds with the mental mechanisms of splitting, identification and projection, defenses best described as unconscious object relations that compose and decompose what is intersubjective in intrapsychic life. I relate the contiguity of psychical life to our uncanny quest for meaning and influence and our susceptibility to searching for ideal objects. However, it is in this meeting that I also see a kernel of alienation carried into our perceptions of conflicts in the structure of schooling, the arrangement of professional knowledge, and the confusion between phantasies of learning, or their ideality syndrome, and the daily imperatives to act with certainty, stay on task, and avoid emotional involvement. I am calling such phenomena uncanny.

For those learning to teach, anticipating the adolescent can feel strangely familiar and the one they bring to their education is an anxious double, or the uncanny adolescent. There are worries with the conflictive nature of school culture that they do know something about because they have been there before. In learning to become the high school teacher they each want to be, they trade uncertainty about meeting the adolescent and thoughts about their own becoming for an idealization of the role of perfect teacher. What is being put forth is super-ego anxiety over education met by a worry that they will have to separate from their positions as learners. Such phantasies have a second defense in the form of an idealization of curriculum that is then symbolically equated with the teacher's authority. Good students simply learn and then leave. Bad students are the fault of others. But the teacher—the one in the classroom and the one in the student's mind—then faces an impossible decision: should one be pedagogical friend or foe? Grossly put, they wish to know as much as they can about how to control adolescents and perhaps avoid the doorstop of developmental theory so that they can just teach their subject and believe in what they know. They wish they could kick the adolescent out of adolescence, just as they felt they too were kicked out. I think this aggression and accompanying suspicion toward the adolescent imaginary does return, but for now I reference an early split between affective and intellectual life repeated in professional education that comes with the question of whether pedagogy must be involved in the student's emotional world and therefore whether the teacher must become an affected teacher. Defenses against the wild side of learning expose the situation of adolescence—the one my students thought they left behind and the one that returns in their idealization of knowledge, the teacher's authority, and the splitting into good and bad. How does the complex of adolescence—as figuration, situation, uncanny double, and drive to know and as subject to displacements, reversals, and substitutions—repeat in the anxieties of professions? Can learning be more than a return of the repressed? Or, does learning rely on the compulsion to repeat?

The Impossible Professions

What can be said of the professions and their psychology is they are impossible. When Freud (1925b) gave recognition to education, governance, and medicine as "the impossible professions," he enfolded psychical life within the intersubjective difficulties of the work and then extended psychical conflict into the professions themselves. With the idea of transference, Freud urged the practitioner's involvement and symbolization. He understood the heart of the helping professions, including their techniques, goals, and language, as affected by forgotten events: remnants of sexual research, infantile wishes, Oedipal conflicts, latency, and return. From these developments in psychical life Freud then supposed that working with others brings to the professions the paradox of symbolizing intersubjective history through intrapsychic dynamics. Our doubts over the veracity of knowledge, our difficulty of knowing the other, and our desire to solve problems and to help, for example, are woven from our own frayed threads of primary helplessness and dependency. Just as individuals defend against these feelings of helplessness, the professions have comparable mechanisms, though they are hardly diagnosed as attachment disorders. But neither are affects and phantasy considered as ordinary pieces of psychological life. Instead they are treated as meaningless outbursts. Nonetheless, the impossible professions are subject to the estranging time of déjà vu and the compulsion to repeat that is founded on what is unspeakable about intellectual and affective uncertainty. If our personal cause effectuates traces of our infantile roots—internal perceptions and their first tendency to hallucinate satisfaction and then cry out to the other—our adolescence introduces to the conflict between pleasure and reality the new tendency of ideality. For the adolescent, the ideal has the flavor of the absolute, a quality of the superego. In the case of the impossible professions, the idealized object is its knowledge of others, while the defense is against the loss of love, displaced into worries over becoming unprofessional. Here the impossible professions are subject to adolescence through the ways in which the passion to know becomes confused with the need to believe. The handling of knowledge, Freud (1915a) thought, conveys as much about our internal world as it does about the conflicts with transference to the mandates of institutional life and the people with whom we work.

At least four of Freud's ideas on the psychical body press upon the vulnerability of experience in education and provoke new narratives for the impossible professions: that consciousness is not the sum of mental life; that there is a fluidity between sanity and madness; that the human subject is divided and affected by both internal conflicts and the ambiguity of external reality; and that education, as our human condition, is an unsolvable and necessary problem. Kristeva (2010b) sees within this design what is most creative: the speaking subject's search for beauty, truth, and thought amid existential anxiety. Hence, if the human professions are impossible, they are also thinking professions and have the added burden of questioning their own learning theories with the responsibility to protect and encourage the freedom to think beyond prescriptions.

It almost seems as though Freud, when speaking about the impossible professions, was really addressing the psychological fact of the human condition as caught between the drive to know objects in the world and the anticipation of its own reception. All this occurs in daily school life, where unconscious human nature flourishes and where people do not make up their minds so much as worry whether their minds are becoming lost, ignored, or rendered irrelevant. So many conflicting desires play in these events, and what then makes psychoanalysis its own impossible profession is that it must begin from the complication that the human is a stranger, difficult to know, and swimming against the tide of perception, itself a passionate affair. Winnicott (1988) describes human nature from this vantage but also insists: "Human nature is almost all we have" (1). Consequently any education inherits a terrific problem: psychical reality is transferred into our procedures for becoming a speaking subject with others. And the teacher's work involves what already belongs to human nature: meeting the desire for truth, beauty, and thought from the situation of ambiguous reality and what feels uncanny about that.

For the psychoanalytic field, school life is thought of as contingent on that exchange between the epistemophilic instinct, or the drive to know, and the ambiguity of reality. But it is our research desire that proposes and registers phantasies of learning and creates our first theory of origin (Walsh 2010). The human, then, is a self-theorizing creature of learning, impressed by what she or he cannot know and, as beholden to her or his own research, is subject to breakdowns and the need to believe against all odds. In the early history of child analysis, psychoanalysis was thought of as a cure for neurosis in school life and as on the side of sexual enlightenment. Anna Freud (1954) broke into this idealization when she generalized the term "education" as "all types of interference with spontaneous development" (9) and then had to conclude, "The emergence of neurotic conflicts has to be regarded as the price paid for the complexity of the human personality" (15).

If education is all types of interference, and plays in the field of neurosis, the teacher, too, is interfered with. Like the psychoanalyst, teachers must greet more than they know. François Roustang (2000) raises this dilemma when he places the difficulty of group psychology into the mix:

> Pedagogy, which seeks to bring everyone to the same level of capacity, nonetheless comes up against collective and individual resistances as it accomplishes its program, and must take those resistances into account. . . . How will it inspire the desire to grow and progress? It will have to bring into play forces that cannot be itemized in books. (83)

The clinical material of child psychoanalysis presents the other side: young patients, while playing with toys, communicate a great deal of what they feel as their misfortunate education. They take on the character of good and bad teachers and punish those other students who have trouble with being told what to do. They are able to play all the roles and perform the fragility of communication as vulnerable to misunderstanding and to feelings of persecution punctuated by narcissistic injury. Even as school life is contemporaneous with psychoanalytic treatment and often the reason why there is an analysis, these phantasies of education propose a history of disunity between feeling and experience (Green 2000a).

For both education and psychoanalysis, however, adolescent revolt presents as a crisis to adult identity. Perret-Catipovic and Ladame (1998) suggest that adolescence raises a theoretical paradox for cure when they claim: "There is no adolescence without a crisis of adolescence" (162). Their view places uncertainty into the heart of moral views that regularly amplify the divide between normality and pathology in developmental theory and between success and failure in pedagogical efforts. Winnicott ([1963] 1994) highlights a more immediate crisis when he argues that it is normal and pleasurable for adolescents to wish not to be understood: "In fact adults should hide among themselves what they come to understand in adolescence" (145). And yet, what precisely is being hidden if part of the dilemma is that one has forgotten one's own adolescence? It may be as simple as stopping oneself from telling adolescents that they too will grow out of it. Winnicott advises that adults must know how to wait. They may accompany the crisis of adolescence but may not cure it (Dethiville 2014).

Impossible Adolescence

For Helene Deutsch (1967) actual adolescence challenges the psychical body and presents a torrential storm dedicated to the other. It creates the sharpest exaggerations of the mind's wishes and defenses, and so Deutsch emphasizes agonies:

> The kaleidoscopically fluctuating changes on the inner battlefield: victories of the instincts over the superego or vice versa; the rejection or revival of previous identifications, the upsetting of the ego ideal; the search for new identifications; narcissistic engrossment and masochistic self-depreciation—all these are examples of the turmoil that occurs during the process of maturation. (22–23)

Just as childhood impresses the adult's mental life, Deutsch suggests there is no final goodbye to adolescence. Adolescent tendencies are eternal and, for the adult, unconscious. In this sense, Kristeva's (1995) view is capacious: "When I say 'adolescent,' I mean less a developmental stage than an open psychic structure" (136).

Anna Freud ([1957/58] 1969) turned her observations on adolescence back to the psychoanalytic field, suggesting why adolescents are so hard to know, and related this difficulty to her observation that "adolescence remain[s] a stepchild in psychoanalytic theory" (141). She identifies two difficulties for psychoanalysis. First, adolescence cannot be reconstructed as one is undergoing it. And second, in adult analysis, even within reconstruction, a history of affects escapes:

> What we fail to recover, as a rule, is the atmosphere in which the adolescent lives, his anxieties, the height of elation or depth of despair, the quickly rising enthusiasm, the utter hopelessness, the burning—or at times sterile—intellectual and philosophical preoccupations, the yearning for freedom, the sense of loneliness, the feeling of oppression by the parents, the impotent rages or active hates directed against the adult world, the erotic crushes—whether homosexually or heterosexually directed—the suicidal fantasies, etc. (143)

Anna Freud's astute observation raises the question, why would any adult want to bring this atmosphere back? Even so, within contemporaneous relations between adults and adolescents, given the uncanny qualities of these relations, can atmosphere ever leave?

Kristeva (2009) draws upon Deutsch's (1967) discussion of eternal adolescence with the insight that, while seemingly a test of maturity, the adolescent answer is vulnerable to the defense of ideality: a splitting of knowledge into either good or bad; where friends are either loyal or pretenders; where adults are either friend or foe; and where the line between convictions and absolutism blurs. There is a desire for paradise. The adolescent, Kristeva proposes, is a believer who has given up on research. Ideality is just a part of the story. As a formulation of the mind, eternal adolescence, Kristeva (2009) writes, "also indicates a certain suppleness of agencies, an adaptability, a capacity to modify oneself according to the environment and the other, as well as against them" (51). Such fluid views of adolescence are difficult to keep in mind, partly because actual adolescents seem to demand justice but to be heard they must break all of the rules.

We can also ask, what does the adolescent demand? One might suspect a release from unbearable drives and the question of belief. Kristeva's (2007) provocative formulation of "the adolescent syndrome of ideality" is where she sees the mind's flexibility becomes rigid. She proposes adolescent belief as a mental constellation mesmerized by the force fields of culture and super-ego cravings, leaving the ego to be captivated by the imaginary choice between beauty and thought. The adolescent, an incredible believer in the need to believe without knowing why, becomes caught in the atmosphere of her or his beliefs in the perfection of the object. The missing element is the actual other and her or his imperfections. Kristeva identifies within the syndrome of ideality

> a new type of speaking subject who *believes in the existence of the erotic object* (object of desire and/or love). He only seeks because he is convinced that *it must exist. The adolescent is not a researcher in a laboratory, he's a believer.* We are all adolescents when we are enthralled by the absolute. (717; italics original)

Kristeva's (2007) argument is that the adolescent trades the ambivalence of childhood research for the absolutism of knowledge. In doing so, the other is always a threat if it cannot be perfectly controlled. Due to the force of belief—its ideality and tendency to foreclose the ambiguity of meaning through the splitting of good and bad—the adolescent defends against her or his own depressive position. The belief is maintained with the painfulness of the paranoid/schizoid position. There is, for the adolescent, a terrible beauty in the belief in perfection: in an ideal object that is totally satisfying and therefore must be true and unchanging. From Kristeva's formulation, one can see the force of certitude in "a rush to paradise" (718) but also a tragedy: a fall into suffering when ideality is disillusioned or fails to stabilize the subject. Kristeva likens these passionate attachments to those exemplary adolescents, Romeo and Juliet, where the couple, in the name of love or ideality, must be destroyed.

Nevertheless must one take sides? This may be the teacher's best waiting question. In his advice for beginning psychoanalytic treatment as discussed in chapter 2, Freud (1913) urged analysts to be modest, expect misunderstanding, avoid suggestions and the urge to prescribe to the patient their own values. Here, technique is impressed with its negativity because meaning is elusive and subject to self-deception and narcissistic gratification. Kristeva (2007) has described how cure is a matter of making "a creative bond with others" (716) that urges an abiding interest in what inhibits our bonds and destroys desire. But to accept this psychical reality and indeed work from within its conflicting desires, Kristeva advises the analyst to share the adolescent's ideality "and thus be capable of metabolizing the need to believe not through acting out but through the pleasure that comes with thinking, questioning and analyzing" (724–725). The same goes for the teacher provided that she or he can recognize that the adolescent ideality has a comparable form in her or his ideality of education.

Entre les murs, or Between the Walls

Psychoanalytic ideas developed throughout this chapter come alive when my students view Laurent Cantet's (2008) film *The Class* (*Entre les murs*). It takes us three weeks to watch the film. My slow-motion pedagogy defers what will happen to make space for what we think has happened to us. The students do feel the touch of their own history of education and the sting of the transference to the characters: sometimes through their identification with the film's teacher; sometimes with the students and the young actors; sometimes with the school rules that must be broken; sometimes with insufferable boredom. Difficult to share, however, are the phantasies of the teacher's education. So they feel relief with exciting lessons and then disappointment when the teacher's good idea falls flat. Like the student characters in the film, my class becomes angry when the teacher is unfair or takes revenge. It is as if my students are watching their doubles. It appears they worry about their own sense of fairness and whether they can avoid feeling conflictive life. Our discussion of the film is slow to shift away from their anxiety of what the teacher should do to avoid mistakes. They cannot give advice to a film's characters and, even if they could, it would only destroy the story. By the second and third viewing the students begin to notice the uncertain dilemma of how they interpret and why, for them, records are being broken. It is the characters' reply to the teacher that both references ideality and wrecks it. The students in my class are amazed at the flashpoint of words exchanged: they are yelled, mumbled, cut off, and overthrown with affect. But they have also experienced these linguistic gymnastics before.

The film follows teachers and ninth-grade students throughout their academic year and focuses on Mr. Marin's French class, from the chaos of the first day, where the teacher worries about losing time to noise and disruption, to the last meeting when, before they say goodbye, he asks students to say what they have learned. By the last scene, viewers are privy to the students' and teachers' secrets but also to the rhythm of sparring matches: from the ways communication fails and is revived, to the young students' strategies for truth, beauty, and thought, and how all these emotional events bring to truth its circuitous motion to convey meaning and the forces that alienate it. As for the students in the film, they challenge the teacher's pedagogy by asking whether he, too, is in search of beauty, truth, and thought. Through talking back, through asking unanswerable questions, through meaning one thing but saying another, the students are also teaching a lesson in language.

The film is set in a large, working-class, multicultural, comprehensive high school in Paris. Mr. Marin, a young teacher of French, is dedicated to the students' progress and to the ideality of innovative pedagogy but spends much of his time trying to decide whether his efforts are wasted. He struggles with his own adolescent syndrome. The film opens with an argument: Mr. Marin is trying to explain to his students that they are wasting thousands of minutes by not settling down to work; yet the students challenge his math. They tell him the class is only fifty-five, not sixty, minutes, and he has to admit his calculations are wrong and feel the disparity between his worded desire and theirs. During one lesson, the students challenge his cultural bias. His examples insult their world. One student advises him: "Just change a little." Viewers are privy to the pleasures of sparring and the painfulness that overtakes the class when the game goes too far and, just as suddenly as it began, dissolves into hurt feelings, revenge, and broken records.

Within the film these fourteen- and fifteen-year-old actors present their character studies, well known to anyone who has been to school: the class clown, the brain, the fidget, the sleeping one, the bored one, the gossiper, the quiet one, the absent one, the bossy one, the vanishing one, the one who will not make it, the one who cannot understand, the one who cannot wait, the one who gets expelled, and so on. There are funny interruptions: exploding pens, bathroom requests, sexual innuendos, and, when frustration erupts, name-calling and humiliation. Mr. Marin is always faced with an impossible decision: will he be friend or foe, stubborn or passive, attentive or ignorant? Must he trade in his own beliefs to comply with school rules?

The character adolescents also have a great many things on their mind; foremost is whether the teacher is friend or foe. Mr. Marin's first assignment asks the students to write a self-portrait, a character sketch, with the focus on what they love and hate. The class is reading aloud a passage from *The Diary of Anne Frank*. Their reply is that they have nothing to say, and he urges them to make something from their nothing. He explains the assignment as a way to practice French grammar and use language as a means "to learn things from your feelings." These students also want to know the teacher's feelings, his loves and hates, and whether they can influence him. Will he share his life with them? What of their divide? Indeed, as the film progresses, as misconceptions pile one upon another, the weight of being a person renders him the adolescent teacher. The difference that Mr. Marin needs, to open some possibilities and foreclose others, to say both yes and no to the students, is momentarily lost. Adolescence has this timeless quality and proposes the paradox of the unconscious as both urging immediate gratification and presenting our greatest adversary to the delay of thinking. Rather than symbolize the students' distress and his own, Mr.

Marin acts out his incredible need to believe and in the process loses the language he needs.

In one uncomfortable scene, student representatives participate in the teachers' meeting on student progress and witness a teacher's frustration with a particular student whom Mr. Marin tried to reach yet also sabotaged. The representatives report to the class what was said. It comes during Mr. Marin's French lesson, and the students confront him with his own words. He loses his temper and angrily tells the young women acting as class representatives that they are behaving like skanks. The young women yell back at him, and Mr. Marin denies the word its wish to hurt. A chain reaction ensues leading to the expulsion of a student. While almost all of the film occurs between the classroom walls, near its end, Mr. Marin marches to the playground—the students' territory—to confront the girls whom he felt caused him trouble. The director employs a close-up shot of a few students standing around a jungle gym. As the camera surveys the playground, suddenly an angry crowd of students surrounds the teacher. They are arguing over words. He tells them, "A teacher can say things a student can't!" and then one of the students calls him an asshole. Though he protests, a girl yells, "You say skank, we say asshole." Through the trade of insults, Mr. Marin has lost this fight. He is not above the law, even as he wishes to speak words without consequence. The teacher cannot be a king. And yet, in becoming too human and because he is both friend and foe, Mr. Marin too must be willing to take his own assignment and "learn things through his feelings."

Cantet's (2008) commentary on the film's reception in France notes that its controversy resided in public debate over whether or not teachers should be emotionally involved in the lives of their students. Part of the debate was whether "modern pedagogy" was too soft and, in consequence, could not make upstanding citizens or kick the adolescent out of adolescence. We are back to the conflict between affect and idea along with a psychoanalytic rejoinder that ideas without affect are useless and affect without intellect is meaningless. But personal involvement is the heart of the alienation between developmental theory and pedagogy and it preoccupies my undergraduate class, so well-schooled in their subject area but so frightened as to whether their future students will find their love of knowledge as relevant. Indeed, that one must pass through the emotional world on the way to a shared reality is something that my students demand when they ask me why they have to do the assignment, when they question its application for their future, and when they ask me to take the time to be affected by their views and just change a little. Our pedagogy develops by way of digression, works against the classroom clock, and presents the uncanny question: What is between the teacher's knowledge and the student's learning?

As for viewing the film, all of us have difficulty remembering we are watching uncanny fictions of education. Perhaps this is due to our transference to the film's verisimilitude, to déjà vu of endless classrooms, and to the velocity of digression that language carries, often to the point of destroying meaning. We have been there before. Ideals are being broken and, if patched together, reveal their fissures and our vulnerability to them. As we discuss the film, my students wonder, what would they have done? Who would they become? Could they tolerate the teacher's mistakes and deceptions and times when the teacher is no longer a charming character mask but an actual human who fails and disappoints? Can their identifications contain the pathos, aggression, and comedy as they too try to learn something more about the inevitable and needed mismatch between teaching and learning and knowing and not knowing?

And what of that other character, namely, the school? The undergraduate students seem surprised that while the school has rules, the students have representatives in the faculty council. They do not think there can be democracy in schools. Nor are they or anyone else prepared for the conflicts that democracy brings to the speaking subjects who now talk back and who do revolt. In this sense, the undergraduate students repeat a variation of Cantet's comments on the film's controversy: adolescents have too much freedom and too much of a say. The students in my class seemed to have forgotten their high school years and the subjective fact that they, as much as their teachers, created subterranean school culture. Yet the students do remember that their teachers regress into adolescence. They remember the teacher's affect but not the idea that each time a teacher insists there is only one way to do things, that order can be perfect and that time is either wasted or valuable—when all of these super-ego demands are felt as the only story—they forget that the rush to pedagogical paradise dissolves the human bond, leaving only the adolescent syndrome of ideality that comes with the acting out of friend or foe. The teacher is both friend and foe and each subjective position carries a transference history of ambivalence, love, and hate. This, too, is the agony and creativity of the impossible professions, so dependent as they are on what cannot be known, and from this ignorance must try to accompany and recommend the human condition with affecting words, questions, and interpretations.

Das Ding

Aggression in teaching and learning also returns though as its study may only be reached by the shock of allegory. One of the curious paradoxes in my course and repeated in the film is that studies of developing relations in education have no endpoint and cannot be perfect. Such uncertainty, too, is a condition of the impossible human professions, where learning proceeds through breakdowns and reparation and, often, it is difficult to decide their differences. Returning to the finger in the pail episode Freud (1914c) recounted, a great deal has to be lost before anyone learns to count. Thus such radical uncertainty may be a gathering point for déjà vu, the uncanny, and phantasies of hostility, as well as disruptions to the adolescent syndrome of ideality, found in institutional life, professional knowledge, and in the traces of adolescence in the teacher's mind that are also needed for the quest for beauty, thought, and truth. What remains is how one breaks through the claustrum of ideality. In my view, we invite more phantasy, or the intolerable education.

Cantet (2008) mentions in the director notes the influence Alfred Hitchcock's 1963 film, *The Birds*, had on his staging of Mr. Marin's march to the playground, the scene where he loses any semblance of a unified, sane teacher and reveals his hysteria. Not many film critics consider Hitchcock's *The Birds* as having much to do with education. Nor is it trotted out as a heroic film for the teacher to emulate. There is a school and a number of adult and child rescue fantasies woven throughout the erotic plot, a number of castrations that are undergone, and Hitchcock films these repressed urges through what comes before: anxiety that all will be destroyed because something bad, something one cannot see but is there all along, will return with vengeance. It is usually something quite small and, in normal times, not scary. For Hitchcock it was birds and, when out of place, they return as horror. I showed an eleven-minute clip of *The Birds* to my class. It creeps up on us viewers and then leaves us frightened.

The character played by the actor Tippi Hedren is concerned about a young girl in school and decides to take her away. There is a long shot of the school and the sound of children singing a repetitive song. Miss Hedren waits on the playground bench, nervously smoking a cigarette. Her back is to the jungle gym. She hears the flutter of wings. One crow lands on the jungle gym and moments later it is filled with hundreds of birds. It is an uncanny scene, and Hedren has spent most of the film fighting with her erotic desire, I mean the angry birds. Hedren runs into the schoolhouse, whispers into the ear of the teacher, and the teacher has the uncanny assignment of getting the children out of the school in the middle of their lesson. The teacher tells the students they have to leave immediately. With great confusion many children ask why. But the teacher insists: act like we are having a fire drill, line up, walk quietly to the door, and when I yell "Run!" do that as fast as you can. The children line up at the door, walk in line, and then the teacher screams: "RUN!" The birds immediately attack the running children, Tippi Hedren, and the teacher. They dive into that human vulnerability: the fingers, the neck, the face, the ears, and the eyes.

It is a terrible, violent, and bloody scene. And it enrages the serenity of the nice classroom with phantasies of destruction, persecution, anxiety, and escape. Hitchcock breaks all of the rules.

In the early part of this chapter I noted that within the wish against adolescents—a wish to kick the adolescent out of adolescence, just as we have felt kicked out—a rather unspeakable phantasy of aggression is being made and forgotten. The letter Freud received about the man who felt his mother cut off his finger/penis and threw it away serves a similar function. Perhaps my use of the Hitchcock film repeated the phantasy but now as a performance of emptying out the ideality of control. If *The Birds* forces the question of whether we must treat the adolescent as the canary in the mine of education, that subterranean thing may be called "attacking birds" or the thing that the ideality of education finds intolerable. Consider the birds as the unspeakable thing that cannot be symbolized. The birds may represent the fallout of our language, what Lacan speaks of as jouissance: the terrible drive excitement always already there but it is an excess we cannot see coming. "From a Freudian point of view," Lacan (1992) notes in his seminar on the ethics of psychoanalysis, "the reality principle is presented as functioning in a way that is essentially precarious" (30). I think we can say the same of our precarious adolescence. And in the case of the impossible professions, there is no reality principal to announce over the loud speaker the order of our days.

5

On the Madness of Lecturing on Gender

We all know that if we detect in ourselves impulses of hate towards a person we love, we feel concerned or guilty. As Coleridge puts it:

> . . . to be wroth with one we love,
> Doth work like madness in the brain.
>
> —Melanie Klein, "Love, Guilt, and Reparation"

Madness

When lecturing on the topic of gender, words lent to the body take on uncanny abundance: there are fights over essentialism, construction, and evolutionary psychology.[1] There are gaps between experience and theory; stories of "gender trouble"; questions over the relations between nature and culture and between phantasy and reality; attempts to correct or defend stereotypical meanings through the splitting of gender into masculinity and femininity; and discord over social, cultural, patriotic, and religious convictions. There are emotional pleas to secure terms such as gender, sex, sexuality, men, and women. There are euphemisms for body parts and heated debate over causality in socialization, biology, and revolt. There are claims for existence, sexual difference, and gender violence. There is disquieting imagination. The gap between biology and meaning grows ever larger or is collapsible. Then come the casualties of hurt feelings and pedagogical failures. But are there second chances?

Yet when lecturing on how gender ought to be, the lecturer is apt to forget that ideas about gender are neither easily received nor are they necessarily experienced as a means for social change or as a mechanism of compliance to normative conventions. We are apt to forget that gender involves a rather complex emotional layering and an intimate resistance to its folds; at times there are also inchoate refusals to involve oneself in a contest of meanings. We may find that the lecture then founders on the bedrock of biology, hormones, chromosomes, and neurons.[2] All this raises questions of the emotional valence of gender, the reach of its psychical and social representatives and their tenacious splitting. But also there is the drive to know. As for the lectures, we are always in pedagogical trouble and this chapter considers a psychoanalytic view on why lectures can invite the symbolization of gender madness.

What does such madness entail? Psychoanalysis proposes psychical life as bearing the additional weight of internal aggression, or bodily drives that seek satisfaction and objects. Aggression is a needed element for the constitution of gender and gives rise to phantasies that complicate problems for its symbolization, always in crisis with prefabricated instruction (Gozlan 2014). When trying to represent the internal world and the object relations that propose an impressive dispersal of the unconscious history of gender, psychoanalysts risk the soundings of a particular madness. They play in the field of the personal and the impersonal, feeling their way into gender as a combine of affects, unconscious phantasies, sexual research, and transitional space. They also propose a constitutive gap between the given meanings and their reception. "The analyst," writes Kristeva (2000), "is led to see sexual difference situated in being. . . . We are at the heart of an unsettling strangeness here, and at the same time this memory, however outrageous, is invested by the narrative that restores it to us, that submits it to the domination of the conscious, that deciphers in language and addresses an Other" (64–65).

One of the first attempts to introduce object relation theories of gender to the general public occurred in 1936, when the London Institute of Psychoanalysis sponsored two public lectures given by Melanie Klein and Joan Riviere, announced as "The Emotional Life of Civilized Men and Women." The title is now dusty yet it still manages to hold an enigma with the suggestion of something uncivilized. A year later they were published under the title *Love, Hate and Reparation*, which was a compromise with Klein's "Love, Guilt, and Reparation" lecture and perhaps might be easier for the eyes in comparison to the negativity of Riviere's opening topic, "Hate, Greed, and Aggression," that seemed to sound the death knell. Indeed, Riviere (1937) worried what the audience would take to heart and concluded her lecture on that note:

An artificial segregation and discussion of the hate in emotional life, such as has been attempted here, is, you must remember, entirely schematic and is no representation of life as a whole. I hope that my presentation of it will not have proved depressing. It is of great importance that this side of our lives should be better understood. (52)

I imagine that worries over depressing our students with discussions on gender continue to this day. Then and now the delicate problem is whether, without having to take a side, we can begin to consider what is so one-sided, or rather so defended against and resisted, in attempts to represent the inside world of gender. The danger that usually goes without much comment is that a psychoanalytic orientation will propose and even act out both the madness of gender and the madness of trying to speak about it.

Riviere and Klein's lectures introduced to a general public about to go to war the concealments and displacements of aggression in emotional life. And they placed the evolution, dynamics, and phantasies of femininity and masculinity there. In doing so they proposed what is most startling about our gender madness and our endless struggles to feel its reasons. Just as Klein ([1959] 1975) would see, years later, the emotional situation of the infant in adults, these lectures gave to aggression a precocious chronology that is best called "phantasy," an inchoate constellation of helplessness, drives, anxieties, defenses, and wishes that compress introjections of the sensate world into the internal world of object relations. Taking the world in, they assumed, and both began with taking in the mother's breast, also involved anxieties over its destruction. While there are a great many ways to think about aggression and gender within the psychoanalytic field, Klein and Riviere were the first to present the force of what they understood as most inevitable about the gendered body—somatic trauma, psychical frustration, loss of the object, and constitutive anxiety. And yet from this negativity, they also suggest the development of creativity, epistemophilia, and symbolization. Along with the entanglements of love and hate, they added one more dimension to aggression: it is poignant in its self-protective postulates and foolhardy in its destructive tendencies. Aggression, they argued, is needed to create the distinction between reality and phantasy and the difference within gender. For Klein and Riviere, there is something impossibly unreal about aggression: it originates interiority; ordains every one of its functions, defenses, and wishes; and reverberates throughout gender and its transference.[3] There really isn't anything civilized in conveying and receiving a kernel of neurosis and psychosis in any knowledge, and trying to know plays with what is most uncivilized, or asocial, about emotional life: symbolic equation, or a tendency to collapse perception with the object, and the pleasure principle with the reality principle.[4]

Jacqueline Rose's (1993) contemporary lectures on Melanie Klein and war consider the problem of symbolic equation, where internal affects collapse into perceptions of an external object. Rose's topics are violence and femininity, war in the nursery, and the death drive. She, too, brought renewed attention to what is most uncivilized and her lectures had to respond to the anxiety that the magnification of phantasy and its negativity in emotional life might exclude, rather than deepen, awareness into the inexplicable and always-terrible hostility found in the social world. Yet in trying to open the imaginary of gender, one must touch the anxieties that the body conveys as its "being" without the consolation of knowing in advance its "doing" and how the other experiences her or his own unconscious history of gender. Rose asked that we consider the problematic of these limits in our theories: "What are the possible connections between an interrogation of problems of self-identification and sexuality in the unconscious and a field that can be called one of (conscious) knowledge and politics . . . ?" (236). In the case of attempting to convey this symbolic reach and the panic made when the world feels lost, we can also ask, what is it to represent phantasy as our human condition? Where, when speculating on the experience of gender, can our madness play?

Here, then, are some considerations on gender madness: the madness involved in conveying gender to the other, the madness of gender itself, and the madness of lecturing on gender. All of this brings me to matters of emotional life that unexpectedly bother, agonize, propose, and surprise our sense of gender as given, as unity, and as cohesion, all idealizations that seem to make gender feel so one-sided. I'll describe what Klein and Riviere make of gender and its aggression but will also press their limits of understanding with Winnicott's approach to gender and aggression. Winnicott was analyzed by Riviere and early in his psychoanalytic training was supervised by Klein (Winnicott [1962] 1996).[5] His views will lead to a new paradox for gender madness: we seem to find gender, destroy it, and then create it. These emotional activities are how Winnicott defines gender. In Winnicott's view, aggression in gender, however, feels as if it has been created before it can be found, and with this paradox a different understanding of destruction will emerge. Another term for destruction is the object's survival: that what is really being destroyed are the illusions created in a good-enough environment. Each of the three analysts—Klein, Riviere, and Winnicott—consider gender's madness differently, even as they maintain the innateness of bodily drives and consider aggressive drives as a constitutive force in emotional and social development. On these matters, we need not take sides since intrapsychic and interpsychic processes are two sides of the same coin. In fact, one intimate dilemma of gender is that if we feel we may only have or occupy one side, we find and create the condition for war.

I turn to the idea of gender madness for three reasons, knowing full well I cannot give reasons to my reasons. First, I have been struck by the strangeness of trying to explain something like why we have gender at all, let alone what it means to attempt to affect its transitory time. And, given the transference, or the ways we unconsciously exchange authority, love, and knowledge in our pedagogical affairs, I have also felt that it is difficult to know when we are not talking about gender. This strangeness can be found in our classrooms, our theories, our activism, and in clinical practice. We can say with some certainty that one cannot be talked into gender or out of it even though gender seems to be an odd combination of given and received ideas, social pressure, cosmetic manipulation, and unaccountable desires. But we never can say, "Have a nice gender." Often, the idea of having or being a gender seems to be akin to meeting what Bion (1993) called "thoughts that have no thinker" (165). Gender is there before the infant's consent; it is an unconscious thought in the minds of those who come before us, and trying to think about the backdrop of gender brings us to what is most archaic in social, cultural, and psychical life.

My second reason for focusing on gender madness emerges from a reconsideration of feminism's poststructural turn and its reliance on the matrix of power, knowledge, pleasure, and performance. We are used to the feminist ideal that the personal is political and now the poststructural one that both the political and the personal are historically structured and resonate as discourse. Along with taking the body through the linguistic turn, we can add what Butler (1990) named early on "gender trouble,'" as identity's performance anxiety. More turns will inevitably be made, as there is no absolute or transcendental theory that can settle once and for all why we seem to care so much about it. However, I am not sure we can sort out just what the historical, the constructed, or the performance does to the tension Alice Pitt (2003) has capaciously named as "the play of the personal" and, drawing upon Winnicott, argues that "there is something of a protest that can trail the pleasures of communication" (83). It may now be time to consider qualities of the personal protest, an ambivalence due to bisexuality, that is deeply impressionable, impressive, secretive, and even excruciatingly impersonal and ahistorical. That is, there is something about gender that is also unconscious.

My third reason is really a hope that a notion of madness, sometimes also referred to as passion, may be a useful frame since gender is saturated with phantasies of one's own body, the body one does not have, and by the transitional space of creative play. The idea of madness conveys this entire scramble. This may seem like a long way from Klein and Riviere's lectures, or from Rose's needed question, but really, these thinkers teach us that there is always a conflict with the creation, transmission, reception, and unconscious meaning of both personal and political knowledge. The personal and the political, all maintain, are also unconscious.

Now these ideas of the phantasy and symbolic space of gender play havoc with the political and every concept that must be taken for granted for something like the political to be postulated. When Rose (1993) attempts to hold the personal and political together, she does so by way of their destructive force, with the interminable question, "Why war?" She brings to this clash the fact that there are three wars at stake: those of the inner world, the external world, and the bodily relation between these realities. Rose illustrates the conflict of these registers when she analyzes the well-documented British Psychoanalytical Society's 1941–1945 Controversial discussions between Melanie Klein and Anna Freud.[6] This little war occurred between schools of thought and erupted in the midst of World War II. It concerned, among other things, whether psychoanalysis itself had to be one-sided and what happens to education in this collapse (Britzman 2003). The other controversy, still active today, concerns just how much the war imagery of psychoanalytic theory affects the psychoanalyst and patient. Rose tells us that war is a terrible breakdown of knowledge and imagination, a foreclosure of the fact that as soon as knowledge becomes tied to absolute authority, described in chapter 4 as the adolescent syndrome of ideality, the limits of knowledge and imagination of it as our ethical resources fail. But authority, as well, has a phantasy life that affects us all: in psychoanalysis it goes under the names of omnipotence, the drives, the super-ego, love and hate, the transference, guilt, and moral anxiety and finds a home in our attitudes toward what is imagined as going right and wrong for gender. All these psychical affairs make gender our last stand, or the thing we can't stand in either others or ourselves.

In entering the personal—what we take too personally—the public lectures of Klein and Riviere have some odd work to do. They take us to the brink of the latency of experience, reason, consciousness, and memory. They begin with what feels to be an unsolvable conflict between love and hate, show how suffering from inexplicable frustration leads to guilt over destroying the object, and then, insist that from this negativity comes the work of gratitude, love, and reparation, the elements for thinking, relationality, symbol formation, and recognition of difference. At times, their claims lean upon the madness of absolutism yet still they manage to propose that knowledge of the emotional world can never be absolute since it may only begin when one can admit its vulnerability to loss, breakdown, frustration, and phantasy. Knowledge of the emotional world may only begin when psychical reality can be acknowledged and enjoyed. Klein and Riviere suggest as well an unavoidable relation between feeling absolutely certain and defending against a primary helplessness. From all of this, they suppose, guilt and ambivalence allows knowledge of the world its transience, incompleteness, and fragility. There is an utter difficulty in learning from (as opposed to defending against) the travails of emotional life.

Affect

Riviere thought of affects as both bodily passions and representations of the force of their drive history. The major affect she discussed is anxiety over loss of love and self. She stayed with negativity as her means for reaching into what is most disclaimed and disavowed about the affect's vicissitudes and stunning outbursts. She also refused to separate affect from its roots in bodily distress. It is a counterintuitive approach since in everyday parlance affect is considered as a product of consciousness. Riviere follows affect along its lines of the logic of psychical reality and the momentous transition between bodily needs and desires for the other.

Riviere's (1937) lecture, "Hate, Greed, and Aggression," kept aggression close to love and hate and linked it to our capacity to fight for what we believe is right. She argued that while hate is allied with destruction, love, too, has its destructive underside: we do not give up the libidinal object easily, the object is so easily lost, and thus love indicates a constitutive dependency on the object, a tie that is also hated. In proposing our right to love and so our fight against its vulnerabilities, Riviere insisted that aggression is never so far away. She kept close to the fact that our emotional life is emotional. Yet this leaves us with bare-bones tautology: that emotions cause emotions. It is probably better to admit that we become entangled in the roots of our emotional life since, to say the least, the roots themselves are insecure because we need someone to water them.

In a clinical essay on bereavement, written just after the Second World War, Riviere ([1945] 1991) argued that when we try to reach the history of our emotional roots, we meet contemporary entanglements. There is a tendency to experience events in later life in terms of earlier "ones . . . [, and] we tend to explain unhappy events in personal terms; that is to say, we attribute them to some personal cause, essentially to some wrong-doing (as with the child to whom the loss of a pleasure means that his parents are punishing him)" (215). These two emotional rules having to do with the anxieties made from personal cause—what we take too personally and that bring the personal into its divisiveness—are the soft foundations of Klein and Riviere's lectures. There, the register of aggression oscillates between the sources, aims, and pressures of bodily drives and the Other's care needed to become a separate subject. In a very special sense, the madness and creativity of our emotional world lean upon this drive/object dilemma, and aggression is both the hallmark of this tiny war and, paradoxically, a destruction needed for symbolization. This emotional world conveys our uneven development: our lifetimes are spent piecing together and fraying again the innumerable threads of what Klein (1937) simply called, in her lecture "Love, Guilt, and Reparation," "the emotional situation of the baby" (58).

The lectures are extraordinary in candor, in their passionate language, in their audacious sense of love and hate, and in the ways in which they magnify the already disproportionate unreason of bodily anxiety and defense, which they call phantasies. They insist that most difficult for the human is coming to terms with the fact of dependency, so linked as it is to the ensuing anxiety of losing the beloved object that, when lost, will be symbolically equated with being abandoned. For Riviere and Klein, the fact of dependency is a frustration that then incurs the hatred of dependency, itself a part of this fact. We can now get to their punch line: our original dependency on the mother will have an afterlife in how men and women imagine—through fears of persecution, punishment, envy and with love, guilt, and reparation—the advent and vicissitudes of femininity and masculinity.[7]

Klein and Riviere tell an incredible story of the natality of gender and sexuality as marked by a constitutive anxiety transferred through its surrogates: from the fact of dependency will come phantasies of destroying and being destroyed. Quite schematically, in Klein's ([1928] 1975) view, humans begin their gender madness with the femininity phase, organized by their identification with and envy of the breast. Dependency on the mother saturates the child's phantasies of femininity, linking its meanings to fear of dependency, hostility toward this condition, and then desire to be separate. Separateness brings feelings of guilt and the awareness that the mother is also a separate whole being. The infant comes to understand that it both loves and hates the same person. With the work of reparation a new meaning of separation and unity comes into being, and Klein proposed this work as the depressive position, marking an awareness of love's fragility, ambivalence, and concern for the other and the self.

Unlike melancholia, where nothing seems to matter at all, the depressive position is the beginning of poignant thinking, the capacity for guilt, and development of concern for the other. It is also the beginning of an awareness of the difference and relation between the internal and external world and a way to symbolize absence into something more than destitution and abandonment. Before all of that, as we will soon see, Klein posits the paranoid/schizoid position, where the world is split into a terrible war between good and bad and attack and retaliation, a mad scramble that creates the need to project into others whatever feels bad in the self and then defend against the other's retaliation. This is what war feels like. There can be no real others since there is no meaning as to why the battle had to begin and since there is no meaning to the fact of dependency. In the psychological logic of the paranoid/schizoid position, dependency is just a bad thing to be defended against. Femininity may languish in this empty space and masculinity will imagine an escape. The tension is that Klein and Riviere locate this conflict within the psychical body.

While Klein presents us with a bellicose tiny subject, it is not as apparent why the baby must be paranoid or why there is this war between love and hate. Indeed, in these lectures, the emotional situation of the baby reads like a miniature war theater: from the beginning of life, the biting, kicking, crying, incontinent baby is always formulating and communicating its anxiety over absence and presence, equating absence with badness and presence with goodness. The baby is burning mad, particularly when she feels and must feel her utter helplessness and dependency. The beginning is painful and devastating. In Riviere's (1937) words:

> If he feels emptiness and loneliness, an automatic reaction sets in, which may soon become uncontrollable and overwhelming, an aggressive rage which brings pain and explosive, burning, suffocating, choking bodily sensations; and these in turn cause further feelings of lack, pain and apprehension. The baby cannot distinguish between 'me' and 'not-me'; his own sensations are his world, the world to him; so when he is cold, hungry or lonely there is no milk, no well-being or pleasure in the world—the valuable things in life have vanished. And when he is tortured with desire or anger, with uncontrollable, suffocating screaming, and painful, burning evacuations, the whole of his world is one of suffering; it is scalded, torn, and racked too. . . . It is our first experience of something like death, recognition of the non-existence of something, of an overwhelming loss, both in ourselves and others, as it seems. And this experience brings an awareness of love (in the form of desire), and recognition of dependence (in the form of need), at the same moment as, and inextricably bound up with, feelings and uncontrollable sensations of pain and threatened destruction within and without. (8–9)

No wonder Riviere worried about her audience's feelings. So did John Rickman (1937), whose preface to Klein and Riviere's book tries to warn readers what they are in for. The conflicts described will be felt and then, perhaps, disclaimed by this very reason. In one way, this was Riviere's worry: that magnifications of hate mean we are liable to lose all perspective. Our hope may dissolve into depression. We may feel there is no way out. These lectures do empower infancy to such an extent that it never seems to go away. More so, they seem to be speaking for the baby who cannot yet speak, and the mother's voice is barely perceptible. Intellectual defenses against their views also follow: neither Klein nor Riviere could prove that the baby has and projects phantasy into the other, that it made a story-feeling about its body and the other body without any knowledge at all, and that there was something already driven, already psychological about its mind. And, in a certain way, we cannot settle this miasma with any ease because, as Riviere worried, an account of our emotional world must be one-sided since so much depends upon what can never be remembered, since emotional life filters our perceptions of the object as our means for making up a mind, and since the exploration of one's emotional world takes its lead from phantasy and play, all of which are subjective experiences of the object that most adults hope to leave behind.

While Riviere worries about the audience's feelings, Rickman turns to a plea for feelings they may have but know nothing about. Rickman's advice and warning resides with the centrality of the unconscious in the lectures: Remember, he writes, that the unconscious is antithetical to reason, to time, and to contradiction. Consciousness will be that struggle against its own unconscious representations. His advice concerns the ways Riviere and Klein move seamlessly between the child and the adult, as if no one can ever rid themselves of infantile despair, omnipotent thinking, and the talisman principle of an eye for an eye that governs the unconscious. Rickman writes: "The fact is that the unconscious of the adult is actually not so very different from the mind of the child; it must be recognized, therefore, that in a certain sense psychoanalysts do attribute infantile thinking to grown-ups" (vi). Something about us does not grow up, and knowing this may return us to our oldest defenses. And yet, his warning is really a plea for the reader's tolerance and open-mindedness, even as he concludes by understating a special difficulty that affects psychoanalysis as well: "Not a little misunderstanding of psycho-analysis is due to a failure to realize that unconscious ways of thought and feeling are not only unconscious but are grasped only with difficulty" (v–vi).

Lest we begin to feel that psychoanalysis plunges us back into solipsism, or worse, the paranoid/schizoid position, notice the ways in which the external world matters to what is being said. The psychoanalyst sees group psychology in each individual, although there are strong disagreements as to how the subject is thought to repeat, with great variation and without prior knowledge, their susceptibility to history, which includes the unconscious emotional history of parents, school, culture, and nation. In speaking about what the historical means in the psyche, André Green (2000a) describes the historical as akin to a dream, "a combination of what has happened, what has not happened, what could have happened, what has happened to someone else but not to me, what could not have happened . . . [and] a statement that one would not have even dreamed of as a representation of what really happened" (2–3). The psychoanalyst is not immune from this dreamy history and indeed, through the transference, learns to lean upon her or his own inspired time (Britzman 2009). Unconscious life exhibits the odd paradox of being both formative and destructive, proposing the future of the ego's conflicts and serving as both blind spot and magnifying glass. So a large difficulty of learning the consequences of the historical, let alone trying to symbolize its destiny, has to do with our capacity to play within the ever-shifting lines of the conscious and the unconscious, masculinity and femininity, and phantasy and reality.

Clinical Knowledge

While Klein and Riviere's lectures give us a sweeping account of development, it is useful to consider how clinical knowledge constructs and conveys these difficult passionate matters. It must be said that its knowledge is not authoritative but vulnerable to the disquieting imagination and the unconscious play between the analytic couple. They only have words. Paradoxically, the creation of clinical knowledge is not so far away from how infants, bit by bit, acquire their sense of the other. Such knowledge takes as its starting point the force of phantasy, anxiety, and desire within the intersubjective space. Constructions made in the clinic are one way to symbolize the relation between the inner and external world, even as their language may return us to what is most disclaimed about both: namely, the gendered afterlife of our fact of dependency. This fact weaves its way into rigid notions of masculinity and femininity that do find confirmation in the external world, but not without having to first pass through our own anxiety over loss of love.

In her discussion of Melanie Klein, Juliet Mitchell (1998) suggests the difficulty the clinician undergoes when trying to understand the other and how the clinician herself is changed. This is because clinical knowledge is made from

> being good at identifying with what one observes in order to follow what is going on in something other than oneself and then describing it [, which] constitutes an intermediary level of conceptualization. . . . Klein identifies and describes what intuitive identification and clinical observation are about: areas of confusion, fusion, lack of boundaries, of communicating without the differential structures of speech. (29)

Mitchell's depiction of Klein's technique of projective identification gives us a primary definition of gender as "areas of confusion, fusion, lack of boundaries, [without] the differential structures of speech" (29). The psychical life of gender is an admixture of masculinity and femininity, an original bisexuality that expresses the ambivalence and conflicts of having and being and wanting both ways. Our private gender is also an ongoing commentary on how we feel others feel about our bodies and pleasures. Projective identification is our permit into this madness. The danger is that in the act of trying to know, knowledge, too, carries a kernel of paranoia made from defenses against the inconceivable.

The clinical relation lives within and creates this emotional tension and, as we will soon see, constructs a mad world where, paradoxically, one can feel sane because emotional experience may take place symbolically. The clinic can be considered as a container, not so much in terms of unifying gender or even aligning it with adaptation to reality, which would be an experience of compliance and actual aggression. Rather, the clinic provides a safe space where thinking can contain the play of the emotional life of gender and where phantasies of destruction can be sounded and symbolized. In this way the clinic contains and repeats the features of the psychical world, but from a new angle because there is the other (Green 2000b, 47).

Clinical Material

One of D. W. Winnicott's (1999) formulations of gender is found in his discussion on the origins of creativity, where he suggests a paradox within the transit between femininity and masculinity, between the analyst and the analysand, and between aggression and frustration. Whereas Klein and Riviere highlight the inner world of anxiety, Winnicott's approach is through observing play as the potential space for symbolizing the inner and external world (Abram 2008). He is famous for his critical quip, "There is no such thing as the baby," a needed reminder to psychoanalysts and to parents that cultural life, environmental provision, and the other create the capacity to be a baby whose right is to be as ruthless as she or he pleases. His idea of ruthlessness concerns the use of the object and this brings him to thoughts on aggression. Destruction, Winnicott believes, allows for creativity, provided that the other can stand the baby as a baby.[8] Here the fact of dependency belongs to the other who can survive, without having to retaliate against the condition of being depended upon. In speaking about Winnicott's contribution to psychoanalysis, Pontalis (1981) observes that his notion of creativity "is the condition for an exchange between inside and outside" (140).

Winnicott understands the problem of love, hate, and aggression through the use of the object rather than as an emanation of ontology. Object use presupposes the other and a shared environment. Because there is no environment without tension and frustration, the child's aggression is first and foremost a matter of object relating and object use. Modes of aggression then are a communication to the environment that must fail yet paradoxically must also be good enough to continue holding, handling, and using the object (Dethiville 2014). Destruction must take place at two levels: the infant's omnipotence and the environment's omnipotence (Scarfone 2005). The paradox is that the environment must frustrate the child, but not so much that the child loses hope in her or his own capacity to find and create the world that already exists. No aggression, Winnicott thought, was a sign of compliance, a giving up on the idea that playing with reality is an activity of the mind needed to release gender phantasy from the rigidities of the inner and outer world.

When reading Winnicott's essay on creativity, which contains quite a mad narrative of the inner world of gender, I found myself asking, what kind of man is Winnicott? And so I went to Joyce McDougall's (2005) lecture, "Donald Winnicott the Man: Reflections and Recollections." I suppose I was asking whether he, too, was a good-enough mother. In a short vignette, McDougall asked Winnicott about his article "Hate in the Counter-Transference." There, Winnicott ([1947] 1992) suggested why the mother must hate the baby, or hates the fact that her omnipotence is of no use. McDougall (2005) wondered how he managed to support deeply disturbed patients that attacked his interpretations and refused to take anything he offered. So she asked him, and then she wondered more:

> Winnicott replied: "We must admit that it is always fatiguing to be a bad breast." He went on to explain that it was also very important that the bad breast analyst survived the attacks of the enraged infant within. In this context, however, I sometimes had the impression that although Winnicott fully accepted counter-transference hatred and used it creatively, he was perhaps sometimes chary of actually dealing with transference hatred. I sometimes wondered if perhaps he very much wished to be loved by his patients. (35)

It really is quite mad to understand that within the bad breast lives an enraged infant who finds again the bad breast analyst. And yet, the wish to be loved originates our capacity for both primal projections of the good and bad breast and our wish to be met.

Winnicott's (1999) essay on the origin of creativity provides another sense of the difficulty of putting the question of gender to the analysand whose own questions are incredibility congealed. Indeed, he speaks of gender as hidden, as secret, and as repressed. And this leads Winnicott to write a very long sentence that indicates the slowness of psychoanalytic technique, followed by a short sentence on its limits:

> While it is the patient who is all the time teaching the analyst, the analyst should be able to know, theoretically, about the matters that concern the deepest or most central features of personality, else he may fail to recognize and meet new demands on his understanding and technique when at long last the patient is able to bring deeply buried matters into the content of the transference, thereby affording opportunity for mutative interpretation. The analyst, by interpreting, shows how much and how little of the patient's communication he is able to receive. (72)

Winnicott then describes his work with a married man of middle age who had had many experiences with therapy, including psychoanalysis, but was left with the feeling that something had been missed. In one session, Winnicott felt something new: the patient was speaking about his penis envy. "I said to him: 'I am listening to a girl. I know perfectly well that you are a man but I am listening to a girl, and I am talking to a girl. I am telling this girl: 'You are talking about penis envy'" (73). Now Winnicott understood his interpretation as akin to playing with reality. His patient replied: "If I were to tell someone about this girl, I would be called mad" (73). But Winnicott went even further in this cross-identification when he then said to his patient: "It is not that you told this to anyone; it is I who see the girl and hear a girl talking, when actually there is a man on my couch. The mad person is myself" (74).

The interpretation introduces separateness: two people are in the same room but have different minds. It is at this point that the patient could then feel sane in a mad environment. Winnicott's phantasy opened a new construction, for in the analytic work the patient felt (but without any proof) that his mother wished for a girl and could not see him as a boy. And in the strange logic of the unconscious, the man could not feel himself as a man. As for the cross-identification, Winnicott occupied the position of the patient's mother who was mad enough to see a girl when there was a boy. However, a few days later the patient fell ill, and Winnicott began to think of what he called, for lack of a better term, "the split off girl element in the male patient" (77).

The essay on creativity becomes stranger. Winnicott adds to the clinical material a brief note on Shakespeare's *Hamlet* to illustrate gender dissociation. Even as he summarizes the play, Winnicott cannot help giving Hamlet some stage directions, knowing full well that the character Hamlet would not be able to go to his own play. Hamlet's question—"To be or not to be?"—gave Winnicott a way to say something about the play and the disorder between "being" and "doing." Even if Hamlet cannot decide whether he should or can exist, he is still only one person. Winnicott links "being," or the capacity to know one's own existence, as a consequence of identification with the mother. Being, or what he calls "the girl element," is the condition needed for the baby to enjoy fusing with the mother's femininity. It is the precondition for any self. While being comes before doing, doing allows for separation. Winnicott links the actions of doing to the boy element, or the masculine element. Separation, Winnicott notes, also contains a deep-seated envy of femininity. A further astounding claim can now be constructed, because both doing and being contain elements of aggression, albeit of a different nature. "It seems," writes Winnicott, "that frustration belongs to satisfaction-seeking. To the experience of being belongs something else, not frustration, but maiming" (1999, 81). Frustration is an inevitable consequence of the search for satisfaction. Maiming is the reaching for existence that involves pushing against objects and therefore incurs both an emotional injury that provides one's place and the pleasure of feeling one's place. In Winnicott's view, the object survives this needed ruthlessness.

Winnicott's formulation defied my expectation, which is to say, stereotypes that, however much I try to rid myself of them, seem to be reading me and so return as paranoid anxiety. I worried that Winnicott, or really, that I, might fall into a rhapsodic view of oceanic femininity, as a unifying force, while masculinity is relegated to discord. And if this is the separation, then only one element was aggressive, only one element valued. But it turns out that "being" not only signifies being with someone—Winnicott's good-enough mother—but the being who is on the way to being a self with someone else who survives the baby's ruthless attempts at both unity and separation. These ruthless attempts to become a self are what Winnicott calls "maiming." Maiming comes before frustration, which sounds a different chord of aggression than the one played by Klein and Riviere. Maiming is now tied to creativity, to pressing on the world and not to hating it, which, for Winnicott, comes much later and is rooted in frustration. The infant will create, from the world presented, what is already there. For the time being, the infant may act as if it can be the mad author of the world but will soon come to be disillusioned by the mother's maiming, her being. Creating, destroying, and finding belong to our gender activities.

Winnicott's ideas about the poesis of gender depend upon the ripples of dependency, not only as an index of our profound helplessness, although we all begin there, but also dependency as a condition located on the borderline of being and doing, between the boy and girl element and between the self and the other. He presents an emerging subject who creates and finds his or her being through maiming and doing, but without knowing it cannot be its own origin. Winnicott proposes this aggression, stemming from permissible omnipotence, as gender's playground and mad scene. At first, the "good-enough mother" provides the infant the conditions to discover, create, find, destroy, and so use what already exists. This permissiveness belongs to the mother's madness, and part of this madness will also entail disillusioning her omnipotence. If this cannot happen, as Winnicott presents in the case of cross identifications, gender dissociation may be one terrible fate. To play with this reality, one must separate from reality and bear the force of ambivalence. Such play involves a destruction of compliance, itself a reaction formation to cultural, social, and emotional impingement. The activity of this little destruction neither splits the self nor the other. Rather the activity is akin to what Winnicott names as "maiming," a word we might use when conceptualizing the transference field between the boy and girl element in any gender.

From Winnicott's clinical example comes the idea that splitting and the hostility toward male and female elements within any gender will agonize the subject's capacity for taking gender pleasure. He attributes these gendered elements as emerging from the human's constitutional bisexuality, and so gender becomes a commentary on the polymorphous nature of desire and object use, and then associated with something that is not gender at all, but still leans upon bodily activity, namely, the capacity to be ruthless in playing with reality. I think Winnicott is suggesting that the afterlife of gender constantly creates and destroys our own otherness, an otherness that must include what is historical about the history of feeling the struggle to be a subject with other subjects. The paradox is that gender both registers the body as other and services the potential space with others. On this view, gender is always active and passive and signifies being and doing. Gender is found before it can be created. Yet the psychic cost of reducing gender to the encasements of biology, stereotype, or even knowledge is depression and rigidity, which translates into a defended organization dedicated to hatred toward the self and the other, a wearing away in the faith that language can matter, and a giving up on the creative work of playing with reality. This is also the condition of war.

Lecture Madness

In a lecture given to social workers, Winnicott ([1963] 1996) offers a definition of illness: "Let me use my friend the late John Rickman's definition: 'Mental illness consists in not being able to find anyone who can stand you'" (218). His definition may have resonance for everyday life; it reminds me of pedagogy as the peculiar muddle made when lecturing on gender. Our pedagogy after all does involve finding others who can stand us as much as it involves our capacity to stand the students. If our lectures implicitly split off masculinity and femininity and only take one side of gender, it is as if we are telling the other side, "No one can stand you." But if we don't take each event seriously and grapple with sexual difference, we lose the potential space for psychological significance within gender's sounding. If we demand compliance with external reality, we have truly become insane and have made another condition for war. If, in our lectures, we reduce gender to proper behavior and compliance, we lose contact with the emotional situation of gender's overabundance of meanings, conflicts, disavowals, and the audacity of becoming a self with other selves. Lost as well is our capacity to link this little war within to attractions of the contemporary wars in our own time.

Later in his lecture Winnicott relates madness to what is most ordinary about life, telling the social workers:

> Think of casework as providing a human basket. Clients put all their eggs into one basket which is you. . . . They take a risk, and first they must test you to see if you may be able to prove sensitive and reliable or whether you have it in you to repeat the traumatic experiences of their past. [Now, here is where the mad part comes.] In a sense you are a frying-pan, with the frying process played backwards, so that you really do unscramble the scrambled eggs. ([1963] 1996, 227)

It's quite something to move inside the scenes of the madness of lecturing on gender. We risk our own madness in doing so. My logic throughout this chapter began with rehearsing Riviere's worries that a lecture might depress the audience. That may still be the case, but it is the character of depression and the eschewal of ambivalence made from loving and hating that may be noticed and symbolized for further use. A psychoanalytic approach, after all, begins with objections to the emotional world, and a psychoanalyst in the classroom considers the transfer of the personal into the political as one of the emotional world's inevitable activities. There is, however, the odd matters of Winnicott's lecture; that we learn to unscramble eggs, an activity that cannot really be accomplished. Nor can we be a frying pan playing backward; though we can try to imagine what comes before the scrambling of gender. Here again is the gender madness and perhaps a new worry that a lecture drives the audience mad, playing, as it must, in areas of fusion, confusion, maiming, and separation. Still, if we can tolerate these mad parts and become curious toward their scrambled play, I believe we can learn a great deal and not only about the madness of lecturing on the lifeworld of gender. We may learn to speak in the strange grammar of gender's emotional logic, become curious with matters of love and hate, ask what aggression has to do with masculinity and femininity, and perhaps play with this knowledge as ruthlessly as it is made while imagining that pedagogy will survive. This would be the new madness: conceptualizing gender as potential space. The large question is whether our lectures on gender, too, can tolerate such indirection, play in the field of ambivalence, and serve as gender's creative playground.

6

The Untold Story of the Writing Block

> It gives you a queer feeling if late in life,
> you are ordered once again
> to write a school essay . . .
> It is strange
> how readily you obey the orders,
> as though
> nothing in particular had happened in the last half century.
>
> —Sigmund Freud, "Some Reflections on a Schoolboy Psychology"

Freud's (1914b) ode to shrinking time tarries with the unconscious. Word by word they sound the sotto voce of writing and release the feel of a dream: *queer feelings, late, ordered, once again, school, strange, obey,* and *nothing happened.* Yes, the school essay is replete with writing's transpositions; it animates our capacity for decomposition and leaves us pleading for more time. Listening for the subjunctive mood, we want to ask what rules the order to write and what, in writing, does the writer both obey and defy *once again?* We shall stay close to the claim that the writer pens the force of her or his emotional situation—conflicts with love and hate—and that however refined writing becomes, our affective fight with and for words carry traces of wishes, anxieties, and defenses. Someone else is always in mind, given the character of good and bad witnesses or judges. The writer's oscillating moods affiliate with these other scenes. We also question the writer under erasure, though neither from the frame of deconstruction nor from discussions on the death of the author. Instead let us picture the erasure of the self under the order and sequences of phantasy.[1]

Recall that a sixty-year-old Freud (1914b) was given a late assignment from teachers no longer and that he used the occasion to notice the transference torrents of his childhood education made from his wishes to both know and please his teachers. But he cannot do that again, and the essay carries traces of that loss. Writing anxiety has a tenuous foothold in that conflicted desire to please and to influence, though the pathos of the writing block mainly belongs to the adult. It is then that the desire to please and influence are at odds, and gradually each conflict takes on greater ambitions along with their dangers: social anxiety (whether others hate the writing), moral anxiety (whether the writing destroys a law or must protect it), and ego anxiety (whether it is the self that must lose respect). For the psychoanalyst in the classroom the writing block reassembles the human condition of separation anxiety, thought of as a constellation of phantasies that plot the loss of experience, the other, the self, the idea, the teacher, the group, the career, and so on. In Freud's schoolboy essay, anxiety erupts as the loss of time. The force of affect carries into his insistence that as a psychoanalyst he must take an interest in unconscious life, an order so emphatic that one may wonder if he would rather have preferred to remain unaffected. Perhaps Freud worried that his teachers would read his late essay as anathema to science, that his greater interest in unconscious life would diminish their respect for him, and that without social approval, he would be left with the terrible question, who cares? Is this why his essay ends with sending his teachers back to the nursery so they too might feel again what the writing writer is up against? Or, does the message open a new demand: read for where anxiety and its phantasy delegates irrupt in order to write before them.

Yet there is discontentment with the attempt to communicate what happens for the writer. And beginnings feel particularly troublesome. In trying to write the untold story of a writing block, I find myself caught in its decompositions, its exorbitant retellings, its repetitive style, and its acting out. While writing this chapter, I lost my interest, felt no one cared, was sure someone else had already written it, and gave up hope that the disparate pieces of thought would take me any further than a description of what everyone already knows. Draft upon draft drove me away from the topic. I lost my train of thought and felt out of focus. Suddenly, I needed to read more. Then I began to hate writing. It was making me suffer. In these symptomatic acts something was missing and needed to be blamed. But I am both culprit and innocent, both omnipotent and helpless. And if this transference to the writing block rather than with communicating the writing of it is part of the writer's neurosis, we have a bare clue that it is quite possible to write without knowing one is blocked. Resistance is an astounding quality of its untold story. So too is its other side that belongs to the creativity of primary process and that Georg Groddeck proposed early on as "the compulsion to symbolize" (qtd. in M'Uzan 2013, 10).

Melanie Klein ([1946] 1975) termed the urgency of feeling thoughts as "paranoid/schizoid mechanisms," our earliest attempts to both know our mayhem and defend against its persecutory anxiety. She proposed the strange term "latent anxiety" to consider an unconscious sequence that suggests one may be in its throes but not realize that such affect has meaning, contingencies, origins, or effects. Defenses against persecutory feelings are being made and emptied of recognition. The latency occurs, she writes, "by the particular method of dispersal. The feeling of being disintegrated, of being unable to experience emotions, of losing one's objects, is in fact the equivalent of anxiety" (21). So again, a sequence of anxiety unfolds: fragmentation, loss, disintegration, and dissociation. Not knowing and needing to know brings the writer to feel wrong but also unable to locate the problem. Then comes a second dilemma: the writing block being written resists its own telling, and this latency is an unusual claim given how often we complain about not being able to write the way we want. The writing may be going well and then, just as suddenly, is treated as worthless. Sounds a bit like a love affair gone wrong. Hard to say what has happened. Readers too are affected. They become quite exhausted by the writer's never-ending battle to settle into a topic while the writer, alone at her desk, suffers from too many beginnings.

There is plenty of frustration to pass around and displacement serves that function, but the sequence of anxiety begins with an unbearable aggression. For Klein, the earliest problem is libidinal and already symbolic in that libido seeks objects. Aggression, perhaps the earliest response to frustration and itself a sign of life, begins with introjection or taking inside parts of the external world only to worry that the act of incorporation, like eating, devastates the integrity of the object who seems to know it is being destroyed. Then come more worries that the object is angry and will return to destroy us. Yet even in this fight to the finish, something new occurs. Within the anguish of the paranoid/schizoid position, new doubts and pining for the object create a mental constellation named the "depressive position": a concern for the object relation, however imaginary. In the act of writing, the sequence may begin with hopes for the potential that writing may promise to create, along with doubts over its goodness and then the desire for making reparation. The self is at odds with the mix-up of desire and frustration as it confronts the currency of psychical reality that, at first, is contingent upon the destruction of the good object. The numerous anxiety situations Klein ([1935] 1975) saw as our emotional situation and as an index of loss may be read as a good-enough allegory of what the writer then faces:

> To quote only a few of them: there is anxiety how to put the bits together in the right way and at the right time; how to pick out the good bits and do away with the bad ones; how to bring the object to life when it has been put together; and there is the anxiety of being interfered with in this task by bad objects and by one's own hatred, etc. (269)

Bad objects and one's own hatred of them is pretty much the same thing. And this leads Klein to her most contentious existential insistence: the basis of anxiety is the hatred of psychical life; itself a phantasy further agonized by the defense of denial of psychical reality. Klein maintains that fear of annihilation and what Freud formulated as hostile impulses are favorable conditions for the bottomlessness of depression and the painful latency at work in all inhibitions.[2]

We still have to ask, what holds the writer back? To stretch Tolstoy's (2000) observation on the family into our topic, we can say that every happy writer is alike; each unhappy writer is unhappy in her or his own way.[3] While there is always more than one story, the writing block shares common affects—unhappiness, frustration, depression, neurosis, obsessionality, and separation anxiety—and its events that go under the sign "nothing happens" occur in voluntary settings such as the university, psychoanalytic institutes, academic journals, conferences, dissertations, and various assignments that call upon the ego's desire to write along with the super-ego's dedicated hostility.[4] In writing, anxiety and desire go hand in hand. The odd part is that one comes to the university, either as a professor or a student, to write and may find the self driving around in the state of a writing block. And it is a guilty state that is ordered by rules, rituals, and courts of law. There are writing police, stop signs, go-directly-to-jail cards, waiting in line, traffic jams, accidents, expired permits, and insurance policies. The writing block is a character world of object relations, mostly suspicious toward the desire to write. "Who cares?" the poor writer says to no one in particular. The worst part is that even if the story is being told, no one is there to listen. Let us admit from its onset that both the desire to write and its blocks carry on our difficulties of love and hate. And let us also suggest some relief: most of us who write know how difficult it is.

Even in nomenclature, "writing block" repeats its conflicts. No one is there. There is little agreement as to its etiology, its precipitating factors, its genetic evolution, its symptomology, its cause, and its subjective predicament. Except for the gigantic disappointment factor, the writing block is hard to read. A psychoanalyst named Edmund Bergler coined the term in his 1947 article "Further Contributions to the Psychoanalysis of Writers."[5] While his nickname has great legs, the article is largely forgotten, not only because it contains a riot of opinion or that it reads as a self-parody of midcentury psychoanalysis and its preoccupation with the analyst as all knowing figurehead. Bergler's dusty work is ignored because he can't help hating the writer in trouble; and readers do receive that hostility. His view is that the writing block is a regression into the oral-cannibalistic phase of libido that leans upon infantile defenses that fend off persecutory anxiety with the weapons of greed and envy. Maybe, but Bergler's explanation seems to repeat these processes and, in his writing fever, it is difficult to know who is doing what to whom. He abandons the suffering writer and cannot say why it is that the writer feels at a loss. A few years later, Bergler (1950) wrote another defense of his theory, "Does 'Writer's Block' Exist?" He answers with certainty that it does by dragging his readers through ten fallacious arguments. He concludes that anyone who cannot agree with him is stupid. Avital Ronell (2003) who wrote *Stupidity* would have a field day. In her praise of slow learners she insists, "Stupidity sets the mood that afflicts anyone who presumes to write" (24), and although she does not mention the famous block because it is not one stupid thing, she does rehearse a long list of flouncing affects or the raw material the writer calls upon: depression, isolation, hostility, revenge phantasies, ambivalence, and anxiety.

My main approach is to pass the act of writing through to its constellations of phantasies—the emotional logic, dramatic personae and delegates, object relations, and sequences of psychical events that animate as well as deaden one's style. However given, the order to write involves both psychical time and the queasy feeling that one has fallen behind. My interest is with meeting such phantasies. Because the writer has to rely upon the self, writing is also a means to create a self who writes. While my observation sounds obvious, the self is oblivious. It is in this nexus that anxiety over loss enters the scene. I think that the writer's dilemma includes the problem of learning to read for anxiety's delegates, by which I mean attending to the often maddening phantasies, neurotic solutions, and defenses that split off the writer from the writing and that render both meaningless. The work is to analyze the power and dispersal of unconscious conflicts that, more often than not, divide passion into warring factions of love and hate and tear the writer into bits and pieces. Whether anxiety opts for the paragraph, sentence, or word, a story is being unwritten, and the writer can become interested in her or his aesthetic conflicts and, in writing, transform phantasy into a commentary on problems in the wider world. But writers drift between inchoate conflicts and their symbolization and this can be maddening. Susan Kolodny (2000) puts the dilemma this way: "Creative work can have problematic unconscious meanings for us and then too can bring about resistance. . . . The work may affirm our separateness, and for some, this is itself a danger" (xv). The paradox is that conflicted psychical life and the obstacles, terror, and desire carried into the world of others are our first resource for disquieting imagination, an intermingling of reality and phantasy, whatever these terms can mean. We are handling what is most abstract or unconscious in the affecting dynamics of writing with the open-ended question of writing as sublimation.

Sublimation, or the symbolization of anxiety that is never completed, is of a different order than technical advice on writing where behavior is detached from an apprehension of the complexities of the inner world. We are urged to "get over" ourselves without a thought as to where would we go. So, for example, while we have learned that editing our work is a matter of improving language, the psychoanalytic conflict suggests otherwise. The editor can quickly change into the censor. Having to put words to things one knows nothing about calls upon and creates the ambiguity of psychical reality. And in writing, facing the decision over what to preserve and what to destroy involves separation and the breaking of our rules founded in phantasies of loss, affiliation, and ideality. The issue is that we creatures of writing are made from what experience cannot complete. Writing may lead to a path beyond Klein's ([1935] 1975) "depressive position," described earlier as a quality of mind that creates from destruction a sense of guilt and a desire to repair what in phantasy feels damaged. For Klein ([1952] 1975) the difficult work is "to acknowledge the increasingly poignant psychic reality" (73). It is in writing then that the self is ordered to make up its mind. In the painful state of being stuck, the order may follow along the lines of the paranoid/schizoid position that call upon defenses against anxieties that are unduly harsh, persecutory, manic, and omnipotent. However strange it is to imagine that when we tear up the page the self too feels in bits and pieces, it is in writing that we have access to the emotional conditions we have faced before and that return again. We owe this formulation to Klein's insistence on a sort of prehistoric emotional situation made from the infant's earliest defenses of introjection, splitting, projection, and identification, which she called the schizoid mechanisms of object relations and also considered as the bare elements for symbolization. Perhaps what feels unreasonable is taking on this assignment and, then, becoming unsettled by the topic.

Ronell (2003) admits, "A writer rarely confides the mood in which an act of writing is established" (63). She was discussing her invitation to a conference presentation where she was given a topic. For all kinds of reasons she accepts the assignment but then feels constrained by it and angry with herself. If everyone, she suggests, "has had the experience of writing in unfreedom," she continues this thought that writing is characterized as being "about the difficult hinge where the mirage of freedom and stark unfreedom meet" (64). And she then notes: "A wave of anxiety emerged with the work at hand" (64). There are, most of us will admit, pressures the writing sustains, and whether we call it our mood or simply our emotional situation, we do have to break free from something we may not know. Even when we feel like writing, we may worry that sequester from the world means we miss out on life or, just the opposite: that due to separation from life, writing becomes lifeless. Klein ([1946] 1975) considers such experiences as interlinked to "the feeling of loneliness and the fear of parting" (13).

Roland Barthes's (2011) provocative lectures, *The Preparation of the Novel*, also picture writing from the side of its emotional experience: writing brings the writer to new realms of difficulties and to novel pleasures. One learns a great deal about the self. The published lectures were a heroic undertaking of a translator and an annotator of Barthes's notes and drawings. The lectures concerned the phantasy of preparing to write a novel, an odd topic since the students had to imagine what goes into and then disappears in writing. Barthes's pedagogical principle for his lectures was simply stated: "I sincerely believe that at the origin of teaching such as this we must always locate a fantasy, which can vary from year to year. . . . The principle is a general one: the subject is not to be repressed—whatever the risks of subjectivity" (3). The risks, Barthes reminds his students, belong to that which captures the writer and holds her back. He proposes a few solutions to keep writing, such as taking drugs or even writing about the breakdown as many writers have done. The neurotic solution, Barthes councils, is to embrace and symbolize the neurosis:

> It's possible to imagine, as a solution, a sort of neurotic stratagem or plasticity: depending on the nature of the problem or of the breakdown, you exploit the different neuroses within yourself; for example, breakdowns at the outset: defeating the page, coming up with ideas, provoking the *spurt*, etc. = hysterical activity ≠ the phase of Style, of Making Corrections, of Protection = obsessional activity. (269)

Barthes's ode to neurosis however, because it is symbolized, creates a transition: from identification with the writer's melancholic introjection and berating of the lost object to "identification of what doesn't work" (270). One can say that Barthes provides a creative writer position: "You exploit the different neurosis within yourself." Then, one is forced to consider one's nervous condition with one's desire for symbolic expressions.

The characters that populate this chapter are psychoanalysts, novelists, and professors. They all write about not being able to write, about their preparation to write, about disquieting imagination, and do so with an eye toward both subjective freedom and its disappearance. It is here that I find a creative approach to analyzing or taking apart the old conflicts that make their way into the so-called writing block. Except for holding to Barthes's idea that we exploit the neurosis, I shall try to set aside an avalanche of advice and technologies of pedagogy that purport to cure the block, partly because writing already involves directions one cannot follow and partly because of my claim that the indefinite character of a writing block means that the writer lacks an object, a dynamic condition for anxiety. The emotional situation any writer must face is that anxiety and desire go hand in hand and obstacles are not only inevitable. They are needed for desire to take hold. The chapter, then, opens a number of lines of inquiry, first by asking why reading for anxiety matters in understanding what happens affectively while trying to write. Our note to anxiety will take us into further discussion on manifest and latent anxiety through examples of writers who articulate and disperse their feelings about writing as they write. From there we trace a third path with the idea that one can write one's way into and out of anxiety provided that one links the dynamics of writing to a constellation of libidinal conflicts that bring to the fore matters of loyalty, affiliation, ideality, and finding one's own way.

Anxiety

"Then and now," Lyndsey Stonebridge (2007) observes in her affecting study of writing in midcentury, wartime British culture, "anxiety fills the gap between reason and imagination" (2). Her question is psychoanalytical: How do we respond in writing to a history we fail to comprehend? Her method is to read into the work of journalists, novelists, poets, and psychoanalysts as presenting "a kind of historiography of trauma" (5) that provokes the imagination needed for thinking the afterwardness of "wartime madness" (2). Her study proposes what is extraordinary. Writing resembles a state of emergency: a crisis for the writer and the emergent response to an event. The desire to symbolize what is out of order, however, affects "the writing of anxiety" (2). At times, the writing will oscillate between exorbitance and depression. Anxiety, Stonebridge points out, "is what we feel when we are caught in a situation" (2) that is beyond our thinking and our knowledge of it. And this catch is where the writer loses and finds herself. Affiliation with anxiety is a part of the danger being written.

Freud's (1915b) essay written during the First World War—"Thoughts for the Times on War and Death"—begins with the incomprehensible: civilian disillusionment of commonality and "an altered attitude toward death" (275). To make sense of the senselessness of death in war and the breakdown of care and social response, Freud turns to writing: "We should seek in the world of fiction, in literature and in the theatre compensation for what has been lost in life . . . in the realm of fiction we find the plurality of lives which we need" (291). Except that this is the plurality that is being destroyed, and Freud argues further that we cannot remember our own murderous hatred, that war between aggression and libidinality. The exorbitant claim is that our hatred is unconscious and founded in what Freud calls a prehistoric killing drive. It is a grave speculation but does bring Freud to think more about how pervasive violence destroys the love of our emotional world so tied to the love of the fragility and plurality of people. Writing and reading, Freud seems to suggest, reminds us of why we need anxiety, missing in times of war and only later returning as war neurosis. In mentioning what writers do, Freud is grasping for a depressive position, a means to sublimate into words the violence of the drives. Stonebridge (2007) as well presents this paradoxical situation. The writer, she insists, feels anxiety, and Stonebridge's case in point is a new reading of writing done during and just after the war that does convey trauma's volatility and sometimes fails from it. This matter of anxiety *writ large* in times of humanly induced destruction forces the writer to account for the desire to write.

It is a difficult transition to move from times of representing war and death to the benign and not-so-benign university classroom, although we can observe that education receives what the social cannot repair, that learning repeats its breakdowns without knowing why, and that students and teachers, before they are able to prepare, are asked to witness the human condition through their crisis in learning. Felman's (1992) breakthrough discussion of crisis in education justifiably links a theory of trauma to the question of pedagogy. She also brings into this mix a clinical sensibility as she notices and becomes witness to her class's distress after they viewed Holocaust survivor testimonies. Felman too needed a witness. After consulting with Dori Laub: "We concluded that what was called for was for me to reassume authority as the teacher of the class and bring them back into significance" (48). Felman acknowledged the students' anxiety as significant and assured them that what they had to wrest from their distress mattered to her. She asked them to write even as they felt they had nothing to say. Yet the problem for pedagogy persists. "The question for the teacher," Felman suggests, "is, then, on the one hand, how to access, how not to foreclose the crisis, and, on the other hand, how to contain it, how much crisis can the class sustain?" (54). The same is true for writing. If writing requires a quota of affect, if anxiety is the fragile link and that which catches on the fraying thread between imagination and reason, as Stonebridge argues, then how much crisis becomes too much? Writing about difficult topics may be one dimension of writing anxiety. Can we be respectful of the pain of others and still have our own say? The writer may either suffer from guilt at not having undergone the trauma or sway into indifference and deny anxiety with the thought that in the face of social collapse and violence writing does not matter. But what then can matter if we have to feel before we understand and write before we know how the other will receive our work? "Bring them back to significance," Felman is advised (48). In other words, do not abandon the writer.

In everyday classroom scenes the little traumas, or narcissistic blows, felt as persecutory, affect the writer and are just as difficult to communicate. They are felt as a collapse of the self. They include responses to the conditions faced such as asymmetrical relations and the teacher's authority and, as Winnicott would insist, much of the trauma of learning and writing involves erasure of the self when the environment demands compliance or loyalty. Then too there is the solution, though it comes with just as much force. Ordinary learning carries on something extraordinary. "The anti-social tendency," Winnicott ([1956] 1994) notes, "appears in the normal or near normal child, where it is related to the difficulties that are inherent in emotional development" (120) and "is characterized by an *element in it which compels the environment to be important*" (123; italics original). When Winnicott writes of the antisocial tendency, he is referencing the vicissitudes of ordinary frustration and aggression and the need for a witness. The antisocial tendency on this view is not a diagnosis but a mechanism for hope that the response to frustration will be of a different order than the provocation the outburst brings and that the environment, meaning the responsiveness of others, will be able to stand the revolt without revenge. Even ordinary times, such as the ones that ordered Freud to write his schoolboy essay and that sent Ronell to a conference, may animate feelings of compliance and push back. To press this point further, if one is to write what is on one's mind, an antisocial tendency that involves aggression is needed. We are moving into an area of how writing is psychically experienced by the writer, and as we shall see the intermingling of phantasy and reality, and love and hate, are major turning points in the untold story of the writing block.

Symptoms

Freud's (1926a [1925]) great statement on anxiety—"Inhibitions, Symptoms and Anxiety"—arrives late in the development of his theory; and it is where he changes his mind. His first topology of libido posited that repression of intolerable ideas and so representation itself creates anxiety. In his second structural theory, populated by the agencies of id, ego, and super-ego, the sequence is reversed: anxiety instructs the ego's many defenses against danger and helplessness. In centering anxiety as both a signal of danger (automatic) and a question of from where the danger comes (phantasmic), Freud's theory of neurosis intertwines the catastrophe of the ego losing love with the problem of the loss of imagination.[6] But his essay suffers from the topic; it has the feel of a little book that argues with itself and, at least for this reader, seems to perform the repetitions of the displeasure of the affect he wishes to grasp. That is one of the transference qualities of anxiety; it makes us nervous or places us in the realm of the anticipation of danger. In writing there is always the worry that one will be misunderstood or that one cannot really understand. The two anxieties are interrelated. Strachey's (1968d) introduction to the essay on inhibitions notes that Freud had difficulty unifying the essay. The writing anxiety irrupts when Freud (1926a [1925]) admits the confusion thirty-seven pages into the beast: "It is almost humiliating that, after working so long, we should still be having difficulty in understanding the most fundamental facts. . . . If we cannot see things clearly we will at least see clearly what the obscurities are" (124).

The obscurities have to do with what is anticipated as danger as the ego's anxiety revolves around the loss of love. Freud's indexing of specific dangers references evolutions of existence as relations to one's body, to other bodies, and to dearly held ideals. They share inevitable separation anxieties of life: birth, loss of breast, loss of the penis, loss of love, loss of the super-ego's love, and death. Such agonies allow Freud to write of id, ego, and super-ego anxiety. Yet his conclusion—"Anxiety is a reaction to a situation of danger" (128)—does not really tell us what anxiety is. He tries again: it is an "affective state" (132), there are physical reactions, the ego anticipates a loss of a beloved object, and finally, "the ego is the actual seat of anxiety" (140). But the problem from where the neurosis comes cannot be finally settled. His second addenda of the essay clears a new path: "Anxiety [Angst] has an unmistakable relation to *expectation*: it is about [before] something. It has a quality of *indefiniteness and lack of* object" (165; italics original). We return to this problem later though for now can note that, in writing, the lack of an object presents as a blank page, missing ideas, loss of words, and the abstention of the self or other. What's left is the sad conviction of the writer's despair. The so-called writing block appears as a terrible punctuation for this entire nothing.

Freud's (1926a [1925]) essay opens some difficulties in nomenclature, and his distinctions between symptoms, inhibitions, and anxiety often read like splitting hairs due to the subjective fact that each motive opens the problem that something is missing. Inhibition has to do with an ego's restriction, though here, too, a story is not quite on pause since the ego is never really alone and the function of an inhibition, Freud tells us, is to keep the ego busy avoiding internal dangers that appear to parade as external ones. There is an attempt of flight, though due to the fact that the ego cannot flee from itself, the self may develop a symptom and be loyal to that. Defenses against anxiety are the ego's last stand. Of interest to our discussion on writing are two of them: undoing what has been done and isolation (119). As for these defenses, for now we can note that in the situation of a writing block or the writing inhibition, undoing the writing—either through endless editing, harsh comments that seem to kill off an idea before its time, and never letting go—are key obsessional activities. Isolation further disrupts by denying the meaning of the block as a piece of emotional life, keeping the writing to oneself, thinking one citation will wreck another so conflicting ideas are kept separate or even forgotten, and being bothered by putting thoughts together. A conflict is being written. The anxiety that animates these defenses, it seems to me, concerns the worry that having one's say can only mean being sent into exile as punishment for one's ideal. Here, the dejected writer believes she will never be published, that there is no place for her work, and that no one cares. It is a paradox that the defense of isolation—keeping things from touching—brings closer the problem of associations that do make up psychical reality. Freud (1926a [1925]) understands the dilemma this way: "The experience is not forgotten, but instead it is deprived of affect, and associative connections are suppressed or interrupted so that it remains as though isolated and is not reproduced in the ordinary process of thought" (120). Touching involves putting ideas together, needed for thought and for erotic activities. It seems that the defense of isolation plays out a prohibition on touching.

The Letter

We can observe the painfulness of admitting these defenses and working through them in a letter Winnicott wrote to Melanie Klein on November 17, 1952 (Rodman 1999). Klein had invited Winnicott to write a chapter for a book she was editing, and the letter he wrote explained why he could not write for her. It had to do with his conviction that Klein only wanted compliance to her theories and that he wished to develop his own views as separate from hers. We can see the antisocial tendency as a needed position but also a hope that the other will respond without further persecutory anxiety. His letter is excruciating to read: he admits a failed analysis with his past analyst Joan Riviere, one of the editors of the book; he is writing to Klein who supervised some of his analytic training; and, he is launching a stringent critique on Klein's views, including his wish to destroy them. It is a letter that declares the personal cost of his freedom of thought:

> I am writing this down to show why it is that I have a real difficulty in writing a chapter for your book although I want to do so so very badly. This matter which I am discussing touches the very root of my own personal difficulty so that what you see can always be dismissed as Winnicott's illness, but if you dismiss it in this way you may miss something which is in the

end a positive contribution. My illness is something which I can deal with in my own way and it is not far away from being the inherent difficulty in regard to human contact with external reality. (Rodman 1999, 37)

We do not have Klein's response and only occasionally through footnotes did Klein mention Winnicott's work. Winnicott, however, will continue to write on the problems he believes that Kleinian formulations repeat; he will admit his hostility through the concept of the antisocial tendency and in his 1947 (1992) argument, "Hate in the Counter-Transference,"[7] where Klein's formulation of the baby's hatred of the mother is reversed. It is the mother who must hate the baby and know this hatred so well that she can surrender to love. And it is the writer who hates the writing and must know this well in order to surrender to words.

Ronald Britton (1994) discussed Winnicott's letter in his article on publication anxiety. Britton was addressing the analyst's anxiety in publishing her or his work: worries about putting forth a declining or unpopular theory, of not being original enough, of being disloyal to one's analyst, and of having to face a matrix of hostility that divides psychoanalytic societies into warring factions. He points out that anxiety also musters an intense epistemophilic desire to communicate to the other what one knows along with a fear that either no one will care or the writer will be condemned as wrong or crazy. The defenses involve a great deal of splitting into good and bad, undoing what has already happened, and isolation. This "no one" may be real, but as agony "no one" is in the writer's mind and may include phantasies of the indifferent audience, the hostile ones who read only to attack ideas, the disappointed ones who cannot be moved, and those the writer may put to sleep. It is important to remember that these bellicose characters wager with the writer's mind, and Winnicott's letter admitted such poignancy when he wrote of his own illness as the "inherent difficulty in regard to human contact with external reality" (Rodman 1999, 37). The fear may well be real angst, as Winnicott's letter shows. And while sadism in both academic and psychoanalytic culture seems to justify the phantasies, the issue is that phantasies themselves justify anxiety. There are phantasies that match this anxiety with the defense that the writer is smarter than anyone can ever understand, that the writer wishes to destroy the other's ideas, that the influence of others is a sign of weakness, and that the writer must go it alone. Britton raises Harold Bloom's (1973) idea of the anxiety of influence, and leaning on the Oedipal situation as discussed by Klein, Britton goes on to argue that the writer is caught in conflicting wishes to create something novel, to join with others, to become one's own origin, and to exceed what has already been done.

There are, for Britton (1994), two external pressures that tear at desire: "One is fear of rejection by the primary intended audience, and the other is fear of recrimination by colleagues with whom the author is affiliated and possible exile from them" (1213). Both involve the anticipation of separation, isolation, and the loss of love. I have already mentioned Klein's view that parting and loneliness go hand in hand, and I understand Britton to be suggesting that the defenses against anxiety in the form of undoing and isolation are also the first places of writing. Britton's contribution turns to the writer's phantasies and he can then describe what happens if the anxiety goes unrecognized by the writer: "If it is denied it may result in a superficial, complacent text" (1213). The writer's feelings of compliance do turn into a "complacent text." The odd part is that one will have written anxiety into the article by way of academic citations that don't belong there, by backtracking on one's argument and slipping it back in, and by offering false homage to one's theoretical parents with stingy reference. Sometimes the enemy is made small through a footnote. It is as if the antisocial tendency so needed to write suddenly goes missing. Britton came to these conclusions after analyzing one of his own articles. It is a turn to the writer as subject. "Sometimes," Britton observes, "it simply corrupts the language; at other times, the meaning of the discourse. I think anxiety about affiliation may be prevalent in psychoanalysis now. . . . There seems to be uncertainty as to whether psychoanalytic theory is in a state of fragmentation or integration" (1222).

To Write or Not to Write?

By the time one arrives at the university, an unconscious history of having to write includes impressions of hostility; compliance, aggression, and revolt are ready at hand. In chapter 3, we met some of their delegates: fear of theory, worries over plagiarism, and not knowing how to begin or finish. Yes, the symptoms are fast and furious as are defenses against them. And in the university, the pressure to write classroom assignments and dissertations, and then articles and books for tenure along with the wish to put all this pressure behind, are abiding dilemmas made exorbitant in phantasy. Many of us are unable to survive what feels like a terrible loneliness agonized by rules that cannot be followed. For the psychoanalyst in the classroom, as I mentioned in the chapter's opening, one of the more puzzling thoughts is whether one comes to the university to experience a writing block. It is hard to imagine, unless one considers that one arrives with a great deal of desire for belonging, affiliation, and having a say, along with doubts over whether such conflictive desires can be sustained or are even what we name as "realistic," a signifier of frustration, isolation, and failure. In chapter 3,

I also suggested the advent of writing inhibitions can be linked to fear of theory or more elemental, as fear of absence indicated by words. Here, I wish to develop the paradoxical claim that what we call the writing block is a constellation of emotional life, and to appreciate the psychical processes at stake, we can look for the sequence of phantasy.

When someone tries to discuss a writing block and the accompanying assignment that is either self-ascribed or demanded by a waiting teacher, employer, or press, one first hears consternation as to why a writing block happens. There are too many words or not enough words. When someone tries to discuss what it feels like to have something hanging over one's head, or feeling that things are out of reach or getting under one's skin, he or she may be referencing forgotten childhood but now with the acrobatics of self-disappointment at wasting precious time. We have heard such warnings before. There follows harsh judgments on the lazy self, trapped in a fortress of doubt as to whether he or she can really write at all. One languishes at the waiting post of thought. The disappointed writer may conclude he or she is best at fooling others and besides, writing is only pretense. Originality and the wish to write something novel seem to bring more danger and then anxieties over copying what others have already said follow suit. The writing block takes cover in passive voice: it makes the subject go missing. And nothing can change.

Advice on how to overcome the block seems to make the matter worse. The old standbys of time management, making lists, and getting out of bed seem to be speaking more to the problem than to the experience of going nowhere. The Internet may only aggravate matters. The endlessly updated blogs on writing blocks multiply. One may read or contribute to an open marketplace of opinions from those who have not suffered, from those who have suffered but have surmounted their doubts and can now give advice, and from those caught in the throes of the maelstrom of mental masochism. All these descriptions come with alarm and at their worst raise the question of whether one is ever meant to become a writer if one suffers by way of words.

Oddly, the writing block is filled with a crowd of thoughts that are often written down, but these thoughts enjoin the would-be author to clean her house, delete emails, go for a run, shop, check emails, go on Facebook, pick lint off the carpet, get a coffee, search for misplaced objects, and imagine all other sundry imperatives. It is the writer who is missing, caught in the glare of the blank page. Literature, philosophy, and psychoanalysis weigh in on these matters and, oddly, they come in the form of books.

Instead of a frenzy of activity, just the opposite occurs as it did with Melville's ([1893] 1997) enigmatic character employed in the dead letter department, "Bartleby the Scrivener"—whose only refrain when asked to do anything was "I prefer not to." One may languish and hardly move. As the story's narrator complains, "Nothing so aggravates an earnest person as a passive resistance. . . . Poor fellow! thought I, he means no mischief; it is plain he intends no insolence; his aspect sufficiently evinces that his eccentricities are involuntary" (28). It is true that no one would elect to possess a writing block; it seems the writing block possesses the would-be writer.

Although not writing about the writing block, Eleanor Catton's (2013) novel *The Luminaries* presents readers with a terrible sense of what it feels like to take on someone's assignment and not want to volunteer. The author is describing the outwardly successful Thomas Balfour, a shipping agent somehow involved in criminal activity and who readily steps into a task someone else has assigned:

> But Thomas Balfour's energies tended to span a very short duration, if the project to which he was assigned was not a project of his own devising. His imagination gave way to impatience, and his optimism to an extravagant breed of neglect. He seized an idea only to discard it immediately, if only for the reason that it was no longer novel to him; he started in all directions at once. This was not at all the mark of a fickle temper, but rather, of a temper that is accustomed to enthusiasm of the most genuine and curious sort, and so will accept no form of counterfeit—but it was, nevertheless, something of an impediment to progress. (82)

William James's ([1890] 1980) study of psychology takes the cake. Much of the topic is busy avoidance. Here is what he does instead of writing a lecture:

> One snatches at any and every passing pretext, no matter how trivial or external, to escape from the odiousness of the matter at hand. I know a person, for example, who will poke the fire, set chairs straight, pick dust-specks from the floor, arrange his table, snatch up the newspaper, take down any book which catches his eye, trim his nails, waste the morning anyhow in short, and all without premeditation,—simply because the only thing he ought to attend to is the preparation of a noonday lesson in formal logic which he detests. Anything but that! (421)

James wrote this passage in the chapter "Attention." He was writing about his own writing block as a constellation of anxieties that waxed and waned over the course of his life. It probably did not help to have as his brother, Henry James, who could not stop writing. But neither could William stop writing about the wandering mind and it lead him to a new theory.

Alison Bechdel's (2012) graphic novel *Are You My Mother?* wrestles with terrible anxiety, spectacular obsessionality, creative inhibitions, and the disappointments, indeed, the loneliness of self cure. She begins to wonder what hostile impulses have to do with the wish to write and dream and comes to the idea that her hostility is defended against and with phantasies of perfection. In a snippet of conversation with her mother, Bechdel complains about the author Joyce Carol Oates, whose memoir, Bechdel feels, is overrun with the writer's liberties. Mother offers to write for Bechdel. This has happened before. As a child Bechdel dictated to her mother stories, or rather, lists of disparate thoughts. The child seems to be saying, "Help. I can't put the pieces together." Or, perhaps she asks, "Mother, why are you stealing my words?" Hostile impulses are a bit like that: they take cover in ordinary ways. These scenes of overwriting repeat when Bechdel sees a therapist. The therapist too writes everything down. Then, in other sessions, Alison too is taking notes. But her symptoms take on new meanings when Bechdel stumbles upon the theories of Winnicott. Her homemade theory of preparing to write is, after all, a piece of mania. And then, she begins writing with Winnicott.

Marion Milner's (1950) self-study, *On Not Being Able to Paint*, brings us to the heart of the matter. Published at a time when the question of creativity for ordinary people was just entering psychoanalysis, Milner's own disappointment with her painting—what she saw as "copies of appearance" (4)—led her to question what the desire for mastery denies and so she had to considered her mood. She was in search of the practical problems: what she took for granted, refused to see, and felt as absence.

> The more I thought about the direction in which this study was leading the more one thing seemed likely: that the original work in painting, if it was ever to get beyond the stage of happy flukes, would demand facing certain facts about oneself as a separate being, facts that could often perhaps be successfully by-passed in ordinary living. Thus it seemed that it was possible, in spite of having lived a life of independent work and travel and earning a living, to have evaded facing certain facts about the human situation, or only given a superficial acquiescence to them. Otherwise why was it so difficult to feel about, as well as think about, the separateness or togetherness of objects? (13)

The "facts" Milner must face, face us all: the human condition involves what we may disclaim about the self and the vulnerabilities that are evaded by anxiety, defenses, aggressions, and phantasies have something to do with how we perceive separation and union. The writer has to put things together as well as take them apart.

Affiliation, Influence, and Misreading

"Influence," Bloom (1997) writes twenty years after the first edition of *The Anxiety of Influence*, "is a metaphor, one that implicates a matrix of relationships—imagistic, temporal, spiritual, psychological—all of them defensive in their nature. What matters most . . . is that the anxiety of influence *comes out of* a complex act of strong misreading, a creative interpretation that I call 'poetic misprision'" (xxiii). Bloom was describing both the ways in which he felt his own text was misread over the years and his view that there is a readerly need to misread as a first experience with any text, person, or situation. But it is also the poet's dilemma. To write poetry at all, the poet misreads those who came before. And something of this affects the reader who must feel that disquieting imagination. The emotional sequence for the reader begins in projective identification, putting into the text a phantasy and function of psychical life where what one wishes to project and meet again is one's expectation. Yet it is hard to distinguish expectations from anxiety's anticipatory urge. The reader's early attempt is to control the page, just as the writer has tried to do. But language is not like that. Another way to consider misprision is through the transference: the anxieties, defenses, and phantasy plays are given over to the other and allow the self to maintain an elusive sense of continuity and disunity. The anxiety, Bloom maintains, belongs more to the text than to the author. On this view, the emotional situation of reading proposes a problem of envy: projections, anticipations, and anxiety that reading must call upon may destroy the text one wished one had written. Of note is that misprision or misrecognition is an affective feature of reading and writing. And it is difficult to decide whether one is being loyal to an ideal or simply taken in.

Affiliation, we have already seen, comes at a cost. And one of the dilemmas of the writing block is that the writer, to return to Stonebridge's (2007) point, has to be disloyal to reality and still understand something more exists than what one feels. Henry James's ([1888] 2007) novella, *The Lesson of the Master*, presents four characters: a young writer who may just be on the verge of fame; an old writer who is famous but no longer writes; the old writer's wife, who administers his life and soon passes away; and a young woman who admires the old writer and may be interested in the young writer who is interested in her. It is the young writer's ambition, or his writer envy, that leads to his acceptance of a deception. Paul Overt arrives at the big house of Henry St. George, the old master, and Paul, who published one book, wants desperately to learn the secrets of writing that lead to becoming a famous writer. St. George tries to warn him off, "Don't become in your old age what I have in mine—the depressing, the deplorable illustration of the worship of false gods!" (33). But the character of Paul cannot make sense of the warning. St. George, who explains that he has been made rich by writing bad books, seems to be advising Paul to take a vow of poverty and, to be a great writer, avoid family life. Yet something is fishy. Paul hears St. George's imperatives as "art or life." Paul is persuaded just enough to leave the young woman behind and go away for many years to write a great book. He does that, returns hoping for his due of fame, and then is enraged to find that St. George, the old writer, is to marry the young woman. The story is an avalanche of dashed hopes, illusions, and writing phantasies.

James wrote his characters wonderfully into a number of tensions a writer must face: art and life, sellout and commerce, domesticity and discontentment, envy and deception, good and bad books, and ego ideal and ideal ego. I group these as aesthetic conflicts over the nature of apprehending beauty, truth, and knowledge, all elusive features of the inner and outer world and all subject to loss and to refinding (Meltzer and Harris Williams 1988). It would be tempting to take James's character study through Freud's (1916) "character types," for example, such as those wrecked by success or the exceptional ones believing they should get away without any pain. Or, even later with Freud's (1931) discussion on three libidinal types, "the main ways of employing libido in the economy of the mind" (219) that he named as the erotic, the narcissistic, and the obsessional. I think James leans upon the human condition but is also on to something else. Recall in chapter 1 that James is interested in developing a series of incidents, learned by overhearing, that lead his characters into emergence. The incidents only become events in their aftermath. The character cannot see coming what she or he has set in motion, and a sequence of phantasy composes the ideality of writing made from the wish for a perfect object (whether that be a partner, a book, a famous author, an experience of the top, the perfect conditions, an unchanging object, and so on) that will forever more protect the writer from any conflicts (such as art or life?). James calls such ideality "the worship of false gods," a sort of wholesale conviction that one has found the answer, provided that one perform a series of obsessional actions. With the character, Paul, readers follow his belief of perfection into its disillusionment, and on this suspension of belief, or the breakup of the adolescent syndrome of ideality, James concludes his story as a lesson in writing.

"Children-No-Longer"

"Every poet," Harold Bloom (1997) insists, "is a being caught up on a dialectical relationship (transference, repetition, error, communication) with another poet or poets" (91). We glimpsed these emotional situations in Winnicott's letter to Klein, in Bechdel's (2012) comic drama *Are You My*

Mother? and, in Britton's discussion of publication anxiety. Being caught in "transference, repetition, error, and communication" is what angles the writing block and makes it hard to see. To write without knowing one is blocked and have that be the essay written is also the dilemma that brings Paula Heimann (1899–1982) to create her term "children-no-longer." She was, for a time, a close friend, coauthor, and analysand of Melanie Klein. It was loss that brought them together: for Klein, the sudden death of her son and the alienation from her daughter, the psychoanalyst Melitta Schmideberg; for Heimann, who trained as an psychoanalyst in Berlin, it was her sudden forced exile to London in 1933, the loss of family, and poverty. From 1934 to 1955, Heimann associated with the Kleinian group in the British Psychoanalytical Society. She was supposed to be what Pearl King (1989) called in her memoir of Heimann "the crowned princess" (6) of the Kleinian Royal Family. Already we can see the conflicts of affiliation broken by Heimann's development of her own views and her turn toward the influence of environment in psychical life as needed for the self's creative position. Heimann formally left the Klein group in 1955 and joined with "The Independent Group" made up of Winnicott, Balint, and others. And in much of her writing after the break with Klein, Heimann's interest focused on the question of freedom in psychoanalytic work: the freedom of the analysand to find herself/himself, the analyst's capacity to move from the depressive position of repairing objects to the creation of new psychoanalytic experiences and techniques, and the analyst's freedom to relax and become a partner in the analytic adventure. Heimann's reorientation is first hinted in the conclusion of her ([1939/42] 1989) early essay on sublimation:

> As I have said, the inner world is a never-ending drama of life and action. Life is bound up with the dynamic process set up by aggression, guilt, anxiety, and grief about internal objects, and by the impulses of love and restoration; love and hate are urging the subject to strive for sublimation. The internal freedom to which I refer is a relative, not an absolute fact; it does not abolish conflicts, but it enables the subject to enlarge and unfold his ego in his sublimations. (43)

Earlier in the chapter I considered Ronell's (2003) insight that the writer is caught between freedom and unfreedom: freedom in the sense of possibilities yet to be known and unfreedom in the sense of the anticipation of constraints that feel as if there is no way out. Bechdel (2012) presents this dilemma as a comic drama and as a story of finding and creating an object. For Britton (1994) one consequence of feeling trapped takes shape in publication anxiety. That concept allowed Britton to understand more about an essay he had written. Winnicott's ([1956] 1994) view of the antisocial tendency is a provision for expressing frustration, provided that the environment can stand it. Barthes's (2011) solution for the writer—"the neurotic stratagem" (269) that James's *The Lesson of the Master* follows from—suggests that all writing (and teaching) locate the emergence of phantasy. Stonebridge (2007) places anxiety in the gap between reason and imagination, and with Klein ([1946] 1975) that we grasp that losing one's beloved objects and the fear they have been destroyed is anxiety. Milner's (1950) view goes one step further and this concerns disquieting imagination. The creator must face the complexities both good and bad in the emotional world. For Heimann, in her last essay described later, the phantasy to disillusion is of ideal beginnings and she uses it to locate the tensions made while trying to write with her concept of "children-no-longer." There she expresses the passing of time and the remnants carried forward that bring her to articulate the difference between children and adults, and freedom and unfreedom. Of special interest is why Heimann spoke of her writing block as an unconscious phantasy repeated throughout her essay until she could notice the latent anxiety contained in her term "children-no-longer."

Heimann ([1979/80] 1989) was eighty years old when she wrote "About Children and Children-No-Longer." She was asked by J.-B. Pontalis to contribute an essay about her work and focus on her responses to being with a child. Her first three sentences will tell the story in miniature:

> I start with the first ideas that came into my mind immediately after reading J-B. Pontalis's invitation to take part in a project that I warmly welcome. The word "ideas" is not quite correct. What occurred to me were pictures, scenes, memories of contact with children outside my professional activities. (324)

The first thing readers may notice is that it takes Heimann quite a while to turn to the clinic. She provides lovely anecdotes of very young children's emotional logic that often seem improbable to the harried adult who has forgotten her or his childhood. She returns to the "warm welcome" of being asked to write the essay in a short section titled "Editorial Demands and Strictures." There, hostility is given air.

> So far, I realize, I have reacted only to J-B. Pontalis's personal letter, and that was easy, child's play so to say. Indeed, without becoming aware of it at the time, I behaved like a child, and by playing showed what I do, in fact, consider characteristic for children: they respond immediately and easily to a benevolent invitation to express their thoughts, to be active and creative. . . . As

> I now study the demands and structures issued by J-B. Pontalis, the editor, things at once become different. I encounter difficulties with which I am only too familiar. An empty page stares at me, and my mind goes blank. (334)

The personal letter has turned into the harsh editor and Heimann's "mind goes blank." There is no other way to present what has happened, except she continued writing and asked herself a question when she noticed her anger and began to "vent criticisms" (335). "Is it significant that they [the ideas] are hostile? I answer in the affirmative" (335). She goes on to write, "Perhaps I have again identified with a child, this time, when confronted with a stranger, not knowing how to start a dialogue, or with parents who for reasons of their own were unable to initiate contact, or respond gladly to the child's attempts at reaching them" (335).

The rest of her essay does play in the land of hostility: she discusses ideas she hates, errors she regrets, and she concludes with her disagreement on the order for the analyst to be neutral and uninvolved.[8] There is, of course, an accrual of incidents that retroactively become the catches of recounting a life history that brought Heimann to become again the child she once hoped she was but is now no longer. Phantasy is written out and used to refine the pleasure in presenting her evolving views. The hostility she mentions and the needed antisocial tendency is only the raw material and its sequence involves the writer's giving way to a phantasy of origin, suspicion as to who is originating what, then blankness in the face of censor, then to an idea one can properly destroy, then to an admission of aggression, and then a communication on the currency of writer's affects and the lifting of repression. Again, Barthes's (2011) rule comes after: "The principle is a general one: the subject is not to be repressed—whatever the risks of subjectivity" (3).

We have in a nutshell the sequence of phantasy and its relation to writing anxiety disclaimed, rendered significant, and worked through. It turns out that the untold story of the writing block is unconscious, a convolution of conflicts that take form in phantasies of origin, affiliation, loyalty, aggression, free association, and desire. We have been there before but without knowing why. Still, we must express our discontentment—that "compulsion to symbolize"—to even begin to write over an index of loss. Writing performs the fallout of separation and union. Perhaps that open secret too was what Freud's ode to time touched upon: *queer feelings, late, ordered, once again, school, strange, obey,* and *nothing happened.* But of course a great deal happens under the sign of nothing. It is after all the portal to the unconscious, to an affecting topic, to the maddening difficulties of communication, and to the disquieting imagination. As for the writing assignment and our sense of the order to write, the antisocial tendency, however schizoid, will be our best resource, provided that we can stand ourselves and find someone else to stand us as we write.

7

The Psychopathologies of Everyday Education

Sleeping, Falling, Forgetting, Lateness, and the Professor's Mistakes

> Indeed, the mistake could not have occurred if the material had not been particularly favourable.
>
> —Sigmund Freud, "The Subtleties of a Faulty Action"

Everyday Material

In any act of pedagogy we express quite a few disturbances of the psychical sort. They come as transient mistakes that break open our intended purposes and leave us to wonder where and who we are and what we think we already know. The professor's language may suddenly crumble. Sentences trail off, thoughts and words go missing, important names are forgotten, the mind wanders far away or momentarily goes blank, and we cannot recall what we have just said or may say the opposite of what we mean. The odd thought pops into the mind. Mishearing is also common. Whether by way of slips of tongue or pen, a misreading occurs; and, too, when we are unable to locate valuable notes or create any assortment of bungled actions—when all these misperformances of attention lose their objects—there is no alibi for becoming senseless. Unmeant events brought Freud ([1915–1917] 1916–1917) in his three lectures on parapraxis to give the term "sense" a special meaning: "Let us once more reach an agreement upon what is to be understood by the 'sense' of a psychical process. We mean nothing other by it than the intention it serves and its position in psychical continuity" (40). But how strange to admit mistakes as having psychical value and that they express other purposes and another mode of continuity. To embrace this affectionate view, we would have to entertain the idea that unconscious mistakes are our little emissaries of desire. They force us to reconsider the raw material of our narrative drive and wonder more about its destiny.

Quite early Freud (1901) named affecting mistakes "symptomatic acts" (191). He placed such subjective subtractions into the question of desire and the book he wrote, *The Psychopathology of Everyday Life*, a year after his *Interpretation of Dreams*, presents a panorama of mistakes—his and others—along with an attempt to trace their blunders to unconscious conflicts of love, hate, and ambivalence. Freud tied these transferences to dreamy behavior, epistemological disorder, subjective gaps, forgetting, wishes, and to split attention. Mistakes seem to return the repressed. James Strachey's introduction to Freud's work had to coin a rather awkward English term, "parapraxis," for the German word *Feheistung* that signifies "faulty function" and misperformance. In a footnote, Strachey (1968a) named the novelty of the subject: "It is a curious fact that before Freud wrote this book the general concept seems not to have existed in psychology, and in English a new word [parapraxis] had to be invented to cover it" (xii). If sometimes a mistake is just a mistake and we already have that word "accidents," it is the affective errors—the slips of the tongue, miscommunications, and flurries of bungled actions—that brought Freud (1901) to notice the poignancy and potential communicative value of associating to unmeant experience. Oddly, Freud shows us not only how mistakes happen but also what drives us to make them.

The conditions for these faulty actions, Freud insisted, are "favorable" and what he meant is that mistakes, as well as our accomplishments, carry on congealed deliberations within psychical reality that manage to grab hold of meanings we may not want to admit or prefer to conceal. Everyday mistakes have an affective sequence. They do not occur just anywhere; their estrangements involve some sort of mixed-up cause, serve some muddled purpose, lean upon conflicts in desire, and call upon some other scene. Like dreams, mistakes depend on that odd combination of the day's residues and forgotten wishes and, so, are open for interpretation.[1] The etymology of psychopathology gives us a clue as to why this word might bother us. It has three roots: "psycho-," or soul; "pathos-," or suffering; and "-ology," or the study. These terms also belong to disquieting imagination and here signify what is extraordinary: a tear or a rent in libido that divides the subject and touches on a kernel of ambivalence carried into our lives with others. The mistake then is a comprise formation in that it joins two competing wishes into one belittling or funny expression.

Freud (1901) kept adding more anecdotes to his book for the next twenty years. *The Psychopathology of Everyday Life* went through eleven editions and reprints in German and five in English. Strachey (1968a) points out that the first English edition, translated and edited by Brill, was published around 1914. Brill cut out a great deal of material, though we can only guess why. The *Standard Edition* contains the complete version, though it seems mistakes keep on surfacing and each generation contributes more of them. We can add to Freud's list our favorable conditions for making mistakes, such as with our modern devices dedicated to attachment, communication, and instant gratification. With virtual reality we now have virtual mistakes. We manage to create them by pushing the wrong button, replying to all, and sending into the ether various catastrophes of immediate gratification that make others mad.

There are still old-fashioned mistakes that Sándor Ferenczi ([1915] 2002) called "mistaken mistakes" (412). These occur when we think we have made one but have not. In a mistaken mistake there are two errors: the thought that one has made a mistake or forgotten something important and a certainty one has made it. Some examples may be thinking one has set one's house on fire because one forgot to shut off the stove, or thinking one is being robbed because one is certain to have forgotten to lock the door. Communication, too, is rife with mistaken mistakes and they have a paranoid flavor. There are common worries that we have (accidentally) insulted someone, that our words were taken in the wrong way, and that we can be accused of something we have never done. Guilt also plays a part, but here, though, it is difficult to settle why someone must feel wronged. Ferenczi settles on the problem of ambivalence: mistaken mistakes are made from that odd mix-up of aggression and feelings of tenderness toward the same object.

Ever since Freud (1901) wrote *The Psychopathology of Everyday Life*, accidents, mistakes, the loss of consciousness, and the destiny of incidental distraction hold a special place for the psychoanalyst. You don't have to be one to laugh at a Freudian slip. I recommend Freud's hilarious index of parapraxes that include: bringing the wrong keys, breaking valuable objects, wrongly dating a check, feeling glued to the stairs, telephoning the wrong person, mashing names, misspelling your own name, not recognizing a beloved, forgetting an important date, self-injuries, going to a lecture on the wrong date, a watch repeatedly left at home, a letter sent with no address, saying idiot for patriot, and the rather startling handshake combined with unfastening a lady's dress. And it is surprising how many examples come from the human condition of education; its favorable conditions are those that urge us to perform, attach, communicate, and understand. The bungled action, Freud goes on to show, leans on both forgetting and memory: "that the forgotten or distorted matter is brought by some associative path into connection with an unconscious thought-content—a thought-content which is the source of the effect manifested in the form of forgetting" (20–21).[2] However absurd or stupid they feel, errors are a rather complicated emotional composition. Two opposing or conflicted ideas are condensed into one action and then displaced into a new event. Old affects transfer or associate to a new scene but paradoxically do not feel familiar. There are, for Freud, sequences to these estranging events; a great many lead back to erotic conflicts, infantile theories of sexuality, Oedipal rivalry, unconscious guilt, unfinished business, everyday neurosis, and just plain jealously, envy, and hostility dedicated to narcissistic demands, disappointments, and group psychology.

I was once asked by one of my students, "But Professor, is there then no such thing as an honest mistake? Do we really mean to make them? Are mistakes really our fault?" Beyond the well-schooled idea that mistakes require someone to blame, we can flip these worries on their side: some sort of honesty, some other truth that may be intolerable, is involved but we don't know what it is. What we do know is that other determinations interfere with the ones we consciously create. And for the psychoanalyst in the classroom, mistakes may be the royal road to phantasies of learning and teaching. They open questions of desire. Mistakes, or the things we don't mean to make, can help us consider the psychical consequences of education and, as I hope to show, how they are noticed and handled, may enliven our pedagogical imagination and the ways we can work.

My interest is with how we may interpret the aftereffects of myriad teaching accidents and mishaps and reconstruct the little disorders of losing words, falling down, lateness, and falling asleep in order to reach the more difficult terms of affecting teaching and learning relations. The challenge of writing how all of this feels and what may or may not be learned from disquieting imagination is usually presented in the world of fiction: for example, the genre of narratives of teaching presented in films, novels and short stories, jokes, and visual art. We do have names for our miscalculations, misperformances, misrepresentations, and missed connections. In common parlance we mess up, forget, get up on the wrong side of the bed, and have a bad day. For the psychoanalyst in the classroom, teaching is carried away by phantasy, the unconscious, transference, anxiety, and desire. But it is the return of the repressed in teaching that warrants an affectionate formulation and a new curiosity toward the recommendations of psychical design. In this chapter, I ask you to accompany the psychopathologies of everyday teaching and imagine their congealed instructions. My method is to freely associate to the vast and unfinished occurrence of affecting mistakes. The chapter concludes by presenting a missing case of the professor's mistakes. In a study of my pedagogical neurosis, the sequence begins with my misprision, or taking things the wrong way. It took me a number of weeks to recognize my defenses as part of the trouble and then how I came to consider anew unconscious matters of love, hate, and ambivalence transferred into the presence of teaching and learning relations.

Sleeping

Perhaps the most radical example that goes beyond the ordinary flummox of bungled actions is "teaching in your sleep," one of those euphemisms that may be received as either a harsh wake-up call or a goodnight kiss that gives way to a dream. As an attempt to escape, "teaching in your sleep" is similar to "talking in your sleep" or "sleepwalking." Such events give us the paradoxical remainder of involuntary actions without memory. The phrasing "teaching in your sleep" is labile enough to invite a teaching phantasy: Wouldn't it be great if we could discover that the secret of teaching is so simple that it can be done with eyes closed? I think that students may believe this about some of their teachers. Those who can do it are geniuses; those who only do that are idiots. For the teacher or professor, however, these feelings in thoughts do reach their apex in phantasies of teaching and learning.[3] We may know them best as they play out in the teacher's dreams. Such projections and defenses may even be needed to tolerate the absurdities and humiliations of institutional life and the endless curriculum checks that do feel we are repeating ourselves. Teaching in your sleep, however, is of a different temporality than when we tell someone: "Let me sleep on it." Then we wish to give time to our waiting thoughts and may well need sleep to do this. Last but not least, if we add anxiety and a tinge of hostility to the phrase "teaching in your sleep" the thought may arise: *Oh no, my teaching, my students, and my colleagues are putting me to sleep.* In this sense, sleep may be our greatest defense against feeling helpless. We can think of these fleeting thoughts as a regression into infantile states. Once upon a time, all that the young child had to do was close her eyes to magically make the world disappear. The phantasy may be stated as: You are gone; I made you disappear; I can't see you; and, by the way, I killed you.[4]

Education is one of those favorable places for bungled actions: for the teacher, there is being late to class, forgetting to bring a lesson plan, losing a dissertation, and recording the wrong grade; and for the student, there is forgetting to raise your hand, calling your teachers Mommy or Daddy, or letting your dog eat your homework. Something slips in, precisely when least expected. When, over the many years of teaching, I admit my anxieties of walking into a class for the first time, more than a few friends have said: "What are you worried about? You can teach in your sleep." In his discussion on patients who sleep during the analysis, and I think we can say something similar about sleeping in class, the psychoanalyst W. Clifford Scott (1952) notes that the wish to sleep or regress is satisfied by "the act of waking up" (465). What I most worry about is sleepwalking through my teaching, becoming terribly stupid again, or running on autopilot. Admittedly anticipating these events cannot get at their experience, though we can turn to those who have written about what I dare to call the "everyday psychopathologies of education": sleeping; narcissism; stupidity; love; bungled actions; lateness; falling; and, more generally, the passion for the transference to learning needed to break open our omnipotent sense of knowledge and authority.

Constance Penley's (1989) groundbreaking essay, "Teaching in Your Sleep," brought the idea of dream life to feminist pedagogy. She raised two problems: whether psychoanalysis and feminism can meet and whether something like an empirical science of pedagogy can be possible. "Teaching in Your Sleep" seems to gather together these contrary predicaments by challenging our psychical sense of pedagogy. And in Penley's hands, the phrasing invites scenarios of pedagogy contingent on nonauthoritative knowledge, or knowledge devoid of the cast of self-possession. She points out that the psychoanalyst relies upon knowledge that does not know its own latency and wonders if the same deferral operates in everyday teaching. If so, and however deferred our pedagogy may be, we can still link what we do in the classroom to our autobiographic impulse, less direct than expected and founded on the pervasive transference of love and knowledge, and hatred and authority.

It is in sleeping, however, that we really do close our eyes. The body goes passive, the ego lets down its guard, though it still manages to maintain some modem of censorship, however disguised by the dream work of condensation, substitution, reversal into its opposite, consideration of representation, and displacement. Judgment recedes and the unconscious comes into play. Sleep is the bare condition for dreaming. And yet, for the teacher or professor, even when asleep, what seems most forgettable about school life returns, but mainly as the theater of the absurd.

Freud's (1900) *The Interpretation of Dreams* has a short section on "typical dreams." He names quite a few: embarrassing dreams of being naked, dreams of the deaths of persons of whom the dreamer is fond, and the dreaded examination dreams. These typical dreams challenge interpretation and all lean upon mistakes, but only in the examination dream do we feel what Freud called "the burden of responsibility" entering into its fiasco (274). Those who have already passed exams typically report these dreams. For no reason, they have to take the exam again, perhaps covering the wish they should never have had to take an exam in the first place. But in the dream something goes wrong: pens are missing, one is unprepared, the exam must be written in a different language, one cannot find the exam room, one goes into the exam and is required to sit in a child's nursery seat, and one forgets the day of the exam or arrives too late. Usually the dreamer wakes up with the thought: But I have already passed my exams. "Not long ago," Freud explains,

> I came to the conclusion that the objection, "You're a doctor, etc., already," does not merely conceal a consolation but also signifies a reproach. This would have run: "You're quite old now, quite far advanced in life, and yet you go on doing these stupid, childish things." This mixture of self-criticism and consolation would thus correspond to the latent content of examination dreams. (1900, 275–276)

Typical dreams are amplifications of early affective impressions. The dream elements return as mood and feeling tone to the day's residues, or what has impressed us but was felt without notice. The dream work or the psychical methods of working over thought perceptions insure disguise. Manifest and latent content intermingle. Things are out of place, nonsensical words are made, and the dreamer is never sure whether she is watching the dream or acting all the parts. These primary thought processes without time, contradiction, or negation are one of the reasons it is so difficult to narrate the dream through to any conventional plotlines.[5] They also make interpretation an adventure in constructions. Freud advises that we treat the dream as if working on a rebus puzzle and try to imagine that images stand in for words and objects. But typical dreams, it seems to me, have one further difficulty and something in common with teaching. It has to do with their overfamiliarity and the defensive thought that follows: But I already know all of this. Barbara Johnson (1987) put the problem into reading: "What the surprise of encounter with otherness should do is lay bare some hint of ignorance that one never knew one had" (16).

Waking Up

Through Kristeva (2000) we can consider these other scenes or what is unconscious in pedagogy as leading to narrative revolts, an overturning of conscious meaning that frees the speaking subject from inhibition. Questions, she maintains, help this work, as does free association where the disparities and displacements made from the tumult of experience may be brought together, symbolized, and rendered significant. And she recommends reading fiction for a lesson in what we cannot see coming. In fiction as with life, that which turns out to be unresolved and even intolerable in our education has a second chance in symbolizing our phantasies of knowledge, authority, and love.

A fine specimen of pedagogical elation, latency, despair, and reparation is found in the literary fiction *Stoner*, a professor's novel written by John Williams ([1965] 2003). Through the lifeworld of one character who often has the feel of a sleepwalker in his undergraduate education and who then becomes a professor subject to bouts of teaching in his sleep and to depression, the novel may also be read as an affected commentary on the historical changes of the North American university between the years of 1910 and 1956. That history as well wavers between sleep and awakening. The university that educated Stoner and where he lived out his career as a student and professor is called the University of Missouri, the place where the author, John Williams, taught. In order to reach into the teacher's phantasy world, our author tells his readers he must take some liberties, just as affect does with historical facts and just what literature does to the duration of imagination. A great deal of what happens to Stoner involves misapprehension. Stoner the character is a late bloomer and significance is a late arrival.

The character called Stoner is sent to the university as a nineteen-year-old; he takes all of his degrees there, stayed on as a professor, and passed away. Our author tells us that Stoner may be a teacher whom no one remembers, a rather extraordinary disruption of the figure of the mythic teacher who is never forgotten. Being forgotten goes against the teacher's fondest wishes, or the idealizations we have been schooled by: that no matter what happens, we teachers are memorable characters for our students no longer. But the university is a fickle place, and through a series of incidents met by students' phantasies that only a winning professor will help their career, Stoner loses the popularity contest. There is too much competition; the students are under the sway of the hearsay of departmental politics, gossip, and various superstitions that shape what they think happen. Besides, Stoner's topic, "The Latin tradition and the Renaissance," had good and bad years. His disappointments and pleasures really belong to him: "He hoped in time to make a reputation for himself as both a scholar and a teacher" (102). As a character study, Stoner's fortitude is memorable, and he lends to teaching his poignancy and the vulnerability entailed in trying to teach. But there were times when he lost his way, fell into depression, and could not wake up.

Perhaps like many of us, the character called Stoner came to the teaching profession by accident. He never thought about becoming a teacher and was slow to fall in love with ideas he did not understand. Over the early course of the novel, much that he does is without volition, and yet, through coincidence, he does try to understand his loves and his limits. Stoner was never meant to go to university. His parents were poor farmers and his father decided that he should go to an agricultural college, just as many girls were sent to the normal school to become teachers. It was to be only a practical training and then a return back home. The utilitarian land-granting colleges were transforming into public universities and began offering PhD degrees. Stoner knew about agriculture and the study didn't ask much of him. He was at first an average student; the course that challenged him to speak his thoughts was literature. But when called upon in class to describe what a sonnet meant, all Stoner could say was, "It means. . . . It means. . . . It means . . ." (13). He could not answer a question his English professor asked. And this mixture of humiliation and elation was the beginning of his education. A few years later, that English professor, Mr. Sloan, asked Stoner about his plans after his bachelor's degree. Stoner had not thought about that: "But don't you know, Mr. Stoner? Sloan asked. Don't you understand about yourself yet? You're going to be a teacher" (20). And then, the only reason: "It's love, Mr. Stoner," Sloan said cheerfully. "You are in love. It's as simple as that" (20). What was not simple is that Stoner did not know this, and, in a sense, the rest of the novel carries on a particular argument on the matter of what it is to love teaching or anything else.

 The years pass in this quiet novel, and the depressive character Stoner marches through his teaching. It wasn't like that at first. He had exciting graduate seminars and loved his material. But due to a series of accidents, departmental jealousy, the rise of academic stars, and his own revolts, Stoner's department chair relieved him of his graduate seminars and assigned him to the endless first year course that everyone had to take and that no one wanted, namely, the required freshman composition. Like many unhappily married, midlife professors, he had a passionate love affair. It was his most intentional act that gave him the gift of having to rethink love and suffer its loss. The novel's omnipotent narrator notes: "Now in middle age he began to know that it was neither a state of grace nor an illusion; he saw it as a human act of becoming, a condition that was invented and modified moment by moment and day by day, by the will and the intelligence and the heart" (195). But it was the ending of the love affair; the loss of love, that opened Stoner to his depressed teaching. He knew that it was not the classes assigned that made him go missing. It was simply that he lost his will to want more than what was demanded. It was the summer of 1937 and Stoner was facing another world at war. He did not sign up for the first one.

 The passion or love of knowledge came back to Stoner as a narrative revolt. On the first day of his freshman composition class, he walked into the room and told the students to take back the books they had bought and throw away the required syllabus. The class will instead study twelfth-century medieval texts to see how the medieval mind thought. A student asked if they were in the composition class. Stoner agreed but continued to discuss the medieval texts. Then he said to his students:

> Certain accidents of history will stand in our way; there will be linguistic difficulties as well as philosophical, social as well as religious, theoretical as well as practical. Indeed, all of our past education will in some ways hinder us; for our habits of thinking about the nature of experience have determined our own expectations as radically as the habits of medieval man determined his. (224)

He gave the first assignment: write a short paper on the question of topics. Stoner's comments to his students had already presented the topos of mistakes.

Lateness

There are certain accidents and things we don't mean and can't understand that do have a second chance in narratives. Harold Rosen (1988) created the captivating term "autobiographical impulse" to discuss desire for our storied lives with the pressing question, what holds us back from saying more? There is a story of this story, and Rosen had in mind an intimate conflict between the desire to make one's world meaningful when speaking to others and the schooled prohibition on worded lives where we are "taught in educational systems how to cover our narrative tracks and even be ashamed of them" (82). We have a clue as to why many hate making mistakes. They call us out.

I've often wondered when writing about education if our research suffers from this malady of erasure and prohibition. Rather than write about our teaching difficulties, rather than interpret the material and sequences of our mistakes, we find it easier to correct others, become ventriloquists for our pedagogical slogans, or imagine our readers are still children, unable to read. Deflecting personal involvement and so extricating the self from one's mental acts, however, has an early start and leaves its trace in nagging thoughts: for instance, whether one is allowed to say what is on one's mind, whether it is alright to use a personal pronoun, and whether one's views have any value at all. Beyond the personal doubts and perhaps the mistaken mistake that nothing can matter, there are also the institutional idealities that diminish desire: we are urged to speak to the topic, be efficient, keep watch over objectives, avoid conflict, and know our plans. We are urged to celebrate best practices and forget our best mistakes. To narrate our malady involves us with mistaken mistakes, filled with anxieties and inhibitions that are common features of life and learning. And we might come to wonder more about what else the autobiographic impulse contains that so affects our worries about it.

Having language is one existential condition favorable to mistakes. Words signify more than we mean and can be used to invoke the breakdown of our meaning. We can draw from the well of the psychopathology of everyday life in education. One need only think about words such as stupidity, love, and accidents, for instance, to wrench education out of its hiding place. But from a personal angle, we all have memories of being at a loss for words. Perhaps this is one reason we fear mistakes. We can recall times when worries over the right and wrong words kept us silent, when the wrong word is blurted out without any cause; and we have all felt the agony of shame in not understanding, in pretending to understand, or simply in closing down. From a symbolic angle language too may cover over its narrative tracks and derail our train of thought. From a psychoanalytic angle however, even if unspoken, remainders of the drive to narrative leave impressions for others to gather. In unexpected ways the other may still interpret hints of a wider world of emerging meaning, seemingly confined in the secret thought (Leader 2000). But it is the ambiguity of words—our dependence on metaphor, synecdoche, and metonymy and our involvement in the logic of language—that lends pathos and pleasure to the subjective gap communication carries forward.

Such silences that Rosen relates to the autobiographical impulse are structural and subjectively felt as obstacles to everyday speech. In literary affairs, we can read portraits of not saying what is on one's mind, such as in long novels of secret thoughts: for instance Henry James's ([1904] 1992) *The Golden Bowl*, Thomas Mann's ([1901] 1994) *Buddenbrooks: The Decline of a Family*, or John Williams's ([1965] 2003) *Stoner*. There readers are privy to life's disguises and the pain of deception that leaves us with a sense that if characters are holding back, a great deal occurs in the plotting of strangulated affect. There is both the wish for words and anxiety over how they are received by the other. In these novels the characters suffer from over correction. They avoid mistakes and mistake avoidance for proper comportment, politeness, and professionalism. The characters make mistakes into tragedy.

A breakthrough narrative for the creativity of the autobiographical impulse is found in Jane Miller's (2010) memoir, *Crazy Age: Thoughts on Being Old*. Miller's impressionistic style gives readers a sense of feeling the ripples of time but also its disappearance. She notes that if in helpless moments the young may wish to be old, they may only be wishing for a magical autonomy they imagine adults already possess. The old, Miller points out, know better and do not want to be young again. But in figuring this out, one has to pass beyond the schooled prohibition that does leave its trace in daily life: "This embargo on old age as a topic reminds me of my early years as a mother, when we tried not to talk about our babies for fear of being thought boring; and the babies themselves were expected to remain as far as possible unseen and unheard" (6). One impossible scene reminds her of another. There is the courage of freely associating with passing time.

Miller's chapter "Reading into Old Age" is ambiguous, referring to both novels of old age and interpreting the presence of old age. For Miller, the memory troubles attributed to the old are really only a feature of the story of memory: "It is not only that one's memories don't match the original, nor even that they either willfully or unintentionally falsify the truth. It is that being old makes being young look quite different" (70). And not only is one's own story affected by passing time. In her chapter "Late" Miller writes, "Old age comes late, but then we are always late for something" (170).

For the literary critic M. Bakhtin, lateness is a feature of language. He argued that words are found in other people's mouths, borrowed, tattered by use, yet can feel anonymous. "Language," Bakhtin (1981) wrote, "is not a neutral medium that passes freely and easily into the private property of the speaker's intentions; it is populated—overpopulated—with the intentions of others" (341–342). And yet the other's intentions are also a riotous crowd, subjected as they are to slips of the tongue, seemingly urged on by language's tendency toward displacement, substitution, condensation, undoing, and reversal of meaning. It is not so much a matter of finding the right words as it is becoming curious about the wrong ones or the slips that permit thoughts their freedom and their desire. One word can refer to so many things; we may wonder for whom we are speaking. In Rosen's formulation of the autobiographical impulse and Miller's insistence on reading into memory, words wager as much with the destiny of communication as they do with the destiny of our feelings. And mistakes, I think, can remind us of this.

Such conflicts have as their pressure point a theory of language joined to erotic life, a binding that is one of the key contributions psychoanalysis brings to the understanding of love and hate in pedagogical exchanges and that must include unbinding in the form of unspoken bits, accidents, and slips transposed into faraway scenes. Our models for writing into this emotional situation are many: memoirs, literary theory, literature, and clinical descriptions of the talking cure (Britzman 2009). These genres of writing have in common their interest in affecting narrative. As for clinical writing in psychoanalysis, the interest is with a subjective gap between the spoken and the unspoken and between presence and absence. The case takes its author as subject of desire with the surprising insistence that the latency and deferral of meaning can become a story we wish to tell.

A Rescue Fantasy

Literary dilemmas founded by the autobiographical impulse find their way into public discussions of psychoanalysis. Anna Freud's early lectures to teachers are a fine example for how learning involves mistaken anxieties and handling various affective obstacles to the drive to narrate. In 1930 a young Anna Freud was invited to address a Viennese audience of teachers and social workers on the topic of psychoanalysis. What they had in common was passion for the creation of new practices: for Anna Freud, it was psychoanalysis for children; for the daycare workers, a citywide pedagogical experiment in afterschool daycare called the Hort programs, which served working-class students between the ages of six and fourteen. While contemporary readers only have Anna Freud's ([1930] 1974) four lectures and not the listeners' responses to them, we can imagine some of the experiences the audience may have had with the request to think psychoanalysis with education. Many of the teachers' objections seem split between Ferenczi's ([1915] 2002) "mistaken mistake," and the anxiety of feeling mistaken when new ideas are met by anticipating a disastrous encounter with the human condition. Psychoanalytic discussion on unconscious education can be a bit like that and affects are invited to come as they are.

By way of some background, the Hort daycare provided children and adolescents help with homework, gave time for games and rest, and provided snacks and dinner. Workers were privy to the children's sense of their school day that must have included a wide range of emotional situations and contingent behaviors expressing the difficulties of transitions from the daily comings and goings among home, school, and daycare. Perhaps, like child analysis, the daycare created a transitional space, and more likely, teachers were confronted with an experiment of group upbringing, a topic that years later took on greater poignancy when in 1938 the Freud family became refugees and went into exile in London. During the war, Miss Freud ran the Hampstead clinic for orphan and refugee children, perhaps with memories of the Hort experiment (A. Freud [1951] 1968). Yet in her early lectures, one may sense that while there are significant differences between child analysis and daycare, these experimental fields of practice do share the work of getting to know the other, learning more about the self, and making some sense from the problem of interpretation and communication. Much of what Anna Freud came to discuss concerned the practitioners' dilemmas with their respective charges that begins with the emotional situation of having to be in charge without understanding what drives their responses and worries.

A close study of the style of Miss Freud's lectures reveals how much she learned from her father, Sigmund Freud, and his approach to introducing psychoanalysis: her lectures articulated the audiences' anticipations for and objections to unconscious life and provided affecting examples that linked the teacher's childhood of education to the currency of the adult/child emotional world, all with the idea that if education is all types of interference—a difference from development yet an address to the child—the teacher's ethical position for interpreting the intersubjective layering of conflict involves a balance between noninterference or permitting the child her idiom and frustration and interference through demanding a delay in satisfaction. From this notion of interference Anna Freud elaborated the idea of education as welcoming the human condition. Her focus was on the inevitability of mistiming, anxiety, and the problem of love. The teacher's pedagogical desire and its myriad frustrations were dominant themes, and Anna Freud zoomed in on the details of estranged desire entangled in the living out of rescue fantasies and the urge to correct misbehavior and turn the child into someone just like the teacher. All these transferences have a long history in the teacher's unconscious childhood of education. The lectures seem to ask the psychoanalytic question, what does the teacher want?

We do know that education wants something from the teacher, but what does the teacher want for herself/himself? There are many desires we may consciously insist upon, such as: the teacher wants the students to learn, only wants to help, give knowledge to others, and be seen as a good teacher. But these mainly concern the wish for an education without being interfered with. We don't often admit the teacher wants more brains, wishes to understand the self within the pedagogical exchange, or desires something wild. Typically, the teacher's persona presents as altruistic, self-effacing, and idealistic. Rarely are these character masks considered as defenses against the fear of the intimacies of autobiography and the chaos of desire. There is much in the imaginary of education that covers over the teacher's narrative tracks and leaves the teacher feeling abandoned. And yet, there is still the surprising encounter made from throwaway lines, accidents, and missed details, and, yes, to the psychopathologies of everyday education that do have a second life in anxiety, dreams, and slips of the tongue.

Miss Freud began her lectures by noting the sheer amount of life's details that the daycare teachers must have encountered: perhaps puzzling scenes, naughty behavior, and secret hopes. Yet the immediacy of the work precluded the needed time for the teachers to make sense of what they and their charges wanted: "You are obliged," Miss Freud noted, "ceaselessly to act" ([1930] 1974, 74). The drawback then is not having the time to wait and the support to think about the riot of meanings in exchange and the push and pull of the child's behavior and the teacher's sense of that. So the lectures requested the pause of thinking, the interest in imagining what goes on without notice, and a curiosity toward what else occurs in pedagogical acts that follow on the heels of the teacher's need to solve problems quickly. We can see that the immediacy of the work is a favorable condition for mistakes and their disavowal.

Her first lecture began: "We are all aware that teachers are still very suspicious and doubtful of psychoanalysis" ([1930] 1974, 73). Miss Freud focused on the question of what psychoanalysis may offer to the practices of education, though she consistently remarked that she had to greatly simplify the complexities and urgencies of both fields. It was a modest way of acknowledging the difficulties education brings to psychoanalysis and that psychoanalysis brings to education. Her four lectures provided a bit of theory peppered by many clinical examples. They are indeed extraordinary for their insistence on the complexity and destiny of the young child's emotional, erotic world in the teacher's life and for the vocabulary psychoanalysis provides for thinking deeply from unconscious ties to this world. From whatever angle she played, Miss Freud was aware that her psychoanalytic approach posed a significant challenge to teachers' and social workers' perceptions of the inner worlds of children and adolescents as well as their own. The lectures would also invite back the audience's childhood neither as regression nor as nostalgia but as a means to remember the ways childhood looks different to those who are "children-no-longer" (Heimann 1979/80 [1989]). Anna Freud's ([1951] 1968) testing point returned to a familiar sentiment the teachers leaned upon and probably felt intimately but now borrowed to justify some of their helplessness: even very young children seemed to be "already finished personalities" (77). What then could pedagogy actually touch if the children were already miniature people with their own minds and desires and if teachers were children-no-longer?

The last lecture, titled "The Relation between Psychoanalysis and Education," raised the question of what psychoanalysis may offer. Here is her summary:

> I maintain that even today psychoanalysis does three things [for education]. In the first place, it is well qualified to offer criticism of existing methods. In the second place, as a scientific theory of the instinctual drives, the unconscious, and the libido, psychoanalysis extends the educator's knowledge of the complicated relations between child and adults. Finally, as a method of therapy, the analysis of children endeavors to repair the injuries which have been inflicted upon the child during the process of education. ([1930] 1974, 129)

I wish to offer a fourth contribution, or perhaps, more modestly, expand upon what I see as one of the most unique possibilities of a psychoanalytic view of education. On the matter of pedagogy, we can sketch the reach of our everyday psychopathologies and our neurotic tendencies—our unconscious afflictions—into a study of anxiety over the loss of love. To notice such anxiety, however, look to our symptomatic acts and why their significance opens mental space for not only what may be intolerable within the autobiographical impulse. We are also involved in disquieting imagination and remembering what we thought we knew but have forgotten. Significance will gradually emerge from the relationship that the symptom congeals. And this is difficult to admit. I must report that my own lectures do not run as smoothly as my description of Anna Freud's lectures that, on second thought and in a chapter on the professor's mistakes, have the flavor of a rescue fantasy. I need my mistakes to imagine how quickly I forget what I already knew.

The Missing Case of the Professor's Mistakes: A Favorable Sequence in Three Acts

Act One

Readers will have met the adolescent teacher course in chapter 4. It is a large, first-year undergraduate lecture course bearing the official title The Adolescent and the Teacher. There are about one hundred students in the lecture hall, and on entering the auditorium in the early morning, I have to walk down the steps to stand in front of the students and they look down to see me. Each week, before I begin my lecture, I make my way through the small passageways of row upon row of desks and greet every student. Sometimes I wave, sometimes I stop to chat, and sometimes, when I see a student reading, I ask for their point of view. The intent is to make some sort of contact before each lecture. But due to this desire, a great many mistakes are in store.

About a month into one particular semester, as I was roaming through the rows of desks, one student, whom I will call "Charlie"—and you will see why in a few minutes—was keen to speak with me. Quite excitedly, as if he was running out of time, Charlie said he wanted me to know that he loved the book we were reading. For him, this was front-page news, though I did not know his urgency. He told me how surprised he was that the book was so affecting since the book had to do with psychology and he hates anything that smells of psychology. He felt, he said, that the author was speaking to him. The book is titled *Inside Lives: Psychoanalysis and the Growth of the Personality* (Waddell 2002). And yes, it does smell like our psychology. At the time of this conversation on the run, I received his good news. On second thought, I wondered what he wanted me to know. His enthusiasm carried what I will treat as an enigmatic proposition, but I also had the feeling of being in the middle of a joke in search of a punch line.

Now in the large lecture, Charlie often raised his hand and had interesting things to say. In one lecture, I was discussing the idea of identifications and tried, in my everyday words, to define something that is like the air we breathe, namely, the unconscious attraction to the other, the characters we introject, and the elusive transference that is acted out before it can be remembered. Of course these are not everyday words, but my point was that only through identifications do we lose and find the exchange of love and hate needed to create the object of desire. So to bring the idea of identification into ordinary life, I gave the example of the "rock star" Lady Gaga, a figure that just popped into my head. A sudden phantasy should have given me some clue about my identifications, but instead I blew it away and I asked the class, "Does everyone know Lady Gaga?" Charlie raised his hand and said, "No. I have never heard of her." So, forgetting the force of identification, forgetting the ridiculousness of my age, forgetting why I even asked that question, then too forgetting that I had little knowledge of what was happening, I launched into my ignorance before I knew I was there. Feeling I was in the middle of something I knew nothing about, I quickly told the students they could see Lady Gaga on the Internet. Being unable to stop myself, I said that many adolescents and adults admired her, wished to emulate her, and enjoyed being called "my little monsters." What was I saying to them?

I recall feeling a bit off track, out of focus, and quite regressed, partly because Lady Gaga was making me speak baby talk and partly because I didn't really know what I was talking about when I tried to talk about this "rock star." I had even forgotten about identification. Something was the matter with my subjective matter. My questions came later, first as consternation and then as guilt. Was Charlie pulling my leg? Had I tumbled into a spectacular ignorance where the professor's desire to move things along ends up keeping her running in place? Where was I? And why didn't I pass my question back to one of the hundred students now staring at me?

Finally the lecture was over, and if it then felt as if I was being lectured to, that may have been due to my projective identifications. They were in overdrive. The students were to remain in the hall to watch the beginning of a film. As the lights were turned off, I began to walk up the narrow stairs to leave the hall. I had to squeeze through the rows of students, and in the second row, I tripped over a student's book bag and fell to the ground. I did hear a collective intake of breath. "The professor fell!" Someone asked if I was all right, and as I tried to quickly get up as if nothing had happened, my foot went into spasm with a "Charlie horse." I limped away.

Over the next few days I thought about my fall. There seemed to be two trips: I lost my footing in my lecture on identifications, and then again in trying to walk away from them. And why had I tripped when I warned myself to be careful as I walked up the steps? Was I sleepwalking? Had I fallen into the unconscious? But, of course, I was suffering a narcissistic injury that could then be displaced onto Charlie. I was angry with him. I felt that he made me take the fall with his unexpected reply that may have also meant: We already know who she is to us but who is she to you? Much later when I described this scene to a friend, she said, "Don't call Lady Gaga a rock star! You set yourself up for that fall."

Act Two

The next week arrived. I greeted each student. I mistook another young man for Charlie and could not help myself from asking, "Have you found out about Lady Gaga?" He said, "Oh, that was not me. I love her." He quickly launched into a little story of his love. I thought, "Oh, here is the good Charlie who does not interfere with me." That week's lecture had to do with what it can mean to open the mind and how opening the mind is opening the mind to other minds and thinking about someone else's views. Closed minds, I said, could not perform this curiosity. Looking back, I wish I could have taken my lecture personally. Then, part two of the film was shown. This time I carefully looked before I leapt and slowly walked up the stairs without having to fall. As I was opening the door congratulating myself on the good escape, there stood Charlie blocking my way. He said quite hurriedly, "Remember when you said there was a problem with closing the mind? That is happening to me!" I said, "Would you like a referral to speak with someone? Send me an email and I will send you the name and number of someone to talk to. But now, you must return to watch the film."

Later I thought I had sent Charlie away and that I had closed my mind. Was this my revenge? Was it a case of hate in the counter-transference? There were my rationalizations: I am their professor and not their analyst. Best not to mix up this work. But these false boundaries only served as the doorstop to my anxiety. I was, after all, stepping away from Charlie's worries and mine. After a few days had passed I wondered if I could invite Charlie to my office for a chat. There seemed to be quite a bit on his mind and on mine. A week went by. I returned to the lecture and as I greeted the students, recognized Charlie. He said he did not send me an email. I knew this and I asked, "Why don't you come to my office today and we can talk."

Act Three

On his way to see me Charlie bumped into his tutorial instructor who said, "Oh, are you coming to see me now?" And Charlie said, "No. I am seeing Dr. Britzman." Much later the tutorial instructor wrote to me that she thought she was now in trouble, that Charlie was there in my office to complain about her. At three o'clock, Charlie was sitting on the couch in my office. He said, "Oh, you have a couch!"

Charlie began our meeting with a torrent of words. "You know how Waddell gives us examples of the paranoid/schizoid? I am a paranoid schizoid! Everything she describes I have!" I thought again of my own identifications and terrors with the material, drifting into memories of training to become an analyst. With each clinical report I read, I had the dreaded feeling that I was being talked about and given a diagnosis. There was that thorny identification with the symptom and the fear that everything talked about was what I had! But why had I forgotten this anxiety when teaching the Waddell text? Had I forgotten everything beautiful and sad about my own human condition? It is indeed difficult to read clinical material and not feel implicated, angry, confused, and at times even relieved that someone else's troubles seem worse than mine. But these resistances to emotional life only lend fuel to more objections to mental pain. Is the material exaggerating the inner world? Can't we get over our childhood traumas? Why should phantasy take such revenge? It took me quite a while to ask something else: Are my objections to the material or to the swirls of my emotional life?

I said to Charlie's self-diagnosis, "Yes, we all have that." He asked, "Is it normal?" I agreed that paranoia is normal and splitting is also painful. Then I asked, "So what's on your mind?" Charlie launched into a series of fights he was having with his mother, and I found again the Freudian cliché, so it is his mother. But for a cliché to come alive, I also thought, *Oy vey ist mir*, I may be his mother too.

Charlie said he could never really talk to his mother about what mattered to him and when he tried, he felt she was not interested. For example, one night he came home late from his girlfriend's house and found his parents watching a movie. With great excitement Charlie announced to them that he wanted to do a master's degree and maybe even a doctorate! At this point I almost stepped into the middle of his story, feeling the urge to give him good advice about graduate school. And I began to wonder, what did I wish to hear? Did I wish to be the good (mother) professor who listened to the excitement of her student (son)? Perhaps this transference resistance, or my urge to give advice, was dedicated to refusing the mother transference. Suddenly the room became quite crowded.

Charlie then said that his announcement of wanting more education was met with his mother telling him he was ruining the movie and had to wait with his news until the movie was over. But I had done the same thing when Charlie followed me out of the class. I had told him not now, not me, and sent him back to the movie. Surely I too was repeating something I knew nothing about.

Charlie told me that he stormed out of the living room while his parents continued watching the film. Later, when his mother came into his room to find out what he wanted, he told her he did not want to talk to her about anything ever again. When she tried to plead with him, he gave her that terrible adolescent rejoinder: "Whatever!" I said, "Oh. You found a way to confirm that your mother does not want to listen to you." He said, "Yes. My girlfriend's mother is the mother I want to have. I can talk to her about Waddell. She is the good mother. I even told her I wished she was my real mother." I said, "So you wish to have a bad mother and a good mother." "Yes," he said. I thought to myself maybe he also has in mind a good and a bad professor and surely this is the same person. I asked him his age. Charlie is nineteen.

We talked quietly for about twenty-two minutes. As he was leaving, he said he did not know if he wanted a referral for counseling but if he did, he would contact me. I handed him a phone number and told him he could use this number as he wished. But I don't think it was a deferral, I mean referral, he wanted. He wanted me to know how much he is feeling affected by the course and by me. And I wanted him to know that he affected me. I think the meeting did that work and, if so, we could forget it as a piece of successful history.

After Charlie left my office he went to the tutorial leader's room and asked for some help on an assignment and some discussion on why, so far, his papers were not as good as they might have been. The tutorial leader gave him the choice of redoing a piece of work for a better grade and, surprised at her flexibility, he gladly accepted.

The Lateness of Interpretation

Interpretation or the creation of new meanings from the mistakes of experience may well be the heart of our narrative impulse. Yet one needs to be persuaded to read into matters of desire as having something to do with the sequences of mistakes. In his most creative essay introducing psychoanalysis to the general public, Sigmund Freud (1926b) wrote a dialogue between two characters: "an impartial person" who asks the maddening question, is it confession? "Freud" the character answers:

We must reply: "Yes and no!" Confession no doubt plays a part in analysis—as an introduction to it. But it is very far from constituting the essence of analysis or from explaining its effects. In confession the sinner tells what he knows, in analysis the neurotic has more to tell . . . than he knows. (189)

Near the end of their conversation the impartial person asked Freud to say more about what happens to all the distortions of the talk that goes on in the analytic session. Freud replied, "In a word, this material, whether it consists of memories, associations or dreams, has first to be interpreted" (219). The word leaves the impartial person burning mad: "'Interpret!' A nasty word! I dislike the sounds of it; it robs me of all certainty. If everything depends on my interpretation who can guarantee that I interpret right?" (219). Who indeed? But Freud then offers a consolation: "Just a moment! Things are not quite as bad as that. Why do you choose to except your own mental processes from the rule of law which you recognize in other people's?" (219). Why indeed?

One of the great tensions in the unfolding of psychoanalysis and education in the writing of our practices is the late arrival of the autobiographical impulse and the capacity to take our work personally. And interpretation does remind us of why we must gamble with mistakes without guarantee, for there is no other way into the stretch of our unreason, our passion, and the things we cannot see. The novel work is to create from each encounter an affectionate and forgiving theory of learning and belongs to the interminability of the professor and psychoanalyst's learning.

Kristeva's (2010b) view is that psychoanalysis—and I would add education—is a treatment for thought, language, and desire. Both are word clinics, places of affecting contact where characters come to lose and make up the mind. It is with the handling of things furthest from the mind and the gathering of them into free associations that we create a story of our autobiographical impulse that can bear the idea that what comes before the impulse is a self-theorizing creature who must borrow language; who forgets what she or he thought is remembered, who slips without knowing why; who sometimes teaches in her sleep; and who, and at the same moment, is capable of both turning away from what is incompatible and disturbing and then, waking up to disquieting imagination. And oddly, mistakes remind us of this feat of human relations, provided that one creates with others an affectionate and forgiving relation to teaching and learning that has the audacity to interpret nonsense, see its repetition in language and social affairs, tolerate the discord of love, and then pick up the pieces of fallout from the psychopathology of everyday education. Then, we might enlarge our view of the favorable human condition.

Notes

Chapter 1. A Psychoanalyst in the Classroom: Character Studies in the Human Condition of Education

1. The opening quote is found on page 355 in the Penguin Freud translation from German of Freud's essay "On the Psychology of the Grammar-School Boy" (see Phillips 2006). It is the collection I use when teaching Freud at the university, and at times we compare the essays in this volume to the *Standard Edition*. There are many differences given that Phillips commissioned translators rather than analysts and with the instruction to lift Freud's prose into literary life, a style with language that inspired Freud. While it is beyond my intent to argue over translations, readers may consult the large debates on this matter, beginning with yet another translation: Ilse Grubrich-Simitis's (1993) *Back to Freud's Texts: Making Silent Documents Speak*. While throughout the rest of this chapter and book, I quote from Strachey et al.'s translation of the *Standard Edition*, on the matter of Freud's 1914 paper, the literary quality of the Penguin collection strikes me as more affecting and direct. The Strachey translation of Freud's schoolboy reads: "As a psycho-analyst I am bound to be concerned more with emotional than intellectual process, with unconscious than with conscious mental life" (1914b, 242).

2. I am grateful to Alice Pitt for her translation of the quote from Freud's 1914 German essay "Zur psychologie des gymnasiasten" from the German edition of Freud's collected works.

3. James Strachey (1968c) made this point in his introduction to Freud's 1915–1917 "Introductory Lectures to Psycho-Analysis" that Freud first gave at the University of Vienna. Strachey was puzzled over Freud's claim that he hated to give lectures since the lectures are written in a style that draws the audience closer. Freud's last lectures of 1933 could not be delivered due to his cancer of the jaw, and in his preface to "New Introductory Lectures on Psycho-Analysis," he writes:

> These new lectures, unlike the former ones, have never been delivered. My age had in the meantime absolved me from the obligation of giving expression to my membership of the university . . . and a surgical operation had made speaking in public impossible for me. If, therefore, I once more take my place in the lecture room during the remarks that follow, it is only by an artifice of the imagination; it may help me not to forget to bear the reader in mind as I enter more deeply into my subject. (1933, 5)

4. Bion's (1993) *Second Thoughts* presents a reconsideration of his early papers. The old papers are reprinted, accompanied by his commentary on them almost seventeen years later. For Bion much has changed, including how he reads his past work. His new question, and one that concerns my own work, is this:

> How is the communication between the psycho-analyst reading and the psycho-analyst writing to be made at least as effective as the communication between analyst and analysand? . . . Transformations of the psycho-analytical experience into formulations which effect communication between the psychoanalyst and the reader, remains an activity to be pursued. . . . No psychoanalyst will be content to leave things as they are. (122)

In returning to his notes, Bion observes, "They resembled nothing so much as a sleepy note that I sometimes tried to make to pin down what I felt to be an important dream for study in the morning. The squiggles remained: the dream was gone. . . . [A]s it is, I do not recognize the patient or myself" (123).

For a contemporary admission of dissatisfaction in the nature of the analytic work, see André Green (2011).

5. Bion's (1993) later discussion "On Arrogance" in *Second Thoughts* home in on the patient's fear that psychoanalytic work will unleash psychotic parts of the self and the shared work of accepting this fear as the price of gaining some sort of relief from suffering. Yet accepting the psychotic parts of the self is also difficult for the psychoanalyst. In a stringent criticism of psychoanalytic training, Bion turns to the psychoanalyst's evasion of her or his own psychotic mechanisms:

> One solution of this problem is particularly dangerous for those concerned with training. The individual seeks to deal with his fear by becoming a trainee, so that his acceptance can be taken as an authoritative declaration of immunity by those best qualified to know. He can proceed with the aid of his psycho-analyst to evade coming to grips with his fear and terminate by becoming a qualified pseudo-analyst. (162)

In Bion's view, what qualifies the analyst and allows the analyst to attempt to be in contact with her or his patients is the capacity to tolerate her or his own emotional pain.

6. For a lively discussion on the uses of the concept of character in psychology, see Ferro (2006, 112–118). Ferro's insistence is that characters need not take figurative form and can be communicated simply through the mind's working.

7. Melanie Klein's ([1961] 1975) *Narrative of a Child Analysis: The Conduct of the Psycho-Analysis of Children as Seen in the Treatment of a Ten-Year-Old Boy* was conducted earlier in 1939 and published posthumously in 1961.

Chapter 2. "An Unexpected Novelty": Freud's Technique Papers Go to the University

1. Sándor Ferenczi (1873–1933) was a Hungarian psychoanalyst in Freud's circle and central to the development of psychoanalytic technique. Known as "the tender analyst," Ferenczi's technical innovations include: mutual or active analysis, flexibility, and his theory of tact and empathy to address inflicted trauma. While it is beyond the scope of this discussion to describe these theoretical and therapeutic innovations that were being worked out as Freud wrote the technique papers, Freud did have Ferenczi in mind when he argued against active treatment, even though, as many have pointed out, Freud's own therapeutic practice involved the derivations he critiqued. Also beyond this chapter is the matter of Ferenczi's kissing of patients and his arguments for this practice in his letters to Freud. For a contemporary discussion of Ferenczi's method and his relation to Freud, see Rudnytsky et al. (1996). For a sense of the ups and downs of their thirty-year relationship, it is best to consult the three volumes of *The Correspondence of Sigmund Freud and Sándor Ferenczi (1908–1933)* and *Sándor Ferenczi–Ernest Jones: Letters 1911–1933*, edited by Erős et al.

2. For example, Jean Laplanche (1989) has argued that psychoanalysis is in crisis and that "the greater part of the analytic world has lost its theoretical bearings" (153) but keeps the idea that crisis may be our most interesting model for change. From the view of Quinodoz and her colleagues (2006) becoming an analyst is "an everyday audacity" (329). Passion ties these views together, and perhaps we may have to lose our theoretical bearings in order to create our audacity.

3. While I have made the case that education is a key signifier in Freud's writing (see Britzman 2011), Sándor Ferenczi's (1949) paper to the 1908 First Psycho-Analytic Congress in Salzburg inaugurated a strong critique of education as an institution.

4. The unstoppable erotic transference is the topic of Jane Gallop's (1997) brave discussion of her teaching that begins with her sentence: "I am a feminist professor who was accused by two students of sexual harassment" (1). She plays in this sensationalism with great passion and invites readers on a rolling tour of her own education and the many kisses involved to ask the question, is kissing after pedagogy wanted or unwanted? University policy as it has evolved since the 1970s sets all this aside and counsels professors to keep their hands off the students. There is no comparable warning to students, though they are not immune from being charged with sexual harassment.

In recounting her own student experience with love affairs with professors, Gallop simply wished to see some of her professors naked, though the devotion was to the naked professor's mind. Of course there is nothing simple here, but her point is that intellectual ideas are erotically exciting and the seduction that sometimes tags along or leads to more kisses belongs to the transference, deeply personal relationships between students and teachers. Gallop calls such passion simply human and admits so much can go wrong. One of her graduate students charged her with sexual harassment:

> In my formal response to the student's complaint, I used the psychoanalytic notion of "transference" to explain her relation to me.... It is a nearly universal response to people whose opinions of us have great authority, in particular, doctors and teachers. The case, the university recommends that in the future I should stop working with any student who has such a transference onto me. Which means I would not work with any student who really believed I had something important to teach her. (1997, 56)

I found Gallop's book exciting and, with this enthusiasm, brought it to a graduate seminar for discussion. Yes, there was my transference to Gallop's mess, but somehow I forgot I was giving her book to my graduate students. What most surprised me was the transference in my classroom: the students hated this book, took the side of the aggrieved graduate student, and refused to examine their feelings. For them, it was obvious that Gallop had hurt her graduate student. Perhaps, too, I repeated this by assigning the book. It took quite a while for me to understand that in introducing Gallop, I was stepping into the middle of something. Years later, one of these graduate students in that seminar became a professor and, perhaps forgetting her first encounter with Gallop, assigned Gallop to her graduate students and then invited Gallop to come to the university.

Chapter 3. What Is the Use of the Theory?

1. It is beyond the scope of this chapter to explore theoretical tensions Kris's case has opened for Lacan, who knew Kris. Much has to do with the large argument in psychoanalysis over the status and consequences of objective reality and what the analyst listens for. I wish to mention Lacan's (2006) use of Kris's work to critique the directions of North American Ego Psychology. See chapters 16 and 22 in *Écrits*.

More interesting for my purposes is Krüger's (2012) discussion of Kris's research into Nazi propaganda in the 1930s and 1940s and how Kris's work in media, art history, and psychoanalysis may have affected his clinical work. Krüger also discusses Lacan's critique. My use of Kris's clinical discussion takes a different tact, and I imagine the writing inhibition through to the question of phantasy, an idea further developed in chapter 6.

Chapter 4. The Adolescent Teacher

1. For an exceptionally fine discussion of the uncanny and déjà vu, see Royle (2003). His chapter 3, "Literature, Psychoanalysis and Teaching," elaborates on what

he terms "haunted teaching" or intellectual uncertainty in teaching as instructive. He asks about the uncanny in teaching psychoanalysis in the university as opening a theory of the return of the repressed in teaching. What is new in Royle's chapter is not so much the claim that the repressed returns, at least for those in the field of pedagogy, but the staging of the theory that does repeats the repressed.

2. Freud hinted at the force of the super-ego across a range of papers, though it had different characters such as the censor, the judge, and the ideal ego. By 1923, his second topology grouped these procedures under the term super-ego or *Über Ich* that has the character of judge and ideal, both of which carry unconscious dynamics of Oedipal crisis. Laplanche and Pontalis's (1973) study of the language of psychoanalysis carries a note in the entry on the super-ego, reminding readers that Freud saw this agency as a cut-off piece of the ego: "Freud insisted on the idea that the super-ego is essentially composed of word-presentations and that these contents are derived from aural perceptions, from instruction and from reading" (438). What is uncanny then, is that school and the university echo and draw upon super-ego demands given that education requires our identifications with instruction and reading. For further discussion, see chapter 5, "The Dependent Relationships of the Ego," in Freud's (1923) "The Ego and the Id."

Chapter 5. On the Madness of Lecturing on Gender

1. André Green (1986) takes on the old word of "madness" this way:

> Rather than characterize it as a disorder of reason, one should on the contrary stress the affective passionate element which modifies the subject's relation to reality, electing a part or whole object, becoming more or less exclusively attached to it, reorganizing his perception of the world around it and giving it a unique or irreplaceable aura by which the ego is captivated and alienated. (223)

Its model is ordered by love, and the use of the term "madness" in this chapter follows along Green's lines of research. For a sensitive account of the history of psychiatric and psychoanalytic orientations to madness, see Leader (2011) and his important distinction between ordinary madness and going mad.

2. See Malabou (2011) for her views on debates over ontological difference and feminism and Rose (2014), who explores the bleak side of personal experience to rethink the uses of the personal to open a creative path for feminism.

3. The psychoanalytic idea of aggression is a variation on the Freudian theme of the life and death drives and the sadomasochistic element in psychical life. Aggression can be thought of as an unconscious wish to destroy the object, although the unconscious logic behind this wish takes great force from any experience of frustration given the human's long maturation process, primal dependency, and radical need for care. Aggression, however, is a needed element for identification and creativity. For a discussion of aggression in cultural life, see Freud (1930). For a discussion on the ordinary and personal uses of aggression in development, see Winnicott (1950–1955). Winnicott considers the confusion of the terms of aggression and

comes to the view that often we could just as well be referencing as spontaneity: "I am suggesting: *it is this impulsiveness, and the aggression that develops out of it, that makes the infant need an external object*, and not merely a satisfying object" (217).

4. For the Kleinians, symbol formation constitutes the mental activity of representation. Hannah Segal (1957) clarified the stakes when she distinguished between symbols proper, or what exists in the world, and symbolic equation, or the psychical tendency to collapse affect and thing. In symbolic equation outside objects are thought as the same as the personifying internal objects relations. The symbol becomes an instance of anxiety, what Segal calls "the original object itself" (393). More than a problem of taking things literally, with symbolic equation there is no separation or difference between phantasy and reality, and no loss needed for symbolization to step into the gap. So symbolic meaning is foreclosed. "The substitute's equation is used to deny the absence of the ideal object, or to control a persecuting one. It belongs to the earliest stages of development" (395). See also Spillius et al. (2011).

5. In 1967, Winnicott ([1967] 1989) gave a talk to senior British analysts on the development of his theories that he titled "D.W.W. on D.W.W." The talk is patched together in his volume *Psychoanalytic Explorations*. Of special notice is his quick description of an abiding paradox that threads throughout his work. The first part of the paradox is that the infant is always a part of the environment but still separate. Given this fusion, the infant cannot differentiate between making an object and finding the object presented. His rule is that we are never to ask the infant whether he or she made the object or found the object, that the area of illusion is to be preserved. My sense is that this question of making or finding is quite central to the poetry of gender.

6. For the key document on the Controversial discussions between Anna Freud and Melanie Klein that occurred between the war years of 1941 and 1945, see King and Steiner (1991). I have also discussed their controversies in Britzman (2003).

7. While it is beyond the scope of this chapter, Riviere ([1929] 1991) further develops the emotional force of splitting masculinity and femininity when she writes about femininity as in conflict with intellectual desire that tends to be considered a masculine possession and, in phantasy, a diminishment of femininity. One outcome of this symbolic collapse, she argues, is an exaggerated femininity, or "a mask of womanliness to avert anxiety and retribution feared from men" (91).

8. In the beginning of his talk to senior British analysts, Winnicott ([1967] 1989) makes a startling admission: "At the beginning there was myself learning to do analysis as a pediatrician having had a tremendous experience of listening to people talking about babies and children of all ages and having had great difficulty in seeing a baby as human at all. It was only through analysis that I became gradually able to see a baby as a human being" (574). We can surmise that Winnicott was not alone in his view and that one of the more devastating aspects of the human condition is that other humans go unrecognized.

Chapter 6. The Untold Story of the Writing Block

1. The concept of phantasy relates to Freud's notion of unconscious wishes and the pleasure principle to which they belong and to Kleinian thinking refer to

the early phantasies of young children created from the problems of annihilation anxiety in life, birth, sex, and death. Both views emerge from the idea of psychical reality always in relation to the external world and the drives. For Klein, phantasies are based on introjections of good and bad objects and projections of them that go on to build the self. In the *New Dictionary of Kleinian Thought* (Spillius et al. 2011) the editors offer a short summary: "In Kleinian theory unconscious phantasies underlie every mental process and accompany all mental activities. They are the mental expression of those somatic events in the body that comprise the instincts, and are the physical sensations interpreted as relationships with objects that cause those sensations. Phantasy is the mental expression of both libidinal and aggressive impulses and also of defense mechanisms against those impulses" (3). For a critical discussion of the term, see the entry on "Phantasy" in Laplanche and Pontalis (1973). For the purposes of this chapter, I follow Laplanche and Pontalis's distinction that phantasy is not an object but "a sequence in which the subject has a role to play and in which permutations of roles and attributes are possible" (318).

2. Klein first mentions the depressive position in her 1935 ([1935] 1975) essay, "A Contribution to the Psychogenesis of Manic-Depressive States." There, she departs from Freud's view of melancholia when she answers his question of why mourning the loss of the object should be so hard for the human. Her answer is startling, as she understands that the infant has mourned before and that any situation of loss, first experienced as weaning, will animate our earliest defenses against psychical life. In Klein's view, "The influence of the early processes of introjection upon both normal and pathological development is very much more momentous. . . . According to our views, even the earliest incorporated objects form the basis of the super-ego and enter its structure" (267). Spillius et al. (2011) have argued that Klein's model of the depressive position gives a greater sense of the work of mourning: "[Klein] links the pain of the work of mourning directly to her dynamic understanding of what bereavement mobilizes: the unconscious loss of the loved parental couple, the depressive anxieties that ensue, the deployment of manic and obsessional defenses and the gradual reinstatement of the loved internal parents, all of which pave the way for sadness proper. This dynamic understanding has more bite . . ." (318).

3. The opening line of Tolstoy's *Anna Karenina: A Novel in Eight Parts*: "All happy families are alike; each unhappy family is unhappy in its own way" (1).

4. I turn again to Klein's ([1935] 1975) frightening discussion on the tremendous forces of super-ego anxiety:

> The persecutions and demands of bad internalized objects; the attacks of such objects upon one another (especially that represented by the sadistic coitus of the parents); the urgent necessity to fulfill the very strict demands of the 'good objects' and to protect and placate them within the ego, with the resultant hatred of the id; the constant uncertainty as to the 'goodness' of a good object, which causes it so readily to become transformed into a bad one—all these factors combine to produce in the ego a sense of being a prey to contradictory and impossible claims from within, a condition which is felt as bad conscience. (267–268)

5. Edmund Bergler (1899–1962) fled Austria in 1937–1938 and settled in New York City. He was prolific in his writing; twenty-five books and about 273 published articles. Bergler insisted on the writer's oral fixations that he traced back to a defense against the unconscious wish for the mother's milk, where words and milk are equated. From there he developed his theory of the withholding writer caught in a masochistic refusal to take and give nourishment and further, will then suffer from super-ego guilt. In one section of the article, Bergler (1947) reprints a *New Yorker* magazine parody of his work. The other arena that Bergler is known for is his virulent obsessive homophobia. He went out of his way to write against homosexuality, argued for its cure, and, eventually, even those of the psychoanalytic establishment had to turn their backs to him. Upon his death, more manuscripts were found. But he was a difficult character and his essays reflect a history of bad faith within the North American psychoanalytic movement. Today he is a footnote for the writing block and, one can say, the footnote is hostile and aggressive.

6. It is well beyond the scope of this chapter to consider a significant critique of Freud's model of libido theory and why this model may have reached its limit for conceptualizing the damaging effects of trauma as an outside event that may be so catastrophic that trauma cannot gain a foothold in earlier events and thus cannot be considered with the temporality of deferred action. I refer readers to the work of Catherine Malabou (2012 and 2013), who considers brain damage and negative plasticity as supplanting Freud's theory of sexuality and the imperishability of psychical structures. In my view, Malabou's thought-provoking research holds great significance for thinking through trauma as social violence and cruelty in our current world. While Malabou's theories write upon the theoretical work of psychoanalysis, philosophy, and neuroscience, in terms of its clinical use, Malabou's speculations may not do away with the transference. In the case of education, a situation we grew up with and keep returning to, the classroom is perhaps one of our most privileged social spaces dedicated to joining the interplay of phantasy and reality as our human conditions for learning. In this sense, education can be taken through to the neurosis and its question of desire as one of our most affecting matters in pedagogy.

7. Winnicott ([1962] 1996), however, wrote a series of critical reviews on Melanie Klein's work, with a main focus on his disagreement with Klein's theory of the infant's innate envy due to Klein's insistence on the death drive. In an unfinished essay, "Roots of Aggression (dated September 9, 1968)," he wrote: "No advance in psycho-analytic theory is made without nightmares. The question is: who is to have the nightmare? The further question—why does he need to have nightmares?" (1989, 458). The two "nightmares" Winnicott notes are Freud's theory of the death drive and Melanie Klein's theory of envy. The essay argues that these concepts should be thrown out and chastises his audience for being loyal to ideas that require rethinking. Winnicott also returns to his disputes with Klein in a talk he gave to senior British analysts in 1967 (1989), "D.W.W. on D.W.W." (see Winnicott's *Psychoanalytic Explorations*).

8. The same year, Heimann ([1978] 1989) wrote another article in honor of Alexander Mitscherlich titled "On the Necessity for the Analyst to Be Natural with His Patient." There, she writes, "We have been freed from the naïve view

that analysis cures symptoms. . . . [Freud's] shortest and most intense formulation of the goal of analysis is the re-creation of the capacity for pleasure and work" (313).

Mitscherlich was a German medical doctor and, along with Fred Mielke, head of the German Medical Committee to the military tribunal in 1946 in Nuremberg, hearing Nazi medical crimes. He trained as a psychoanalyst and was one of the leading figures in the restoration of psychoanalysis in postwar Germany. Alexander and Margarete Mitscherlich are most known for their study of the aftereffects of National Socialism in postwar German group life, *The Inability to Mourn*, originally published in German in 1967 and translated into English in 1975.

Chapter 7. The Psychopathologies of Everyday Education: Sleeping, Falling, Forgetting, Lateness, and the Professor's Mistakes

1. See Freud (1935) where he discusses attention to the affective sequence in "The Subtleties of a Faulty Action." There he notes the limits of self-analysis, and in the short essay it is Anna Freud who, after listening to her father's mistake, gave him an interpretation.

Paula Heimann's ([1975] 1989) essay "Sacrificial Parapraxis—Failure or Achievement?" considers how a parapraxis while belonging to the subject may usher in deeper consideration of a larger history of cultural functions and that the fault lines of culture may be just as significant as the fault lines of psychical life. She points to a thin line between mental health and mental illness, and we may extend this to the intermingling of culture and psychical life: "By diminishing the sharp divisions between mental health, neurosis, and psychosis, both works open new dimensions to the understanding of psychical life" (278). Heimann was working out a new theory of accidents that may serve to preserve and restore a forgotten history in both psychoanalysis and the conflicts its Jewish members faced. In this way, a parapraxis may be an achievement of the ego's self-assertion.

2. It should not surprise us that education is a favorable place where parapraxes and forgetting are usually staged. Freud (1901) gives the example of a doctoral examination:

> When I was being examined in philosophy as a subsidiary subject I was questioned by the examiner about the teachings of Epicurus, and after that I was asked if I knew who had taken up his theories in later centuries. I answered with the name of Pierre Gassendi, whom I had heard described as a disciple of Epicurus while I was sitting in a café only a couple of days before. To the surprised question how I knew that, I boldly answered that I had long been interested in Gassendi. The result of this was a certificate *magna cum laude* [with distinction], but also unfortunately a subsequent obstinate tendency to forget the name Gassendi. My guilty conscious is, I think, to blame for my inability to remember the name in spite of all my efforts; for I really ought not to have known it on that occasion either. (27)

3. Roger Simon (1992a) has written of "disruptive daydreams" needed to think otherwise. He notes, "Wishes do nothing. . . . Yet for many teachers daydreams are not something that deserve special celebration" (3, 4), partly because many teachers may feel daydreaming is a problem of their students. Simon's interest is in disruptive daydreams where possibility for what is not yet becomes desired. My orientation, however, does admit that wishes indeed do something to the realm of desire and sexuality; they carry on the libido our bare excitement and when missing, our worst depression.

4. For a more elaborate view of such phantasy life, see Pitt (2006) on matricide in education, where she links the phantasy of killing the teacher not so much due to fear of authority but to the problem of loss of love. "In this story," Pitt observes, "the unbearable loss of a beloved object causes suffering but also allows for the creation of an internal psychical reality . . . and what it means to bring the mother into representation" (88). Readers may want to keep this in mind when they read the analysis of my teaching that ends this chapter. For a Lacanian analysis of the problems of love and control that underpin phantasies of teaching, see Taubman (2006).

5. Karl Abraham's ([1913] 1955) short essay "Should Patients Write Down Their Dreams?" agreed with Freud that the process is useless. There is, Abraham argued, "a powerful tendency to repress" (34). He gives an example of a woman patient's frustration at having a repeating dream she could not remember upon waking. And then, even as Abraham advised otherwise, she became dedicated to writing the dream down. What she handed to Abraham the next day was a scribbled note: "Write down dream despite agreement" (34). She did eventually remember the dream: it was that her analyst approached her sexually. At that point, she could appreciate why the dream was repressed.

References

Abraham, Karl. (1913) 1955. "Should Patients Write Down Their Dreams?" In *Clinical Papers and Essays on Psycho-Analysis*, edited by Ernest Jones, 33–35. London: The Hogarth Press and the Institute of Psycho-Analysis.

Abram, Jan. 2008. "Donald Woods Winnicott (1896–1971): A Brief Introduction." *International Journal of Psychoanalysis* 89: 1189–1217.

Aichhorn, August. 1990. "The Transference (1935)." In *Essential Papers on Transference*, edited by Aaron H. Esman, 94–109. New York: New York University Press.

Arendt, Hannah. 1958. *The Human Condition*. Chicago: University of Chicago Press.

Aulagnier, Piera. 2001. *The Violence of Interpretation: From Pictogram to Statement*. Translated by Alan Sheridan. Philadelphia: Taylor & Francis.

Bakhtin, Mikhail. 1981. *The Dialogic Imagination: Four Essays*. Edited by Michael Holquist. Translated by Caryl Emerson and Michael Holquist. Austin: University of Texas Press.

Barthes, Roland. 2011. *The Preparation of the Novel*. Translated by Kate Briggs. Text established, annotated, and introduced by Nathalie Léger. New York: Columbia University Press.

Bechdel, Alison. 2012. *Are You My Mother? A Comic Drama*. Boston: Houghton Mifflin Harcourt.

Bergler, Edmund. 1947. "Further Contributions to the Psychoanalysis of Writers." *Psychoanalytic Review* 34: 449–468.

———. 1950. "Does 'Writer's Block' Exist?" *American Imago* 7: 43–54.

Bion, Wilfred R. 1993. *Second Thoughts*. London: Karnac Books.

———. 1994. *Experiences in Groups and Other Papers*. New York: Routledge.

———. 2000. "Making the Best of a Bad Job, 1979." In *Clinical Seminars and Other Works*, edited by Francesca Bion, 321–331. London: Karnac Books.

Bloom, Harold. 1973. *The Anxiety of Influence: A Theory of Poetry*. New York: Norton.

———. 1997. *The Anxiety of Influence: A Theory of Poetry.* Second edition. New York: Oxford University Press.
Bollas, Christopher. 1991. *Forces of Destiny: Psychoanalysis and Human Idiom.* London: Free Association Press.
———. 1992. *Being a Character: Psychoanalysis and Self Experience.* New York: Hill and Wang.
Brabant, Eva, Ernst Falzeder, and Patrizia Giampieri-Deutsch, eds. 1993. *The Correspondence of Sigmund Freud and Sándor Ferenczi, Volume 1, 1908–1914.* Translated by Peter T. Hoffer. Cambridge: The Belknap Press of Harvard University Press.
British Psychoanalytic Society. 2012. "Encounters Through Generations. A Production of the Audio-Visual Project." The Institute of Psychoanalysis. London. DVD. 53 min.
Britton, Ronald. 1994. "Publication Anxiety: Conflict between Communication and Affiliation." *International Journal of Psycho-Analysis* 75: 1213–1224.
Britzman, Deborah P. 2002. "Theory Kindergarten." In *Regarding Sedgwick: Essays on Queer Culture and Critical Theory,* edited by Stephen M. Barber and David Clark, 121–142. London: Routledge.
———. 2003. *After-Education: Anna Freud, Melanie Klein, and Psychoanalytic Histories of Learning.* Albany: State University of New York Press.
———. 2007. *Novel Education: Psychoanalytic Studies of Learning and Not Learning.* New York: Peter Lang.
———. 2009. *The Very Thought of Education: Psychoanalysis and the Impossible Professions.* Albany: State University of New York Press.
———. 2011. *Freud and Education.* New York: Routledge.
———. 2013. "Between Psychoanalysis and Pedagogy: Scenes of Rapprochement and Alienation." *Curriculum Inquiry* 43 (1): 95–117.
Brooks, Peter. 2011. *Enigmas of Identity.* Princeton: Princeton University Press.
Butler, Judith. 1990. *Gender Trouble: Feminism and the Subversion of Identity.* New York: Routledge.
Cantet, Laurent (producer). 2008. *The Class.* Originally published as *Entre les murs.* Culver City, CA: Sony Pictures/Home Entertainment. DVD.
Catton, Eleanor. 2013. *The Luminaries.* Toronto: McClelland and Stewart.
Cavell, Marcia. 1993. *The Psychoanalytic Mind: From Freud to Philosophy.* Cambridge: Harvard University Press.
Certeau, Michel de. 1986. *Heterologies: Discourse on the Other.* Translated by Brian Massumi. Minneapolis: University of Minnesota Press.
De Man, Paul. 1989. *The Resistance to Theory.* Minneapolis: University of Minnesota Press.
De M'Uzan, Michel. 2013. *Death and Identity: Being and the Psycho-Sexual Drama.* Translated by Andrew Weller. London: Karnac.
Dean, J. Todd. Spring 2013. "'What Does Not Change': Technique and Effects in Psychoanalysis." *Division 39/Review: A Quarterly Psychoanalytic Forum* 7: 20–26
Dethiville, Laura. 2014. *Donald W. Winnicott: A New Approach.* Translated by Susan Ganley Lévy. London: Karnac.

Deutsch, Helene. 1967. *Selected Problems of Adolescence: With Special Emphasis on Group Formation.* Madison: International Universities Press.

Egan, Jennifer. 2011. *A Visit from the Goon Squad.* New York: Alfred A. Knopf.

Erős, Ferenc, Judit Szekacs-Weisz, and Ken Robinson, eds. 2013. *Sándor Ferenczi–Ernest Jones: Letters 1911–1933.* London: Karnac Books.

Esman, Aaron, ed. 1990. *Essential Papers on Transference.* New York: New York University Press.

Falzeder, Ernst, and Eva Brabant, eds. 1996. *The Correspondence of Sigmund Freud and Sándor Ferenczi, Volume 2, 1914–1919.* Translated by Peter T. Hoffer. Cambridge: The Belknap Press of Harvard University Press.

———. 2000. *The Correspondence of Sigmund Freud and Sandor Ferenczi, Volume 3, 1920–1933.* Translated by Peter T. Hoffer. Cambridge: The Belknap Press of Harvard University Press.

Felman, Shoshana. 1987. *Jacques Lacan and the Adventure of Insight: Psychoanalysis in Contemporary Culture.* New York: Routledge.

———. 1992. "Education and Crisis, or the Vicissitudes of Teaching." In Shoshana Felman and Dori Laub, *Testimony: Crises of Witnessing in Literature, Psychoanalysis, and History*, 1–56. New York: Routledge.

———. 2003. *Writing and Madness: (Literature/Philosophy/Psychoanalysis).* Translated by Martha Noel Evans and Shoshana Felman, with the assistance of Brian Massumi. Appendix translated by Barbara Johnson. Palo Alto: Stanford University Press.

Ferenczi, Sándor. (1915) 2002. "On Supposed Mistakes." In *Further Contributions to the Theory and Technique of Psycho-Analysis*, compiled by John Rickman and translated by Jane Isabel Suttie et al., 407–411. London: Karnac Books.

———. 1949. "Psycho-Analysis and Education." Translated by M. Balint. *International Journal of Psychoanalysis* 20: 220–224.

Ferro, Antonino. 2006. *The Bi-Personal Field: Experiences in Child Analysis.* London: Routledge.

———. 2011. *Avoiding Emotions, Living Emotions.* Translated by Ian Harvey. London: Routledge.

Fink, Bruce. 2014. *Against Understanding, Volume 1: Commentary and Critique in a Lacanian Key.* London: Routledge.

Freud, Anna. (1930) 1974. "Four Lectures on Psychoanalysis for Teachers and Parents." In *The Writings of Anna Freud, 1922–1935, Volume 1: Introduction to Psychoanalysis and Lectures for Child Analysts and Teachers*, 73–137. New York: International Universities Press.

———. (1951) 1968. "An Experiment in Group Upbringing." In *The Writings of Anna Freud, 1945–1956, Volume 4: Indications for Child Analysis and Other Papers*, 163–229. New York: International University Press.

———. (1952) 1968. "Answering Teachers' Questions." In *The Writings of Anna Freud, 1945–1956, Volume 4*, 560–568. New York: International Universities Press.

———. 1954. "Psychoanalysis and Education." *The Psychoanalytic Study of the Child* 9: 9–15.

———. (1957/58) 1969. "Adolescence." In *The Writings of Anna Freud, 1956–1965, Volume 5: Research at the Hampstead Child-Therapy Clinic and Other Papers*, 136–166. New York: International Universities Press.

Freud, Sigmund. 1956. *The Origins of Psycho-Analysis: Letters to Wilhelm Fliess, Drafts and Notes, 1887–1902*. Edited by Marie Bonaparte, Anna Freud, and Ernst Kris. Translated by Eric Mosbacher and James Strachey. New York: Basic Books.

———. 1968. *The Standard Edition of the Complete Psychological Works of Sigmund Freud*. Translated and edited by James Strachey, in collaboration with Anna Freud, and with the assistance of Alix Strachey and Alan Tyson. 24 Volumes. London: Hogarth Press and Institute for Psychoanalysis.

———. 1900. *The Interpretation of Dreams (First Part)*. SE 4: xxiii–338.

———. 1901. *The Psychopathology of Everyday Life (Forgetting, Slips of the Tongue, Bungled Actions, Superstitions, and Errors)*. SE 6: 1–310.

———. 1911. "The Handling of Dream-Interpretation in Psycho-Analysis." SE 12: 91–96.

———. 1912a. "The Dynamics of Transference." SE 12: 99–108.

———. 1912b. "Recommendations to Physicians Practicing Psycho-Analysis." SE 12: 111–120.

———. 1913. "On Beginning the Treatment (Further Recommendations on the Technique of Psycho-Analysis I)." SE 12: 123–144.

———. 1914a. "Remembering, Repeating, and Working Through (Further Recommendations on the Technique of Psycho-Analysis)." SE 12: 145–156.

———. 1914b. "Some Reflections on a Schoolboy Psychology." SE 13: 241–244.

———. 1914c. "Fausse Reconnaissance (Déjà raconté) in Psycho-Analytic Treatment." SE 13: 201–207.

———. 1915a [1914]. "Observations on Transference-Love (Further Recommendations on the Technique of Psycho-Analysis III)." SE 12: 159–171.

———. 1915b. "Thoughts for the Times on War and Death." SE 4: 275–300.

———. 1916. "Some Character-Types Met with in Psycho-Analytic Work." SE 14: 311–333.

———. [1915–1917] 1916–1917. *Introductory Lectures on Psycho-Analysis (Parts One and Two)*. SE 15: 9–239.

———. 1916–1917. *Introductory Lectures on Psycho-Analysis, Part 3*. SE 16: 243–463.

———. 1917. "A Difficulty in the Path of Psycho-Analysis." SE 17: 135–144.

———. 1918 [1914]. "From a History of an Infantile Neurosis." SE 17: 7–122.

———. 1919a. "The Uncanny." SE 17: 219–256.

———. 1919b. "A Child Is Being Beaten: A Contribution to the Study of the Origin of Sexual Perversions." SE 17: 179–204.

———. 1919c [1918]. "On the Teaching of Psycho-Analysis in Universities." SE 17: 169–174.

———. 1923. "The Ego and the Id." SE 19: 12–68.

———. 1925a. "Negation." SE 19: 235–239.

———. 1925b. "Preface to Aichhorn's Wayward Youth." SE 19: 273–275.

———. 1925c. "An Autobiographical Study." SE 20: 7–74.

———. 1926a [1925]. "Inhibitions, Symptoms and Anxiety." SE 20: 87–172.

———. 1926b. "The Question of Lay Analysis: Conversations with an Impartial Person." SE 20: 183–259.
———. 1930 [1929]. *Civilization and Its Discontents*. SE 21: 64–157.
———. 1931. "Libidinal Types." SE 21: 217–220.
———. 1933. "New Introductory Lectures on Psycho-Analysis." SE 22: 5–182.
———. 1935. "The Subtleties of a Faulty Action." SE 22: 233–238.
———. 1937a. "Analysis Terminable and Interminable." SE 23: 216–253.
———. 1937b. "Constructions in Analysis." SE 23: 257–269.
———. 1939 [1934–1938] *Moses and Monotheism: Three Essays*. SE 23: 7–137.
———. 1940 [1938]. "Some Elementary Lessons in Psycho-Analysis." SE 23: 279–286.
Freud, Sigmund, and Joseph Breuer. 1893–1895. *Studies on Hysteria*. SE 2: 2–319.
Fromm, M. Gerard. 2012. *Taking the Transference, Reaching into Dreams*. London: Karnac Books.
Gabbard, Glen O., and Thomas Ogden. 2009. "On Becoming a Psychoanalyst." *International Journal of Psychoanalysis* 90: 311–327.
Gallop, Jane. 1997. *Feminist Accused of Sexual Harassment*. Durham: Duke University Press.
Gozlan, Oren. 2014. *Transsexuality and the Art of Transitioning: A Lacanian Approach*. London: Routledge.
Green, André. 1986. *On Private Madness*. Madison, CT: International Universities Press.
———. 2000a. "Experience and Thinking in Analytic Practice." In *André Green at the Squiggle Foundation*, edited by Jan Abram, 1–15. London: Karnac Books.
———. 2000b. "On Thirdness." In *André Green at the Squiggle Foundation*, edited by Jan Abram, 39–68. London: Karnac Books.
———. 2005a. *Key Ideas for Contemporary Psychoanalysis: Misrecognition and Recognition of the Unconscious*. Translated by Andrew Weller. New York: Routledge.
———. 2005b. "To Love or Not to Love: Eros and Eris." In André Green and Gregorio Kohon, *Love and Its Vicissitudes*, 1–41. New York: Routledge.
———. 2011. *Illusions and Disillusions of Psychoanalytic Work*. Translated by Andrew Weller. London: Karnac Books.
Grimbert, Philippe. 2007. *Memory: A Novel*. Translated by Polly McLean. Toronto: Simon & Schuster.
Grubrich-Simitis, Ilse. 1993. *Back to Freud's Texts: Making Silent Documents Speak*. Translated by Philip Slotkin. New Haven: Yale University Press.
Hawthorne, Nathaniel. 2004. *The Scarlet Letter*. New York: Pocket Books.
Heimann, Paula. (1939/42) 1989. "A Contribution to the Problem of Sublimation." In *About Children*, 26–45.
———. (1975) 1989. "Sacrificial Parapraxis—Failure or Achievement?" In *About Children*, 295–310.
———. (1978) 1989. "On the Necessity for the Analyst to Be Natural with His Patient." In *About Children*, 311–323.
———. (1979/80) 1989. "About Children and Children-No-Longer." In *About Children*, 324–343.
———. 1989. *About Children and Children No Longer: Collected Papers of Paula Heimann 1942–1980*, edited by Margaret Tonnesmann. London: Tavistock Routledge.

Hitchcock, Alfred (director). 1963. *The Birds*. Universal Pictures, USA. Released August 28, 2012. DVD.
Ishiguro, Kazuo. 2005. *Never Let Me Go*. Toronto: Alfred A. Knopf.
James, Henry. (1888) 2007. *The Lesson of the Master*. London: Hesperus Classics.
———. (1897) 1987. *The Spoils of Poynton*. New York: Penguin Books.
———. (1904) 1992. *The Golden Bowl*. Toronto: Alfred A. Knopf.
James, William. (1890) 1980. *The Principles of Psychology, Volume 1*. New York: Dover Publications.
Johnson, Barbara. 1987. *A World of Difference*. Baltimore: Johns Hopkins University Press.
Joseph, Betty. 2000. "Agreeableness as Obstacle." *International Journal of Psychoanalysis* 81 (4): 641–649.
King, Pearl. 1989. "Paula Heimann's Quest for Her Own Identity as a Psychoanalyst: An Introductory Memoir." In *About Children and Children No Longer: Collected Papers of Paula Heimann 1942–1980*, edited by Margaret Tonnesmann, 1–9. London: Tavistock Routledge.
King, Pearl, and Riccardo Steiner, eds. 1991. *The Freud-Klein Controversies, 1941–1945*. London: Routledge.
Klein, Melanie. (1928) 1975. "Early Stages of the Oedipus Conflict." In *Love, Guilt, and Reparation and Other Works, 1921–1945*, 186–198. London: Hogarth Press.
———. (1935) 1975. "The Psychogenesis of Manic-Depressive States." In *Love, Guilt, and Reparation and Other Works, 1921–1945*, 262–289. London: Hogarth Press.
———. 1937. "Love, Guilt, and Reparation." In Melanie Klein and Joan Riviere, *Love, Hate and Reparation: Two Lectures*, 57–119. London: Hogarth Press.
———. (1946) 1975. "Notes on Some Schizoid Mechanisms." In *Envy and Gratitude and Other Works, 1946–1963*, 1–24. London: Hogarth Press.
———. (1952) 1975. "Some Theoretical Conclusions Regarding the Emotional Life of the Infant." In *Envy and Gratitude and Other Works, 1946–1963*, 61–93. London: Hogarth Press.
———. (1959) 1975. "Our Adult World and Its Roots in Infancy." In *Envy and Gratitude and Other Works, 1946–1963*, 247–263. London: Hogarth Press.
———. (1961) 1975. *Narrative of a Child Analysis: The Conduct of the Psycho-Analysis of Children as Seen in the Treatment of a Ten-Year-Old Boy*. London: Hogarth Press.
Klein, Melanie, and Joan Riviere. 1937. *Love, Hate and Reparation: Two Lectures*. London: Hogarth Press.
Kolodny, Susan. 2000. *The Captive Muse: On Creativity and Its Inhibition*. Madison, CT: Psychosocial Press.
Kris, Ernst. 1951. "Ego Psychology and Interpretation in Psychoanalytic Therapy." *The Psychoanalytic Quarterly* 20: 15–30.
Kristeva, Julia. 1989. *Black Sun: Depression and Melancholia*. Translated by Leon S. Roudiez. New York: Columbia University Press.
———. 1995. *New Maladies of the Soul*. Translated by Ross Guberman. New York: Columbia University Press.
———. 1998. "Psychoanalysis and Freedom." Translated by Charles Levin. *Canadian Journal of Psychoanalysis* 7 (1): 1–21.

———. 2000. *The Sense and Non-Sense of Revolt: The Powers and Limits of Psychoanalysis, Volume 1.* Translated by Jeanine Herman. New York: Columbia University Press.

———. 2007. "Adolescence, Syndrome of Ideality." *Psychoanalytic Review* 94 (5): 714–725.

———. 2009. *This Incredible Need to Believe.* Translated by Beverley Bie Brahic. New York: Columbia University Press.

———. 2010a. "Liberty, Equality, Fraternity and . . . Vulnerability." In *Hatred and Forgiveness*, translated by Jeanine Herman, 29–45. New York: Columbia University Press.

———. 2010b. *Hatred and Forgiveness.* Translated by Jeanine Herman. New York: Columbia University Press.

Krüger, Steffen. 2012. "Fresh Brains: Jacques Lacan's Critique of Ernst Kris's Psychoanalytic Method in the Context of Kris's Theoretical Writing." *American Imago* 69 (4): 507–542.

Lacan, Jacques. 1992. *The Ethics of Psychoanalysis, 1959–1960.* Book VII of *The Seminar of Jacques Lacan.* Translated by Dennis Porter and edited by Jacques-Alain Miller. New York: W. W. Norton & Company.

———. 1998a. *Encore. On Feminine Sexuality: The Limits of Knowledge, 1972–1973.* Book XX of *The Seminar.*

———. 1998b. *The Four Fundamental Concepts of Psycho-Analysis.* Book XI of *The Seminar.*

———. 2006. *Écrits: The First Complete Edition in English.* Translated by Bruce Fink. New York: W. W. Norton & Company.

Laplanche, Jean. 1989. *New Foundations for Psychoanalysis.* Translated by David Macey. Cambridge, MA: Basil Blackwell.

Laplanche, Jean, and Jean-Bertrand Pontalis. 1973. *The Language of Psycho-Analysis.* Translated by Donald Nicholson-Smith. New York: W. W. Norton & Company.

Leader, Darian. 2000. *Freud's Footnotes.* London: Faber and Faber.

———. 2011. *What Is Madness?* London: Penguin.

Lear, Jonathan. 2009. "Technique and Final Cause in Psychoanalysis: Four Ways of Looking at One Moment." *International Journal of Psychoanalysis* 90: 1299–1317.

Leffert, Mark. 2013. *The Therapeutic Situation in the 21st Century.* New York: Routledge.

Loewald, Hans. 2000a. "Some Considerations on Repetition and Repetition Compulsion." In *The Essential Loewald: Collected Papers and Monographs*, 87–101. Hagerstown, MD: University Publishing Group. First published 1973.

———. 2000b. "The Waning of the Oedipus Complex." In *The Essential Loewald: Collected Papers and Monographs*, 384–404. Hagerstown, MD: University Publishing Group. First published 1979.

Malabou, Catherine. 2011. *Changing Difference: The Feminine and the Question of Philosophy.* Translated by Carolyn Shread. Malden, MA: Polity Press.

———. 2012. *The New Wounded: From Neurosis to Brain Damage.* Translated by Steven Miller. New York: Fordham University Press.

———. 2013. *Ontology of the Accident: An Essay on Destructive Plasticity.* Translated by Carolyn Shread. Malden, MA: Polity Press.

Mann, Thomas. (1901) 1994. *Buddenbrooks: The Decline of a Family*. Translated by John Woods. Toronto: Alfred A. Knopf.

McDougall, Joyce, and Serge Lebovici. 1969. *Dialogue with Sammy: A Psycho-Analytic Contribution to the Understanding of Child Psychosis*. Translated by Joyce McDougall. Edited by Martin James. New York: International University Press.

McDougall, Joyce. 1986. *Theatres of the Mind: Illusion and Truth on the Psychoanalytic Stage*. London: Free Association Books.

———. 2005. "Donald Winnicott the Man: Reflections and Recollections." In *Donald Winnicott the Man: Reflections and Recollections* (The Donald Winnicott Memorial Lecture), 17–37. London: Karnac Books.

Meltzer, Donald, and Meg Harris Williams. 1988. *The Apprehension of Beauty: The Role of Aesthetic Conflict in Development, Art and Violence*. London: Clunie Press.

Melville, Herman. (1893) 1997. "Bartleby, the Scrivener: A Story of Wall Street." In *The Complete Shorter Fiction*, 18–51. New York: Alfred A. Knopf.

Miller, Jane. 2010. *Crazy Age: Thoughts on Being Old*. London: Virago Press.

Milner, Marion. 1950. *On Not Being Able to Paint*. Madison, CT: International Universities Press.

Mitchell, Juliet. 1998. "Introduction to Melanie Klein." In *Reading Melanie Klein*, edited by John Phillips and Lyndsey Stonebridge, 83–113. New York: Routledge.

Mitscherlich, Alexander, and Margarete Mitscherlich. 1975. *The Inability to Mourn: Principles of Collective Behavior*. Translated by Beverley R. Placzek. New York: Grove Press.

Oelsner, Robert, ed. 2013. *Transference and Counter-Transference Today*. London: Routledge/Taylor and Francis Group.

O'Shaughnessy, Edna. 1996. "Words and Working Through." In *Melanie Klein Today: Developments in Theory and Practice, Volume 2: Mainly Practice*, edited by Elizabeth Bott Spillius, 138–151. London: Routledge. First published 1983.

Penley, Constance. 1989. "Teaching in Your Sleep." In *The Future of an Illusion: Film, Feminism, and Psychoanalysis*, 165–184. Minneapolis: University of Minnesota Press.

Perret-Catipovic, Maja, and François Ladame. 1998. "Normality and Pathology in Adolescence." In *Adolescence and Psychoanalysis: The Story and the History*, translated by Philip Slotkin and edited by Perret-Catipovic and François Ladame, 161–172. London: Karnac Books.

Phillips, Adam, ed. 2006. *The Freud Penguin Reader*. New York: Penguin Books.

Pirandello, Luigi. 1921. *Six Characters in Search of an Author: A Comedy in the Making*. Translated by Edward Storer. New York: E. P. Dutton. http://www.eldritchpress.org/lp/six.htm

Pitt, Alice. 2003. *The Play of the Personal: Psychoanalytic Narratives of Feminist Education*. New York: Peter Lang.

———. 2006. "Mother Love's Education." In *Love's Return: Psychoanalytic Essays on Childhood, Teaching, and Learning*, edited by Gail Boldt and Paula Salvio, 87–105. New York: Routledge.

Pontalis, Jean-Bertrand. 1981. "The Birth and Recognition of the 'Self.'" In *Frontiers in Psychoanalysis: Between the Dream and Psychic Pain*, translated by Catherine

Cullen and Philip Cullen, 126–147. New York: International Universities Press.

———. 1993. *Love of Beginnings*. Translated by James Greene and Marie-Christine Réguis. London: Free Association Books.

Quinodoz, Danielle, Candy Aubry, Olivier Bonard, Geneviève Déjussel, and Bernard Reith. 2006. "Being a Psychoanalyst: An Everyday Audacity." *International Journal of Psychoanalysis* 87: 329–347.

Rachman, Arnold William. 1997. *Sándor Ferenczi: The Psychotherapist of Tenderness and Passion*. Northvale, NJ: Jason Aronson.

Reeder, Jurgen. 2008. "The Enigmatic 'Nature of the Subject.'" *The Scandinavian Psychoanalytic Review* 31 (2): 114–121.

Rickman, John. 1937. "Preface." In Melanie Klein and Joan Riviere, *Love, Hate and Reparation: Two Lectures*, v–vi. London: Hogarth Press.

Riviere, Joan. (1929) 1991. "Womanliness as Masquerade." In *The Inner World and Joan Riviere: Collected Papers, 1920–1958*, edited by Athol Hughes, 90–101. London: Karnac Books.

———. 1937. "Hate, Greed, and Aggression." In Melanie Klein and Joan Riviere, *Love, Hate and Reparation: Two Lectures*, 1–53. London: Hogarth Press.

———. (1945) 1991. "The Bereaved Wife." In *The Inner World and Joan Riviere: Collected Papers, 1920–1958*, edited by Athol Hughes, 214–226. London: Karnac Books.

Rodman, F. Robert, ed. 1999. *The Spontaneous Gesture: Selected Letters of D. W. Winnicott*. London: Karnac Books.

Ronell, Avital. 2003. *Stupidity*. Urbana: University of Illinois Press.

Rose, Jacqueline. 2014. *Women in Dark Times*. London: Bloomsbury.

———. 1993. *Why War? Psychoanalysis, Politics, and the Return to Melanie Klein*. London: Verso Press.

Rosen, Harold. 1988. "The Autobiographical Impulse." In *Linguistics in Context: Connecting Observation with Understanding*, edited by Deborah Tannen, 69–88. Norwood, NJ: Ablex Publishing.

Roustang, François. 2000. *How to Make a Paranoid Laugh: Or, What Is Psychoanalysis?* Translated by Anne C. Vila. Philadelphia: University of Pennsylvania Press.

Royle, Nicholas. 2003. *The Uncanny*. Manchester: Manchester University Press.

Rudnytsky, Peter, Antal Bókay, and Patrizia Giampieri-Deutsch, eds. 1996. *Ferenczi's Turn in Psychoanalysis*. New York: New York University Press.

Scarfone, Dominique. 2005. "Laplanche and Winnicott Meet . . . and Survive." In *Sex and Sexuality: Winnicottian Perspectives*, edited by Lesley Caldwell, 33–54. London: Karnac Books.

Scott, W. Clifford M. 1952. "Patients Who Sleep or Look at the Psycho-Analyst during Treatment: Technical Considerations." *International Journal of Psychoanalysis* 33: 465–469.

Segal, Hannah. 1957. "Notes on Symbol Formation." *International Journal of Psychoanalysis* 38: 391–397.

Seulin, Christian, and Gennaro Saragnano, eds. 2012. *On Freud's "On Beginning the Treatment."* London: Karnac Books.

Sedgwick, Eve Kosofsky. 1997. "Paranoid Reading and Reparative Reading; Or, You're So Paranoid, You Probably Think This Introduction Is About You." In *Novel Gazing: Queer Readings in Fiction*, edited by Eve Kosofsky Sedgwick, 1–37. Durham: Duke University Press.

Shelley, Percy. 1921. "In a Defense of Poetry." In *Peacock's Four Essays Ages of Poetry and Other Essays*, edited by H. F. B. Brett-Smith, 21–59. Oxford: Blackwell Press.

Simon, Roger. 1992a. "On Disruptive Daydreams." In *Teaching Against the Grain: Texts for a Pedagogy of Possibility*, 3–12. Westport, CT: Bergin & Garvey Press.

———. 1992b. "The Fear of Theory." In *Teaching Against the Grain: Texts for a Pedagogy of Possibility*, 79–100. Westport, CT: Bergin & Garvey Press.

Spillius, Elizabeth Bott, Jane Milton, Penelope Garvey, Cyril Couve, and Deborah Steiner. 2011. *The New Dictionary of Kleinian Thought*. Based on R. D. Hinshelwood, *A Dictionary of Kleinian Thought*. London: Routledge.

Stonebridge, Lyndsey. 2007. *The Writing of Anxiety: Imagining Wartime in Mid-Century British Culture*. New York: Palgrave Macmillan.

Strachey, James. 1968a. Editor's Introduction to Volume 6 of *The Standard Edition of the Complete Psychological Works of Sigmund Freud*. Translated and edited by James Strachey, in collaboration with Anna Freud, and with the assistance of Alix Strachey and Alan Tyson, ix–xiv. London: Hogarth Press and Institute for Psychoanalysis.

———. 1968b. Editor's Introduction. SE 12: 85–88.

———. 1968c. Editor's Introduction. SE 15: 3–8.

———. 1968d. Editor's Introduction. SE 20: 77–86.

Svevo, Italo. 2003. *Zeno's Conscience*. Translated by William Weaver. New York: Vintage Books.

Taubman, Peter. 2006. "I Love Them to Death." In *Love's Return: Psychoanalytic Essays on Childhood, Teaching, and Learning*, edited by Gail Boldt and Paula Salvio, 13–32. New York: Routledge.

Tolstoy, Leo. 2000. *Anna Karenina: A Novel in Eight Parts*. Translated by Richard Pevear and Larissa Volokhonsky. New York: Viking.

Türcke, Christoph. 2013. *Philosophy of Dreams*. Translated by Susan H. Gillespie. New Haven: Yale University Press.

Waddell, Margot. 2002. *Inside Lives: Psychoanalysis and the Growth of the Personality*. London: Karnac Books.

Walsh, Julie. 2010. "Freud's *Wissbegierde* and the Research Projects of Childhood: Revisiting Little Hans." *Sitegeist: A Journal of Psychoanalysis and Philosophy* 5: 55–74.

Williams, John. (1965) 2003. *Stoner*. New York: New York Review Books.

Winnicott, D. W. (1947) 1992. "Hate in the Counter-Transference." In *Through Paediatrics to Psycho-Analysis: Collected Papers*, 194–203. New York: Brunner/Mazel.

———. (1950–1955) 1992. "Aggression in Relation to Emotional Development." In *Through Paediatrics to Psycho-Analysis: Collected Papers*, 204–218. New York: Brunner/Mazel.

———. (1952) 1992. "Anxiety Associated with Insecurity." In *Through Paediatrics to Psycho-Analysis: Collected Papers*, 97–100. New York: Brunner/Mazel.

———. (1956) 1994. "The Anti-Social Tendency." In *Deprivation and Delinquency*, edited by Clare Winnicott, Ray Shepherd, and Madeleine Davis, 120–131. London: Routledge.

———. (1962) 1996. "A Personal View of the Kleinian Contribution." In *The Maturational Process and the Facilitating Environment: Studies in the Theory of Emotional Development*, 171–178. Madison, CT: International Universities Press.

———. (1963?) 1989. "Fear of Breakdown." In *Psychoanalytic Explorations*, edited by Clare Winnicott, Ray Shepherd, and Madeleine Davis, 87–95. Cambridge: Harvard University Press.

———. (1963) 1994. "Struggling Through the Doldrums." In *Deprivation and Delinquency*, edited by Clare Winnicott, Ray Shepherd, and Madeleine Davis, 145–155. New York: Routledge.

———. (1963) 1996. "The Mentally Ill in Your Casework." In *The Maturational Process and the Facilitating Environment: Studies in the Theory of Emotional Development*, 217–229. Madison, CT: International Universities Press.

———. (1967) 1989. "D.W.W. on D.W.W." In *Psychoanalytic Explorations*, edited by Clare Winnicott, Ray Shepherd, and Madeleine Davis, 569–584. Cambridge: Harvard University Press.

———. (1968) 1989. "The Use of an Object and Relation through Identifications." In *Psychoanalytic Explorations*, edited by Clare Winnicott, Ray Shepherd, and Madeleine Davis, 218–227. Cambridge: Harvard University Press.

———. 1988. *Human Nature*. Bristol, PA: Brunner/Mazel.

———. 1989. "Roots of Aggression (Sept. 9, 1986)." In *Psychoanalytic Explorations*, edited by Clare Winnicott, Ray Shepherd, and Madeleine Davis, 458–461. Cambridge: Harvard University Press.

———. 1999. "Creativity and Its Origins." In *Playing and Reality*, 65–85. London: Routledge.

Young-Bruehl, Elisabeth. 1991. *Creative Characters*. New York: Routledge.

Index

Abraham, Karl, 160n5
adolescence, 13, 25, 70–71, 77–78; and regression, 73, 74, 84, 93; and revolt, 77; and syndrome of ideality, 73–75, 78–80
aesthetic conflicts, 50, 56, 60, 66, 70, 109, 119, 133
affect, 5, 9, 19, 36–37, 61, 78, 93–94, 106. See also anxiety
affiliation, 112, 118, 122, 123
aggression, 155–156n3; and drives, 23, 25; and gender, 88–89, 90, 93, 98–99; and psychical reality, 23, 25, 74, 83; and teachers, 46, 64, 83–85; and theory, 51; and writing, 35, 107, 113, 126. See also Klein, Melanie; Riviere, Joan; and Winnicott, D. W.
Aichhorn, August, 41
ambivalence, 2–3, 71, 91–93, 103, 130–131; and guilt, 93–94
antisocial tendency, 26, 114, 116, 118, 125–127. See also Winnicott, D.W.
anxiety, 23, 26, 44, 51–52, 54, 61, 64, 93, 97; and compulsion to repeat, 36, 41, 62, 65–66, 68–69, 74, 75; and latent anxiety, 107–108; and types of, 106, 115; and writing, 46–47, 106, 112–113, 116
Arendt, Hannah, 17–18
Aulagnier, Piera, 34–35

Bakhtin, Mikhail, 140
Barthes, Roland, 54, 111, 126
Bechdel, Alison, 121, 124
belief, 25; and authority, 38, 44, 123; and ideality, 78–79; in teaching and learning, 50, 73
Bergler, Edmund, 108–109, 158n5
Bion, Wilfred, 4, 9–10, 72, 91, 152n4, 152n5
Bloom, Harold, 117, 122, 123
Bollas, Christopher, 14, 38, 43
Britton, Ronald, 117–118, 124. See also publication anxiety
Brooks, Peter, 14–15
Butler, Judith, 91

Cantet, Laurent, 72, 84; and *The Class*, 80–83
Catton, Eleanor, 120
Cavell, Marcia, 55
Certeau, Michel de, 36

character, 13–15, 123; in the classroom, 16–17, 144–148; and the clinic, 8–11, 18–21, 59–61; and in film, 80–83, 84–85; in novels 15, 55–56, 58–59, 119–120, 121, 123–124, 136–138; and types of, 8, 14–15, 72, 123, 136, 155n2. *See also* literature
clinical knowledge, 97–98
compulsion to repeat, 36, 41, 62, 65–66, 68–69, 74–75
constructions, 62, 97
creativity, 13, 35, 43, 50, 75, 89, 98–101, 107, 121

De Man, Paul, 52–53
death, 95, 100, 112–113, 165
déjà vu, 67–71, 75, 83–84, 154–155n1
dependency, 3; and fact of 7, 94; and frustration, 93–95; in learning and teaching, 3, 22, 34, 46, 75; and primal frustration, 155n2, 155–156n3; in relationships, 3, 18, 41–42, 93, 101, 102; on words, 19, 21, 55, 56
depression, 5, 12, 18, 58, 94, 103, 108, 160n3
depressive position, 79, 94–95, 107, 110, 124, 157n2. *See also* Klein, Melanie
Deutsch, Helene, 73, 77–78
doctoral examination, 158n2
dreams, 11, 27, 40, 58, 60, 130, 160n5; and examination dreams, 134–135; and dream work, 134–135
drives, 23, 78, 88, 89, 90, 93, 113, 143, 155–156n3, 156–157n1

Egan, Jennifer, 56–56
ego, 13, 42, 79, 106, 114–115, 155n2; and defenses, 115–116. *See also* anxiety

Felman, Shoshana, 37, 53–54, 113–114
femininity, 25–26, 87–89, 90, 94–95, 98–99, 156n7; and masculinity, 94–95, 98–99, 156n7. *See also* Klein, Melanie, Riviere, Joan, and Winnicott, D. W.
feminism, 91, 134, 153–154n4, 155n2
Ferenczi, Sándor, 31, 42, 131, 153n1, 153n2
Ferro, Antonio, 14, 153n6
Fink, Bruce, 10
forgetting, 2, 7, 10, 36, 44, 77, 131–132, 159n2
free association, 5, 21–23, 29, 31, 34, 37–38, 57, 149
freedom, 4–5, 11, 22, 34, 42, 52, 54, 110, 124–125
Freud, Anna: on adolescence, 78; on education and psychoanalysis, 76, 141–144; on teacher questions, 43–44
Freud, Sigmund: on affective difficulties, 10, 38–39, 62; on anxiety, 114–116; and characters, 8–9, 14–15; on childhood and forgetting, 1–3, 68–69; on constructions, 62; and dreams, 134–135; on education, 34, 42–43, 49; and everyday mistakes, 129–132; and examinations, 158n5; on interpretation, 148–149; on listening, 40; and mistaken perceptions, 68–69; and negation, 57–58; on phantasy, 62–63; on psychoanalytic treatment, 31–32; on repeating, 35–36, 62, 64, 68; on transference-love, 32, 35, 39; on the uncanny, 70; on the unconscious, 1, 40, 105, 143; on writing, 7–9, 37–38, 112–113; on working through, 64–65
frustration: and aggression, 23, 89, 98–99, 107, 114; and dependency, 46, 94, 155–156n3; and guilt, 92; and learning, 34, 44, 50, 82, 142; and libido, 15, 42, 101; and writing, 38, 108, 118, 160n5

Gabbard, Glen and Thomas Ogden, 3–4

Gallop, Jane, 153–154n4
gender, 25, 87–88, 99, 102; as boy and girl elements, 99–102; and internal aggression, 89, 99–102; and madness, 90–93; and natality, 94–95; as paradox, 102; and phantasies of, 89–90; as psychical, 9. *See also* femininity and masculinity
good-enough mother, 101–102; and bad breast, 99; and weaning, 95
Green, André, 7, 33, 37, 96–97, 155n1
guilt: and castration, 68–69; characters, 15; and the depressive position, 110; and destruction, 92; and love, 87, 92–93, 94; and separation, 94; and super-ego, 70, 158n5, 159n2; and teaching and learning, 30, 46–47; and writing inhibitions, 12, 59–60, 108, 113. *See also* Klein, Melanie

hate, 46–47, 87, 89, 94, 99, 113, 117
Hawthorne, Nathaniel, 12
Heimann, Paula, 124–126, 158–159n8, 159n1
Hitchcock, Alfred, 84–85

ideality: and adolescent syndrome, 12–13, 25, 75; and education, 22, 25, 43, 64, 74–75, 80–84; as ego defense, 73, 78–79; and gender, 92; and self help, 32; and writing, 123. *See also* Kristeva, Julia
identifications, 71–72, 77, 80, 94, 100, 110, 145, 155n3; and cross identification, 100, 102; and projective identification, 97–98, 100, 122
imagination, 10, 17, 55, 97, 112, 114, 122, 125
impossible professions, 74–76
infantile sexuality, 68–69
influence, 1, 3, 11–13, 22, 32, 45, 60–61, 70, 83, 108, 116, 122, 132, 167. *See also* transference
inhibitions, 63–64, 108, 115–116

interpretation, 52, 100, 140, 148–149
isolation, 115–116, 117, 118

James, Henry, 15, 122–123
James, William, 120

King, Pearl, 124
Klein, Melanie: and the depressive position, 94–95, 107, 110; and Heimann, Paula, 124; on infancy, 89; on latent anxiety, 107–108, 157n4; on loneliness, 111, 125; and the paranoid/schizoid position, 94–95, 107, 110; on phantasy, 54–55, 89, 157n2; and Riviere, Joan, 25, 88–89; and Winnicott, D. W., 116–117
Kolodny, Susan, 109
Kris, Ernst, 60–61, 154n1
Kristeva, Julia: on adolescent syndrome of ideality, 12–13, 25, 78–80; on cure, 79–80; on eternal adolescence, 78; on inner freedom, 10–11, 21–22, 75; on listening, 52; on psychical change, 5–6, 78, 135–136; on psychoanalysis, 52; on sexual difference, 88; on suffering, 13–14, 18
Krüger, Steffen, 154n1

Lacan, Jacques, 53–54, 85, 154n1
Laplanche, Jean, 153n2; and J.-B. Pontalis, 155n2
Leader, Darian, 22, 155n1
Lear, Jonathan, 42
learning, 3–4, 9–10, 24–35, 113–114; and delay, 44; and doubts, 62, 75; as paradox, 30–31, 51; and phantasies of, 71–74, 76; and psychoanalytic sensibility, 29; and the transference, 35, 41–42
listening, 5, 12, 14, 38, 40, 52, 57, 100, 105
literature, 13–15, 50, 54, 58, 112, 136–137, 139
Loewald, Hans, 59–60, 64

loss: and anxiety, 52, 97, 107; of good object, 13, 69, 73, 115, 160n4; of imagination, 114; of love, 2, 33, 35, 43, 65, 75, 93, 115; of mind, 4, 131; and mourning, 62, 64, 157n2; and teaching, 63; of time, 1–3; 106, 120; in writing, 26, 37, 106–107, 109, 126

love, 2, 13–14, 24, 35, 39, 63, 93, 113; and hate, 24, 48, 89, 124; and loss of, 106; and madness, 99–101; and reparation, 94

Malabou, Catherine, 155n2, 158n6
McDougall, Joyce, 13, 99; and "Sammy Y," 18–21
Melville, Herman, 119–120
Miller, Jane, 139–140
Milner, Marion, 121, 125
mistakes, 26–27; and 'mistaken mistakes', 131; and parapraxis, 129–133
Mitchell, Juliet, 97–98
Mitscherlich, Alexander, 158–159n8
Modern Language Association, 52–53

negation, 57–58, 61

O'Shaughnessy, Edna, 65–66

paranoid/schizoid position, 79, 94–95, 97, 107, 110. *See also* Klein, Melanie
parapraxis, 130
passion, 33–34; and madness, 155n1; and writing, 37–38
pedagogy: and crisis, 53–54; and developmental theories, 71; and gender, 87–88; and ideality, 42, 74; and kissing, 153–154n4; and object relations, 56–57; and the professor's mistakes, 144–148; and psychical disturbances, 129; and theory, 52–54
Penley, Constance, 134
Perret-Catipovic, Maja, 77
phantasies, 54–55, 89, 90, 100, 108; and gender, 25, 87, 99; and reality,

11, 26; and sequences of, 27, 62–64, 92, 119, 122, 156–157n1; in teaching and learning, 4, 22, 46–47, 85,123; and writing, 106, 109–114, 125–126
Pirandello, Luigi, 2
Pitt, Alice, 59, 91, 160n4
Pontalis, J.-B., 48, 98, 125–126
publication anxiety, 116–118, 124–125. *See also* Britton, Ronald

Quinodoz, Danielle, 4

Reeder, Jurgen, 5
regression, 23, 25, 68, 72–73, 109, 133, 143
resistance: as ego defense, 9, 13, 41, 65, 76, 147; and forgetting, 35, 68–70; to learning, 41, 53–54, 63, 66; to psychoanalysis, 4, 10, 31; and theory, 49, 54, 53–54, 57; and transference-love, 30, 35, 39; and to writing, 43, 107, 109
Rickman, John, 95–96, 102
Riviere, Joan, 88–89, 93–96, 156n7
Ronell, Avital, 109, 110–111, 124
Rose, Jacqueline, 54, 90, 92, 155n2
Rosen, Harold, 138
Roustang, François, 76
Royle, Nicholas, 154–155n1

schizoid mechanisms, 110
Scott, W. Clifford, 134
Sedgwick, Eve, 54
Segal, Hannah, 65, 156n4
separation anxiety, 68–69, 106, 115, 118
Shelly, Percy, 58
Simon, Roger, 62–63, 160n2
sleeping, 133–135
splitting, 13, 19, 26, 64, 74, 78–79, 100, 102, 117
Strachey, James, 40, 115, 130, 151n3
Stonebridge, Lyndsey, 37, 112–113, 122, 125
sublimation, 110, 113, 124

superego, 70, 74, 92, 155n2, 157n4
Svevo, Italo, 58–59
symbolic equation, 89, 94, 156n4

theory, 50–52; and fear of 62–64; and resistance, 53–54; and words, 56–58
thinking, 9, 19, 57, 64, 79–80, 94
transference, 30, 32, 33, 39, 75; and countertransference, 41, 46; and phantasies, 63–64; as playground, 36; and transference neurosis, 35, 45; and writing, 18

the uncanny, 25, 68–70, 154–155n1, 155n2; and déjà raconté, 23, 67, 69, 70
the unconscious, 1–2, 7, 31, 40, 52, 69, 72, 96–97; and the conscious, 1, 7, 75, 157n4; and mistakes, 130–132. *See also* dreams, and wishes
undoing, 115–116, 117, 118
university education, 5–6, 136–138; and classroom life, 11–12, 69–70, 113–114; and a novel, 136–138; and psychoanalysis, 42–50; and theory, 24; and writing blocks, 118–119

Waddell, Margo, 72
waiting, 7, 12, 15, 18, 24, 27, 29, 37, 40, 45, 51, 77, 108, 119, 142–143
Williams, John, 136–138

Winnicott, D. W.: on adolescence, 77; on aggression and gender, 98–102; and antisocial tendency, 114–118; and baby, 23, 98, 156n8; and gender paradox, 90–91, 99–100; on hate, 46, 99, 117; on human nature, 76; on Klein, Melanie, 116–117, 158n7; on madness, 102–103; and McDougall, Joyce, 99; on object relating, 51–52; on object use, 24, 51–52, 98–99, 155–156n3; and paradox of learning, 51, 98, 156n5; on primal agonies, 23
wishes: for autonomy, 4, 139; for certainty, 11, 46; to cure, 62; as ego defense, 11, 46, 55, 66; to know, 74, 139; to learn, 29–30, 43, 63; to lose, 15, 46, 63; for love, 37, 50, 99; and mistakes, 27, 130; for originality, 59, 117; for perfection, 55, 66, 123; and secrets, 36, 77; and the unconscious, 7, 155–156n3, 156–157n1, 158n5; 160n3; and to write, 63, 105, 119, 121
working through, 64–65
writing, 7–9, 61, 112–113, 122–123, 126
writing blocks, 26, 61, 111, 108–109, 118–121; and inhibitions, 58–61, 115–116; and neurosis, 106–107, 111

Young-Bruehl, Elizabeth, 13